BLITZKRIEG

BLITZKRIEG

From the Ground Up

NIKLAS ZETTERLING

CASEMATE
Philadelphia & Oxford

First published in the United States of America and Great Britain in 2017.
Reprinted in paperback in 2021 by
CASEMATE PUBLISHERS
1950 Lawrence Road, Havertown, PA 19083, USA
and
The Old Music Hall, 106–108 Cowley Road, Oxford OX4 1JE, UK

Copyright 2017 © Niklas Zetterling

Paperback Edition: ISBN 978-1-63624-055-8
Digital Edition: ISBN 978-1-61200-461-7

A CIP record for this book is available from the British Library

Printed and bound in the United States of America by Integrated Books International
Typeset in India by Lapiz Digital Services, Chennai

First published in Swedish as *Blixtkrig: 1939–41* (Månpocket, 2009)

For a complete list of Casemate titles, please contact:

CASEMATE PUBLISHERS (US)
Telephone (610) 853-9131
Fax (610) 853-9146
Email: casemate@casematepublishers.com
www.casematepublishers.com

CASEMATE PUBLISHERS (UK)
Telephone (01865) 241249
Email: casemate-uk@casematepublishers.co.uk
www.casematepublishers.co.uk

CONTENTS

PREFACE

The German Blitzkrieg has been the subject of many books, but a clear definition of the term has not yet emerged. Some authors have regarded it as tanks and aircraft conducting mobile operations in close cooperation. The image of tanks storming across open fields, supported by Stuka aircraft with howling sirens diving towards their targets, has often epitomized the Blitzkrieg campaigns of 1939–41. However, that image is at odds with the German operations conducted during the initial years of World War II. Admittedly, there are examples of successful cooperation between tanks and air power, but this was far from the norm. Most importantly of all, operations rarely hinged upon successful air–ground cooperation. Still, there is no lack of books emphasizing tanks and air power as the key to the German victories of 1939–41. However, this book approaches the Blitzkrieg from a different point of view; it presumes that the word "Blitzkrieg" simply denotes German warfare as it was conducted on the battlefields in 1939–41 and attempts to find out how it appeared from the eyes of the junior commanders and enlisted men.

Any historical work depends on the sources used. For various reasons, sources from the opposing side in a military conflict are often used and books on the Blitzkrieg are not different. Estimates, judgments and assumptions made by those who confronted the Blitzkrieg have been used in many books. Another widely used source are memoirs of the German generals who participated in the Blitzkrieg campaigns. These sources are certainly not without problems. In war, the understanding of the enemy is hazy. Even when the intelligence may present accurate data, an accurate understanding of the enemy does not follow automatically. Memoirs are widely known for often being self-serving, and the books written by the German generals are no exception. In addition to the less-than-perfect accuracy provided by such sources, they also tend to view the events from a certain perspective. This is of course evident in memoirs, as generals and other high-ranking officers are much more likely to write books or be interviewed after the war than ordinary soldiers. As they are no more than humans, they tend to explain success or failure predominantly from their point of view, which may or may not be the most important perspective.

The German victories were as surprising as they were swift. Allied decision-makers wanted to uncover the Germans' secrets quickly—they had to do something very soon or risk larger defeat. Consequently, the Allies had to rely on the incomplete information available to find answers. In such circumstances, false conclusions often follow, which may turn into myths lingering for decades.

Previous authors such as Robert A. Doughty, James Corum, and Karl-Heinz Frieser have argued that the German victories in the early part of the war rested less upon tanks and aircraft and more on German military traditions predating the invention of the tank and the aircraft. Rather than creating a new way of war based on recent technological developments that differed radically from previous concepts, the Germans fitted the new weapons into their existing strategies. They focused on independent action, initiative, flexibility, decentralized decision-making and mobility. At the core of the concept was how men acted on the battlefield; this emphasis was particularly pronounced in the lower levels of the military structure. The German victories rested upon the quality of the small units.

Given the scope of the operations conducted in 1939–41, it is impossible to cover them all in detail. I have chosen to focus on how the Blitzkrieg operations were experienced by the enlisted men, the junior officers commanding platoons, companies and battalions, and other men who worked together with them, such as surgeons and field chaplains. Such descriptions are less common in the literature than the generals' perspective.

In the last decade, I have been fortunate to spend much time at the German military archive in Freiburg. Gradually, I have found documents of a kind that is difficult to find—war diaries, debriefing reports and other papers from the battalion and company level. Most of these papers were destroyed in 1945, but some did survive. Unfortunately, they cannot be located by the standard search aids, but with time, I have found several documents of the kind needed to write a book like this. The reports and war diaries written soon after the events are the main source used, but private diaries have also been important, as well as printed sources. A significant part of the sources on which this book is based have never been used before. They have allowed me to describe how a company commander led his tanks, how a crew worked inside a tank and the role of the repair services, to name a few examples. The experiences of the individuals are highlighted, but when taken together they also form part of the greater perspective.

The book is divided into seven chapters. The first provides a brief outline of the development of the German warfare concept up to 1939. Chapters 2, 3 and 4 deal with the campaigns in Poland, Norway and Western Europe from 1939 to 1940. Chapter 5 discusses the strategic situation between the German victory over France and the attack on the Soviet Union. Chapter 6 is devoted to Operation *Barbarossa*, the huge German assault on the Soviet Union. The seventh and final chapter is a reflection on the German Blitzkrieg campaigns. Those parts devoted to the campaigns are longer, allowing for the reader to follow individual soldiers and small combat units. However, I have endeavored to fit such narratives into a broader perspective to convey an understanding of the factors that shaped the Blitzkrieg. Thus, I hope the reader will better understand why the Germans reaped their succession of victories 1939–41.

PROLOGUE

The cold and the snow gave the landscape outside Moscow a character befitting the time of year, with the dark night sky contrasting against the white ground. The silence was almost palpable to the sentries of the German 21st Panzer Regiment, who kept a vigilant eye on the surroundings while their comrades tried to snatch some sleep. However, it was difficult to sleep in the bitter cold unless one could find shelter in a building.

The next day was Christmas Eve, signalling the beginning of a festival the soldiers would normally enjoy, but this time the situation was very different. The attack on the Soviet Union had been launched in beautiful summer weather and tremendous success had been achieved; innumerable prisoners and huge quantities of booty had been captured. The Germans constantly appeared to be on the verge of victory, but somehow it eluded them. When the fall was imminent, the Germans at last launched the great offensive towards Moscow. It was expected that the campaign would be over before the winter, thus allowing the soldiers to return home for leave at Christmas. However, these hopes came to nothing. The Germans did not capture Moscow, and the attacking units became stuck in the positions they had reached at the beginning of December.

Rumors of a Soviet offensive reached the soldiers of the 21st Panzer Regiment. They were not immediately involved because they were stationed behind the front; they were even allowed to wash, a luxury they had not experienced for two weeks. The lull did not last long, as they were soon sent to the area near Klin and Volokolamsk, where other German units were hard-pressed. The tanks were repeatedly sent to support the riflemen hunkering in their foxholes while trying to ward off enemy attacks. The low temperature—the thermometer showed -30 degrees Celsius—claimed many victims among the poorly dressed German soldiers.

The winter solstice meant short December days and brief lulls between further action. The German soldiers' minds wandered—particularly during the evening of December 23. They felt bitter; they had hoped the campaign would be over by Christmas, allowing them to return home, but their hopes had been dashed. Their only remaining wish was that the enemy would remain silent during Christmas Eve—but even this hope would be unfulfilled.

Sergeant Bahls was awoken at 3 a.m. by the arrival of a report. It said that Soviet forces had captured the village of Aristovo, 3 kilometers away. An unsuspecting German baggage unit had defended the village, but it had obviously been unable to put up any lasting defense. A motley force had rapidly been assembled for a counterattack, but it failed to recapture the village. Bahls had been thus called for to stage a counterattack. Aside from his own tank, a Panzer IV, he was also allotted a Panzer II. Bahls and his soldiers would not enjoy a peaceful Christmas Eve.

It was still pitch dark when the two tanks began to move. The road was concealed by snow, but after an hour, Bahls had found his way and could discern the outskirts of Aristovo. A few riflemen saw the two tanks and helped Bahls find the commander of the battalion committed to the fighting at Aristovo. He presented a grim picture of the situation. The so-called battalion consisted of only thirty-five men clinging to three buildings at the western end of the village. Soviet forces controlled the remainder of Aristovo. The Russians had captured most of the baggage, as well as the food and gifts to be distributed during Christmas.

Despite the adverse situation, Bahls decided to attack. He and his soldiers climbed aboard their tanks, but they immediately discovered that the turret mechanism of the light tank had frozen; it would be able to provide token fire support at most. Despite the setback, Bahls stuck to his decision to attack. He presumed that the element of surprise and the cover of darkness would assist him. As he only had one fully operational tank, there was perhaps no other option.

On the intercom, Bahls ordered his driver to advance east along the main street. The noise from the revving engine was loud, but as the tank moved swiftly it reached the village before any Soviet soldier opened fire. The loader had placed a 7.5-cm high-explosive shell in the breech and ensured that the machine guns worked properly. Bahls yelled for the gunner to fire at the buildings along the main street. The gunner immediately pulled the trigger and the first 7.5-cm shell left the short barrel with a crashing sound. At point-blank range, the shell hit the target almost instantly, tearing apart a wall. Flames soon began to consume the building while the Panzer IV proceeded up the street with guns blazing at the other houses. The roar from the engine and the rattle from the machine guns merged with the crashes from exploding shells and the crackling noise from burning buildings.

The Soviet defenders hastily fled from the houses that had been set ablaze; after all, the stern cold was less menacing than the heat from the fires. Bahls did not bother much with the Soviet soldiers; he urged his crew to continue along the main street while the tank fired at buildings that had not been damaged yet. He finally reached the eastern end of the village as the first rays of sun appeared above the horizon and began to dispel the darkness. Bahls could see brown shadows fleeing across the fields east of Aristovo; he saw how they struggled in the snow, which reached up to their knees, but he decided to cease firing as he was low on ammunition.

It was not until after the action was over that Bahls realized they had been fighting on Christmas Eve. His conscience was untroubled by fighting a bloody operation on such a day, as it was very important to assist the riflemen in their distress. However, it was clear that the operation and its purpose—to halt the Soviet advance—was far removed from the expectations the German soldiers had nurtured when the war broke out.

CHAPTER I

THE TURBULENT INTERWAR YEARS

The word had existed for a long time, but it was hardly well-known. A few writers had used it in their texts and some had even used it in book titles, but it was not used on the front pages of the major newspapers. However, this changed in the fall of 1939, as the media and propaganda introduced the word to a broader audience. It began to be said that Germany had defeated Poland by using something called "Blitzkrieg."[1]

With time, the word would prove catchy—despite the fact that it was unclear what it actually meant. The lack of a clear definition allowed various writers and commentators to ascribe the term to whatever they saw fit, and the striking nature of the word meant it was frequently used. This meant the word "Blitzkrieg" came to have a vague meaning that could differ considerably depending on who used it.

The German armed forces did not use the word themselves, except possibly in publications by individual officers. Still, they had created something regarded as revolutionary by their contemporaries, even though a mere four years had elapsed since Hitler denounced the Treaty of Versailles. The peace treaty signed after World War I had forbidden Germany to possess modern weapons such as submarines, tanks and aircraft, also drastically curtailing the size of the German armed forces.

It may appear puzzling that an armed force that had been fettered not only expanded rapidly but also created something that appeared revolutionary. Furthermore, this revolution was accomplished by a country lacking most of the raw materials needed for modern warfare and recovering in the wake of a worldwide economic depression.[2] Several circumstances influenced the process, but some were perhaps more important than others. One of these was the German effort to circumvent the Treaty of Versailles, a process that had been initiated in the early 1920s. The German armed forces clandestinely cooperated with the Soviet Union, allowing them to experiment with modern weapon systems such as tanks and aircraft. The Germans also carried out projects in their home country—for example, constructing tank prototypes under the disguise of agricultural tractors. Several theoretical studies were undertaken and the developments in foreign countries were followed closely.

However, one could argue that the German Blitzkrieg was not revolutionary at all. Perhaps it can be better understood if it is not regarded as a break with the past, but rather a development of existing German military concepts. If the Blitzkrieg is conceived as an almost logical continuation of existing lines of development, it is easier to understand how the Germans could go to war in 1939 and swiftly conquer Poland, Norway, Denmark, Belgium, the Netherlands and France despite the fact that conscription had not been introduced until 1935.

Another notion to be called in question is the idea that tanks and aircraft formed the core of the Blitzkrieg. Admittedly, these weapons played a prominent role in German propaganda as well as in many foreign assessments, but the German warfare concept did not emanate from them, nor from any other weapon system. Instead, the Germans had a fairly clear idea of how to conduct operations and battles, and the tank in particular happened to fit quite well into the concept. Still, the infantry divisions remained the backbone of the German Army—a result of economic constraints rather than deliberate design. Germany simply lacked the industrial resources and the raw materials needed to create and sustain a completely mechanized army. Neither was a large strategic air force—akin to what Britain and US would later employ during World War II—a realistic alternative. The Germans could only proceed from their basic concepts and try to fit modern weapons into them.

Hitler has often been described as a propelling force behind the Blitzkrieg concept. His responsibility for the outbreak of the war in 1939 is unquestioned, and it is conceivable that the state of the German armed forces would have been very different at a later date, but there are more fundamental objections to the notion of Hitler's importance. He clearly pushed for a rapid expansion of the armed forces, but he had relatively little influence over how they were composed and, in particular, how they were trained to fight. A study of the period before Hitler assumed power is revealing in this respect.

The Legacy of World War I

World War I has often been regarded as an example of stagnated warfare, but such a view is misleading. In fact, the officers in Germany—as well as in other countries—had tried to understand the implications of rapidly developing technology before the war began in 1914. However, it was difficult to envisage war in the future as much had changed since the Franco-Prussian war of 1870–71. However, it would be even more misleading to claim that little changed during World War I.[3]

Perhaps the major operational limitation encountered by the combatants during World War I was the almost impenetrable defense lines. Unless the enemy defense lines were broken through, operational freedom of maneuver could not be attained. The Germans and the other combatants tried to solve this problem in multiple ways; unsurprisingly, the Germans attached the greatest importance to their own solutions, of which the so-called "stormtrooper" tactics were the most important. In many ways, the German stormtrooper tactics developed during World War I epitomize the conclusions and lessons preserved by the Germans after World War I.

The German approach to breaking the stalemate on the Western Front is indicative of the German art of war, as the process was very decentralized. Local initiatives led by many officers—many of them low-ranking—were vital. After these efforts had proved their worth in battle, the higher command echelons quickly paid attention to them and introduced extensive training programs to capitalize on the ideas conceived by the low-ranking officers. Thus the most useful ideas were put into general practice in the Army.[4]

As can be surmised from the term, the stormtroop tactics were mainly a solution to a tactical problem—how to break through a strong enemy defense. It was necessary to begin at the tactical level as no significant operational results would be attained unless tactical success had created freedom of action for the higher commanders.

The German stormtroop tactics were made up of several components. The underlying principle was decentralization, which was applied in many ways; the most important of these was decentralized decision-making, but this was not a novel idea. The Germans had previously tended to delegate authority, but with the stormtroop tactics this trend was extended further down in the organization and applied more consistently. It was obvious to the Germans that the modern battlefield demanded rapid decisions made according to the fluid situation on many parts of the battlefield. Junior commanders had to act independently and exercise initiative, and this kind of decentralization was facilitated by another kind. At the beginning of World War I, the combat units were rather uniformly equipped—an infantry battalion was mainly composed of riflemen. The introduction of stormtroop tactics also meant that the composition of these combat units changed due to the reliance on the principle of combined arms. Junior commanders therefore had more options to choose from when they decided how to act in battle. Additionally, less time was wasted when the local commanders could, for example, arrange fire support on their own.[5]

The stormtroop tactics were mainly developed by German forces fighting the western powers, but the Germans also gained valuable experience from the Eastern Front, where the number of units was much smaller relative to the size of the theater. The lower troop density made it much more difficult to create the kind of strong defenses that thwarted offensives between the English Channel and Switzerland. Consequently, it was easier for the Germans to break through the Russian defenses, and mobile operations ensued—strongly suggesting that future war need not resemble the stalemate experienced in the west.

It can be argued that most major aspects of what would subsequently be known as Blitzkrieg had already been available to the Germans in 1918. The most important was the command philosophy. Commanders at all levels would make decisions and act on their own initiative. This was the fundamental principle on which the Germans relied when conducting operations and fighting battles. The combined-arms principle as expressed by the stormtroop units fitted well with the decentralized decision-making. Alongside decentralized decision-making and the combined-arms principle, the third important lesson upon which Blitzkrieg was based was the experience on the Eastern Front, which strongly suggested that mobile operations were feasible.

The fourth major lesson actually stemmed from a failure. The stormtroop tactics enabled the Germans to break through the strong defenses on the western front—as in March 1918, for example. However, the Germans did not manage to exploit their initial success, and this was mainly due to logistical shortcomings. The Germans lacked the capacity to bring forward artillery, ammunition, reinforcements and supplies needed to sustain their momentum, while their opponents could rely on the rail network to bring reinforcements to the endangered sector.

The legacy of World War I was thus composed of both positive and negative lessons learned, but in a sense, the peace treaties of 1919 can also be regarded as part of the legacy. In fact, harsh as they were, they might nevertheless have been beneficial to the German development in the interwar period. As the German Army was limited to 100,000 men (of whom 4,000 were allowed to be officers), the Army could select the best people for the job, especially as the military profession remained attractive in Germany.

The lessons learned by the Germans were mainly confined to the tactical and operational levels. However, there were some strategic lessons the Germans would have benefited from paying more attention to; one of these was the fact that very little was gained by the war—even by its winners. France and Britain were economically exhausted and the human cost had been appalling. They would be hard-pressed to maintain the powerful position they had held before the war. Italy was also weakened by the war, despite being one of the victors. It could be argued that the US and Japan had improved their positions, but, significantly, they had avoided most of the costly battles. Thus it can be concluded that the use of military force may have resulted in such immense costs that the fruits of victory could not be enjoyed. However, the Germans would not pay as much attention to this as to the tactical and operational lessons.

A Shackled Army

As intended, the terms imposed by the Treaty of Versailles made the German armed forces very weak. Their low number of weapons and lack of important ones made them incapable of fending off an earnest attack, but the clauses of the treaty could not prevent German officers from pondering on future war. The Germans immediately initiated an extensive program to study the experiences of World War I. Most of the just over 400 officers involved were veterans very familiar with the progress that had taken place between 1914 and 1918 and not least the stormtroop tactics.[6]

The experiences were thoroughly studied, but the process was completed quickly enough to produce an entirely new Army field manual by 1921. It was known as *"Führung und Gefecht der verbundenen Waffen,"* or by its abbreviation *"das FuG."* The manual was thus written less than three years after the end of World War I and served as a guideline for the German Army eighteen years before World War II broke out. The latter observation is particularly important as the foundations laid by the field manual of 1921 remained until 1945.[7]

The 1921 field manual emphasized offensive operations, mobility and decentralized decision-making down to the lowest possible level, allowing officers and NCOs to act independently and exercise initiative on the battlefield. However, there was a latent problem with such emphasis on independence—the actions on the battlefield might become dissipated. The German solution to this dilemma was thorough and extensive training. This would ensure that a common method of thinking would be instilled, guiding decision-making across the battlefield.[8]

The German Army could emphasize the training of its limited personnel during the interwar period, but this training was hampered by the lack of important weapons systems. However, that problem should not be exaggerated. Training, intellectual activity and ideas are often more fundamental than equipment, and the German armed forces were no exception during this time. The process of development that took place did not spring from certain weapon systems or technology; instead, there was an intellectual framework into which the new weapons were included. The legacy and the analysis of World War I were very important elements of the framework.

Occasionally, the French Army has been criticized for preparing for another round of World War I in 1939, while the Germans are said to have used the interwar years to create the prerequisites for fighting a future war. Such an argument would be a gross simplification, as the Germans also used the experiences of World War I as the basis for their preparations for future war. The differences between the approaches of the two countries (which became clear in 1940) stemmed from differences that had existed even before 1918. To regard the French as conservative and the Germans as far-sighted is a simplification that conceals more than it reveals. However, it seems that the German Army accepted diverse opinions and an open debate to a notably greater extent than the French Army. Most likely, such an attitude facilitated the creation of an armed force whose art of war was at a higher level than the opponents, though not necessarily revolutionary.[9]

The German Army's broad acceptance of diverse opinions was apparent in reports submitted by the Swedish military attaché in Berlin, Lieutenant-Colonel Juhlin-Dannfelt, to his superiors in Stockholm. He was clearly surprised at how German soldiers acted during discussions after exercises. On several occasions, in different units—and even in the presence of foreign officers—the commanders had been interrupted by subordinates who argued back while the commander was criticizing the subordinate's performance during a recently concluded exercise. Such behavior had not been commented upon until the commander-in-chief of the Army, Colonel-General von Fritsch, addressed the issue in a speech at the *Kriegsakademie*.[10]

Nevertheless, the inhibitions imposed by the Treaty of Versailles were not inconsequential. The Germans had to study modern weapons, such as tanks, from afar. The tanks that had appeared on the battlefields of World War I were fraught with technical problems that limited their impact—they were hardly harbingers of the future, and they had to be improved considerably to allow them to play an important part in a future war. However, the Germans were banned from conducting the necessary development work. The cooperation with the Red Army in the wake of the 1922 Treaty of Rapallo provided an important opportunity for the Germans to gain knowledge.[11]

Another way to gain knowledge was to monitor development in other countries. The Germans observed exercises as well as production, also managing to learn much from various publications in many countries. Obviously, the major powers—such as Great Britain, France and the Soviet Union—attracted most interest from the Germans, particularly as they were seen as potential enemies.

The German journal *Militärwochenblatt* was a German military journal widely distributed in the Army, dealing with many important issues pertaining to the development of Army equipment, doctrine, training, command, organization and so on. It contained several articles discussing or describing important trends or occasions abroad. For example, there were articles on military exercises in other countries, such as the British fall maneuvers of 1925. Issue 14 and 16 (1927–28) provided extensive coverage of the British exercises conducted in August 1927, when mechanized units participated. However, the Germans were not content with following activities in Europe. Tanks were used in conflicts in other parts of the world—for example, by the British in India and by the French in Morocco and Syria. Also studied were seldom-discussed military conflicts such as the Chaco war in South America (1932–35). Nevertheless, World War I and the battles fought 1914–18 were the most frequent topics. In November 1927, the Battle of Cambrai was discussed in an article entitled *"Ein Vorläufer der Zukunftschlacht"* ("A Harbinger of Future Battle"). On this occasion, the British had committed the first large concentrated tank force. Wars where tanks had not contributed significantly were also studied, such as the war between Greece and Turkey from 1919–22.[12]

Technological trends in other countries were observed. For example, the heavy French Char 2C tank was covered in articles in 1924, 1925 and 1927.[13] New, experimental American tanks were discussed in March 1925, and new light American tanks were described in spring 1928.[14] Despite the difficulties, the Germans managed to remain updated.

It can be argued that the shackles of the Treaty of Versailles were mainly physical rather than mental, but the mental aspects are, in many ways, more important. Furthermore, military technology advanced rapidly in the interwar years. Weapons that had been brand new in the 1920s were often regarded as obsolete by the 1930s, and this was particularly true of tanks and aircraft. Consequently, it was more important to develop a useful foundation for the art of war. The Germans did this mainly by capitalizing on their experiences from World War I and even concepts and trends dating from before 1914.

Hitler Seizes Power

Before the Great Depression, Hitler and his NSDAP had been a rather insignificant factor in German politics. However, the depression and the attendant mass unemployment provided Hitler with a previously unforeseen opportunity. His simplified messages provided him with spectacular success in the 1930 elections. After various political maneuvers and further elections, Hitler managed to assume power in Germany. Soon the new regime would promote substantial changes to the German armed forces, but at the time it remained unclear what lay in the future.

In several respects, Hitler's intentions coincided with ambitions nurtured in many parts of German society, including the armed forces. Perhaps the abolition of the Treaty of Versailles and the reintroduction of conscription were the most clear-cut examples. Hitler's ideas of "Lebensraum" (living space) in Eastern Europe were not unique, although the practical matters—such as timing, means to be used and at what pace the ambitions should be pursued—could result in disagreements.

Initially, Hitler had to focus on securing his position within Germany. However, from 1934, when his power was almost undisputed, he could begin to realize his more far-reaching ambitions. He obviously needed strong armed forces to fulfil his dreams, and in 1935 he officially denounced the Treaty of Versailles and reintroduced conscription. Few German officers objected to this move, although they may have been worried about the reaction in other countries.

The first three German Panzer divisions were formed in October 1935. At the time, Germany lacked battle-worthy tanks. The light Panzer I tank had entered production one year beforehand, but it had been designed mainly for training purposes. The German Army would have to contend with these light tanks (in addition to the only slightly heavier Panzer II) until other types had been produced in sufficient numbers.[15]

The light Panzer I and Panzer II were produced in large numbers and they made up most of the German tank fleet when the war broke out in 1939, while the heavier Panzer III and IV were comparatively rare. The chief of the general staff, Colonel-General Ludwig Beck, foresaw this situation. He had been appointed as commander of the *Truppenamt*, which was effectively the general staff in disguise. The Treaty of Versailles had forced the Germans to abolish the general staff, but when Hitler officially repudiated the treaty in 1935, the general staff again received its proper name.

Beck has been depicted as a reactionary with scant understanding of the value of armored troops, not least in the memoirs of Heinz Guderian. However, the reality was different. Beck was optimistic about the potential combat value of tanks, but he also realized that technology advanced rapidly. He did not believe that Germany could win a war in the near future. If many tanks were immediately procured, they might be obsolete by the time Germany could engage in a war she could win. According to Beck, it was better for the time being to obtain only those tanks needed for training and testing. Meanwhile, development of more powerful types would be carried out to allow them to be produced in time for a war that Germany could win. History certainly does not contradict Beck. When the war broke out a few years later, Germany had almost 2,700 Panzer I and Panzer II tanks with marginal combat value. It would probably have been better to husband some of the resources spent on these models and save them for the increased production of the Panzer III and Panzer IV, which were to enter production very soon.[16]

Beck's cautious approach stemmed from his belief that many years were required to create a powerful army, but this conflicted with Hitler's desire for rapid results. Their disagreements also sprung from differing assessments of the posture the major powers would assume. For example, would the British and French go to war on the Czechoslovakian issue? Hitler believed they would not, but Beck was not easily convinced. Nevertheless, Hitler had the power to enforce his intentions despite Beck's misgivings. The latter realized that the rapid German rearmament would arouse animosity in other countries and also impose great strain on the German armed forces and the economy.

It may appear surprising that the German rearmament efforts were not geared towards Blitzkrieg campaigns of the kind conducted in 1939–41. Such brief campaigns, with lulls in between, would allow the Germans to replenish stocks of ammunition and fuel; thus investments in projects aiming to improve Germany's ability to sustain protracted war would not have been proper. In fact, substantial investments were made in fields that could only be motivated by a desire to increase the ability to fight a protracted war. For example, great emphasis was placed on improving the raw materials situation. By using lower-grade ore and building plants capable of turning out synthetic fuel, textiles, rubber and so on, the Germans compensated for their lack of raw materials. However, such solutions were very expensive and siphoned off resources that might otherwise have been spent on weapons production. Also, it might appear surprising that investments in the Westwall—Hitler's counterpart to the Maginot Line—consumed a share of the budget twice as large as the share allotted to armored forces.[17]

Hitler's assumption of power meant that a breakneck expansion of the armed forces was undertaken, but also that extensive resources were spent on preparing the German economy for protracted war. Such aims were not novel—they had been nurtured since before Hitler became Chancellor and Führer—but he imposed a pace that was quite extreme. He did so despite grave misgivings voiced by many influential people, and the wisdom of his ambitions can certainly be called into question.

Expansion

When the German Army began to expand, it could rely on its well-trained officers and men. Most soldiers in the 100,000-strong Army

Hitler took over in 1933 were trained for higher positions than they actually held. The Germans expected heavy officer casualties in battle and subordinated men would have to be able to step forward and assume command, and thus men had to be trained for a higher position than they were appointed to. Additionally, the German emphasis on initiative meant that junior officers and NCOs had to understand the broader perspective they acted within. Furthermore, as the junior officers were expected to employ many different kinds of weapons in battle, they had to be very well trained. Finally, officers and men trained for positions higher than those actually held would facilitate a future expansion of the Army.

When Hitler decided to expand the Army very rapidly, the well-trained cadre provided by the 100,000 men proved too small. In the years that followed the introduction of compulsory military service, training standards fell. Officer training suffered particularly badly; many years were needed to provide the candidates with the training and experience they required. In contrast, the training of enlisted men could be completed in less time.

The Swedish officer Captain Berggren attended German artillery exercises at Wildflecken in 1938 and reported his experiences and impressions. He noted the confidence the Germans had in their NCOs; for example, several battery commanders were NCOs, which was uncommon in other countries. Berggren was impressed by the display, concluding that the training standards were excellent and the conscripted men were particularly impressive.[18]

Berggren's impressions were gained at a time when the German Army had expanded for three years. The lower echelons could be given adequate training in such a timespan, but it was more difficult to provide battalion commanders and above with the experience and training required, and the kind of warfare the Germans were striving for meant that well-trained and experienced commanders were essential.

Berggren also discussed the firing techniques used by other countries with the German officers. The latter expressed esteem for the more complicated fire-control methods employed by the French artillery, but they did not want to use similar methods in the German Army. Berggren summed it up sententiously: "The Germans have a terrible dread of time-consuming procedures" (underline in original). This was reflected in the exercises conducted, where the ability to quickly deliver fire support was regarded as more important that absolute accuracy.[19]

The Germans probably placed greater emphasis on time than the other powers did; it was crucial for the Germans to act more quickly than their opponents if they were to compensate for their numerical inferiority. In principle, poorly trained men could also act quickly, but probably not in a way that was conducive to success. Furthermore, a poorly trained and inexperienced person was unlikely to have the confidence required to take initiative, which was a prerequisite for the swift action the Germans strived for.

The rapidity of the German expansion is perhaps best illustrated by the increased number of officers. On October 1, 1933, the German Army comprised 3,800 officers, which increased to 6,533 by October 15, 1935. This was a modest increase compared to what was to come; by March 15, 1941, the number of officers had increased to no fewer than 129,645. In little more than five years, the number of officers increased almost by 2,000 percent. As a battalion or regiment commander ought to have at least a decade of experience, it is easy to see that the rapid expansion made it difficult to train officers sufficiently.[20]

These difficulties were clearly considerable, but it should not be forgotten that the German training must be judged in comparison to that of their opponents rather than according to some abstract rule established by the German military. The senior German officers were very worried, but they also seem to have upheld very high standards of training. Furthermore, the duration of the training is not the only indicator of success; if a considerable amount of time is spent on activities not conducive to improving combat power, the number of months in military service matter little. One example is the Red Army, where the men spent much of their time erecting buildings and farming.[21]

It is arguable that the Germans founded their training on a more realistic perception of the demands of war, enabling them to obtain more combat power for each hour spent on training. To some extent, this alleviated the negative effects of the rapid expansion. After all, the aim was not to spend as much time as possible on training, but rather to raise the quality of the units.

Such considerations notwithstanding, it seems clear that the German might have been able to create more powerful armed forces had the pace of expansion been reduced somewhat. Not only did training suffer, so too did the procurement of equipment; the tanks delivered around 1935 faced the possibility of becoming obsolete soon, a consequence of rapid technological advances. This was one of the most important arguments on which Beck based his misgivings against the breakneck rearmament.

In his memoirs and in conversations with Basil Liddell-Hart after the war, Guderian depicted Beck as a reactionary who obstructed the armored troops, but this image seems exaggerated. Guderian and Beck did differ on many occasions. For example, Beck wanted to create Panzer divisions as well as tank battalions for infantry support; he did not, for the time being at least, want to stake everything on a single alternative. He advocated a model in which several options were tried simultaneously and rejected according to experiences from larger maneuvers. Furthermore, Beck believed that the independent tank battalions could be used to quickly create further Panzer divisions if they were needed. In fact, he was proven right, such as when the 10th Panzer Division was formed in 1939. Guderian opposed this, but the alternative recommended by Beck was not a dead end and would have caused trivial delays at most. Beck's stance appears actually quite reasonable in such turbulent times.

Beck also wanted to create tank formations as well as independent antitank units. He argued that future enemies might well possess large tank formations, and thus some means to combat them was needed. Indeed, the Germans did quite successfully use those kind of units to fight enemy tank formations in 1939–42. Guderian opposed this scheme, but again Beck appears to have assumed a fairly balanced position.

It is difficult to expand armed forces and even more difficult to do it rapidly. As we shall see, later shortcomings in the German war machine can be attributed to this rapid expansion, but it must be remembered that other countries also rapidly expanded their armed forces. For example, the United States would conduct an expansion with a speed that rivaled that of the Germans. Another example would be the armored forces of the Soviet Union; in 1930, the country possessed very few tanks, but by 1941 Stalin had approximately 23,000 tanks at his disposal. This enormous figure is ample testimony of a very rapid expansion. The British Army also began to expand rapidly in the latter half of the 1930s. Hence, Germany might have experienced problems caused by rapid expansion, but she was not alone in this respect.[22]

The Horizon Darkens

The tension in Europe rose when Hitler repudiated the Treaty of Versailles, but it is unclear to what extent fears mounted. There were many in Britain, for example, who believed that the clauses were either exorbitant or impossible to uphold. However, it soon became clear that the repudiation of the treaty was only the first step in Hitler's plans. In 1936, German military units drove into the Rhineland, which had been a demilitarized area. The specter of war loomed ever larger. Poland had regarded the Soviet Union as the primary military threat since the failed Soviet attempt to conquer Warsaw in 1920. Since then, the Polish defense plans had been designed primarily to counter an attack from the east; however, as Hitler continued his military buildup, the Polish high command had to develop new defense plans.

Hitler did not make any dramatic moves in 1937. The German armed forces were not yet strong enough to allow adventurous foreign policy. He did not dare an obvious confrontation with the western powers, especially as the expansion of the armed forces ran into difficulties. However, in 1938, Hitler again raised his voice. His first move was to annex Austria in March. He subsequently set his eyes on Czechoslovakia; the so-called "Munich Agreement" saw the British and French agree that Czechoslovakia should cede the Sudetenland to Germany as the majority of the Sudeten population was German and the area was located next to the German border. Simultaneously, Poland seized the opportunity to occupy the Cieszyn area, a territory that had been claimed by both Poland and Czechoslovakia since World War I.[23] The Slovaks also availed themselves of the chance to demand independence from Prague.

In 1937, Stalin expanded the great purge to include the armed forces. Approximately 35,000 officers were executed, imprisoned or discharged.

Thus his military capabilities were reduced, and many commentators in other countries believed that the Soviet military had become too weak to significantly influence a major conflict.

When regarding the situation in Europe at the time, one must not forget that there were five major powers—Britain, France, Germany, the Soviet Union and Italy. It was hardly possible for Britain and France to put great pressure of any of the other three without the support from one of the dictatorships. However, it was not evident—at the time—which of the three dictatorships was preferable or dependable. When Stalin decimated his armed forces, he appeared neither trustworthy nor in possession of a sharp sword. Hence, a firm stance against Hitler seemed to require at least tacit support from Italy. However, Mussolini's involvement in the Spanish Civil War, 1936–39, and his war in Ethiopia in 1935–36, clearly suggested that he was not the kind of player preferred by the western powers.

In addition to the situation in Europe, France and Britain had to consider the threats to their colonial empires, particularly in the Far East. Japanese aggression against China clearly showed that there were danger spots outside Europe. The Soviet Union also had a tense relationship with Japan; several border intermezzos took place along the border between Siberia and Manchuria. Evidently, the international situation was very complicated, and the decision-makers were hard-pressed to find workable solutions, such as a coalition against Hitler. Neither were the French and British military resources sufficient to ensure victory against Germany through swift offensive action. Britain lacked a powerful army and the French Army, while substantial in size, was mainly designed for defensive operations rather than a lightning offensive into Germany.

Thus several circumstances conspired to limit the opposition to Hitler's aggressive foreign policy. Within Germany, many feared that the Führer would drive Germany into a war against a coalition she could not defeat, but this did not occur immediately. Nevertheless, the shadows of war loomed ever larger, especially after Hitler occupied the remains of Bohemia and Moravia in March 1939. However, Hitler's thirst was not quenched; during the summer of 1939, he increased the pressure on Poland.

Kriegsmarine

From a Blitzkrieg perspective, the German Navy may appear anachronistic. It was mainly designed to wage war against British transatlantic commerce— by halting the flow of raw materials and other imports, Britain could be brought to her knees. The German submarines were clearly intended for such use, but the German surface fleet was also mainly intended for that purpose. As such tactics could hardly produce rapid results, they did not fit well into any Blitzkrieg concept. Furthermore, to regard Great Britain as the main enemy was dubious on many grounds. The countries Germany had to defeat were first and foremost neighboring powers. Germany would gain little from war with Britain and it was better avoided.

The role of the German Navy appears more plausible if we disregard the notion that Germany had a particular Blitzkrieg strategy. On the other hand, if we see the German efforts as resulting from an ambition to create efficient combat units allowing operational liberty of action in many different types of war, the German naval buildup appears more sensible. Overall, the Navy received a small share of the funding, but, considering Germany's geographical position, there was hardly any alternative. As we shall see, the German Navy could be used for operations in other areas than the Atlantic.

In the summer of 1939, the German Navy, like the other services, was still preparing for war. Far more warships were projected than those available for immediate service. A major naval power could not be challenged on the open sea, but the German Navy could at least provide some assistance to the other services. As East Prussia was separated from mainland Germany, any military forces in the eastern province had to be supplied by shipping on the Baltic, which had to be protected by the Navy. Nevertheless, it was clear that the Navy could not be expected to have a prominent role in any kind of Blitzkrieg operation.

Completed Warships

Two battleships
Three pocket battleships
One heavy cruiser
Six light cruisers
Twenty-one destroyers

Fifty-seven submarines
Zero carriers
Two obsolete battleships (from 1908).

In Production

Two battleships, one carrier, four heavy cruisers, no light cruisers, five destroyers, fifty-five submarines.

Luftwaffe

The German Air Force was officially created in 1935, but the Germans had clandestinely prepared for this event long before. The cooperation with the Soviet Union had included activity at the flying school at Lipetsk. Additionally, sailplaning had been encouraged within Germany as a means to create a cadre of experienced aviators. Civilian air transport was encouraged and, of course, many theoretical studies on the employment of air power were conducted. All these efforts meant that the Germans did not begin with a blank slate when the Luftwaffe was created.

Many different opinions on the use of air power were voiced in the interwar years. The most extreme position was that wars would virtually be decided by air power alone, through strategic bombing. The idea was that the civilian population would not be able to stand up to the strain and that they would demand their government to make peace. Such an argument was—roughly—put forward by Giulio Douhet. It would perhaps be an exaggeration to claim that he had a large number of proselytes closely adhering to his prophesies, but many shared his emphasis on strategic bombing.

At first, the Germans remained tentative. The choice between a strategic air force and one that was an integrated component in joint operations was perhaps unintentionally delayed. When the Luftwaffe was created, strong voices promoting a strategic air force were raised, but the planning before 1933 had mainly presupposed an air force that would support the Army. By appointing Hermann Goering as "*Reichskommissar für die Luftwaffe*" and Erhard Milch as Undersecretary of State for the Air Force, the foundation for an independent air force was laid.[24] Robert Knauss created the first draft on the structure and tasks for the Luftwaffe, favoring a strategic air force not far removed from the ideas proposed by Giulio Douhet. However, the focus gradually shifted to joint operations and particularly cooperation with the Army.[25]

Given the German strategic situation, there was perhaps little choice but to settle for an air force mainly cooperating with the Army. The closest and most dangerous enemies—France, Poland, Czechoslovakia and the Soviet Union—were land powers. In addition, experience from the Spanish Civil War (in which the German Legion Condor had supported Franco) suggested that the emphasis should be placed on inter-service cooperation. Douhet's beliefs that the morale of the civilian population was fragile were not supported by the events of 1936–39. Exercises conducted in Germany suggested that protective measures could reduce the effects of air attacks on cities considerably.[26] Later, the events that took place during World War II would show that the effects of strategic bombing became clear only after prolonged and very extensive efforts; however, the Germans had neither time nor strong availability of resources. It was wiser for them to devote more resources to an air force designed to cooperate with the Army.

It has been argued that the Germans made a mistake by not creating a powerful long-range air force, but given their strategic situation it is doubtful whether such a project was realistic. During the 1930s, the most important enemies were not Britain, the Soviet Union or the US; rather, the German armed forces had to be able to defeat their closest neighbors, such as Poland and France. Unless Germany could defeat these countries (and preferably swiftly), any long-range striking capability would be quite irrelevant. To develop such a capability would have consumed too many resources to allow success against her immediate neighbors. Indeed, it is questionable whether Germany had the industrial resources to create the long-range air force proposed, and particularly whether she could provide it with sufficient fuel.

Eventually, the German Air Force mainly consisted of single-engine fighters with relatively short endurance, twin-engine fighters with slightly longer range, medium bombers with good but unremarkable range and a substantial number of reconnaissance and transport aircraft. The Ju 87 Stuka, which would become famous, was, in fact, not particularly numerous.

The Luftwaffe of 1939 had three main tasks. The first was to gain air superiority, for example by attacking enemy airfields. The second was reducing the enemy's capability to conduct operations, which could be achieved by attacking communications, depots and similar targets. The third was to support the efforts by other German forces, for example by reconnaissance, air transport and fire support.

These tasks should not be regarded as a strict list of roles to be adhered to by the Luftwaffe. Rather, a flexible approach was preferred, allowing the Air Force to effectively engage in various kinds of conflicts. However, the Luftwaffe did not prepare pilot training in sufficient numbers to cope with the heavy losses that would occur later. World War II would prove to be a war of immense attrition, and the Luftwaffe did not manage to prepare sufficiently for it.[27]

The Luftwaffe's combat units did not only comprise aircraft. Most of the German antiaircraft artillery belonged to Goering, although it often cooperated with the Army. In general, the flak available was both numerous and of high quality. The Germans spent a comparatively large amount of resources on antiaircraft artillery.

Airborne troops were an important component of the Luftwaffe. The parachutists were included in the 7th Air Division, commanded by Lieutenant-General Kurt Student. Thus far, paratroopers were untested in battle, but the Germans decided to place their faith in them.

Generally speaking, the composition of the Luftwaffe allowed it to influence many scenarios in war. The main shortcomings could be attributed to lack of experience. It was not yet understood how costly air operations would be, and the swiftness of rearmament did not allow sufficient inter-service training. However, it is doubtful that any other air force did a much better job in these respects—unrealistic expectations and insufficient training were widespread in other countries too.

The German Air Force

257 long-range reconnaissance aircraft
356 short-range reconnaissance aircraft
366 dive-bombers
1,176 bombers

40 ground-attack aircraft
552 transport aircraft
95 twin-engine fighters
771 single-engine fighters

The Army

The Army remained the most important component in the German armed forces, although this was not necessarily reflected in its influence within Germany. Goering's position in the Nazi hierarchy allowed him to secure resources and influence for his Luftwaffe; however, the most likely scenarios of war suggested that the Army would play the most important part. Enemies such as Poland and France were first and foremost land powers, and they could only be subdued rapidly by a swift offensive on the ground.

In the summer of 1939, the German officers were not yet convinced that Germany could win a quick victory except against a single, weaker opponent like Poland. Technically, the German Army was not particularly mobile. The number of motor vehicles was far from sufficient to create a motorized army quite simply because the German economy was unable to produce sufficient trucks and cars. Only the US and Great Britain had the means to create fully motorized armies. Furthermore, the scant availability of crude oil suggested that Germany would be hard-pressed to keep all the vehicles needed for a motorized army moving. Between 80 and 90 percent of all crude oil production in the world was controlled by the US or Great Britain, either as a result of territorial possession or trade agreement. The Soviet Union controlled more than half of the remainder.[28]

Quite simply, very few major powers had the resources needed for a completely motorized army or large long-range air force. Furthermore, a motorized army required a motor industry of vast capacity, and only the US possessed such a capacity at the time. The fact that Britain could fully motorize its Army was partly attributable to the fact that her Army was quite small.[29] Among the remaining powers, Germany probably had the most motorized armed forces.

The chief of the general staff, Ludwig Beck, had resigned in protest against Hitler's dangerous foreign policy before the Czechoslovakian Crisis. Colonel-General Franz Halder assumed the position, but Beck's fears that the German Army would enter war with mostly obsolete tanks came true. The lightly armored and poorly armed Panzer I and II made up most of the tank force in August 1939. The Panzer I was only armed with machine guns, and the Panzer II was fitted with a 2-cm gun with projectiles that weighed less than 0.2 kilograms. These two types made up approximately 80 percent of the tanks in the German Army.[30]

Perhaps the weaknesses of these two models could have been accepted if their mobility had been excellent, but they were not far above average in that respect. The combat power of the German Panzer troops owed little to the technical performance of the tanks. Neither could the German officers expect that production of new tanks would alleviate the situation significantly. In 1939, a total of 743 tanks were manufactured in Germany. At that pace, three and a half years would elapse before all Panzer Is and IIs could be replaced by more powerful models. This might not seem an undue amount of time, but it must be remembered that other countries were also producing tanks at the time; for example, 969 tanks left British factories in 1939, with the Soviet Union producing no fewer than 3,110 in the same year. Clearly, time was not working in the Germans' favor.[31]

Neither did the Germans possess a qualitative edge in other weaponry. Like their predecessors in 1914, the infantry divisions dominated the German Army of 1939, but there were significant differences within the infantry divisions themselves. However, it seems that the most important changes were introduced during World War I. Before 1914, a German infantry regiment contained twelve rifle companies and one machine-gun company. In the rifle companies, all the soldiers were armed with rifles, while there were six machine guns in the machine-gun company. Thus the infantry regiment was an almost "pure" rifle unit. World War I witnessed substantial changes. By the end of 1916, there was already one machine-gun company per infantry battalion, which also included a mortar platoon and an additional fire support platoon. Additionally, other weapons were often attached to the battalion, such as flamethrowers and assault engineers.[32]

As a result of all these changes, a 1916 battalion commander had a far more diversified arsenal to coordinate than a regiment commander had been responsible for in 1914. In some cases, the trend was carried further down in the organization. The assault battalions created in the German Army during World War I contained mixed companies and even mixed platoons.

The importance of combining several different weapons was one of the most important lessons the Germans absorbed from World War I. Equally important was the conclusion that coordination of them should occur far down in the organization. These principles were adhered to when the Germans created new units in the interwar years, be it infantry divisions or armored formations.

As the German equipment was hardly much better than the weaponry possessed by their opponents, the German Army had to rely on some other kind of advantage. Little else remained except what can be termed "intellectual capital." This included the basic perception of the essentials of war, and the Germans put added emphasis on personnel rather than equipment. This was clearly stated by the basic German Army field manual, the *Heeresdienstvorschrift 300*, which was usually known as *"Truppenführung:"*

> The importance of the individual soldier remains decisive, despite technology; his importance has increased as battles are fought dispersed.
>
> The emptiness of the battlefield demands independently thinking and acting fighters, who consider every situation and utilize them determinedly and daringly, fully aware that success depends upon each man.
>
> The quality of the commander and his men determines the combat power of the unit. Superior combat power can offset numerical inferiority.
>
> From the youngest soldier to the highest commander is in all situations the greatest, independent commitment of all spiritual, mental and physical powers demanded. Only thus can the unit attain its maximum performance in a coordinated way. Only thus emerge men who even in the gravest situations maintain their courage and determination, thereby bringing weaker comrades along in daring deeds.[33]

Such emphasis on independence, decision-making and keenness to take initiative was not empty words; German soldiers frequently displayed these traits in action. This supports the notion that the most important component in the German efforts to create battle-worthy units was the personnel, something that is also evident in the German views on command and decision-making on the battlefield. A few paragraphs from *Truppenführung* are illuminating:

> 36. The mission and the situation constitute the basis for command. The mission indicates the aim to be achieved. He who has received it must not lose sight of it. A mission that contains several assignments may divert attention from the main task.
>
> *Uncertainty remains the rule. Seldom can precise knowledge on the enemy be obtained. It is demanded that clarity should be strived for, but to wait for intelligence in a tense situation is seldom a sign of strong-willed leadership, rather it is often a serious error.*

> 37. From the mission and the situation, the decision is derived. If the mission is insufficient as basis for decision, or if the situation has changed, a decision must reflect these circumstances. Anyone who cancels or changes a mission assumes responsibility and has to report it. He must however act in accordance with the overall situation ... When the decision has been made, it should not be changed unless good reasons exist. However, in war, rigid adherence to a decision can result in serious errors. To identify the proper moment and circumstances to make a new decision is art of command.[34]

The following is stated in paragraph 75:

> Orders may only be binding to the extent that circumstances can be foreseen. However, orders must often be issued in unclear situations.

Paragraph 3 provides an explanation, based on the German view on the character of war, for the content of the paragraphs above:

> The situations that can occur during war are of infinite multiplicity. They change often and unexpectedly. Seldom can they be foreseen. Incalculable entities often influence the events substantially. The own will conflicts with the independent will of the enemy. Friction and error are commonplace.

The three initial sentences in paragraph 37 are particularly interesting as they clearly prioritize assessment of the situation before orders are received. However, given the view on the uncertainty of war expressed in paragraphs 3 and 75, it is virtually a logical conclusion.

The *Truppenführung* can be regarded as an update of the older *Führung und Gefecht der Verbundenen Waffen* from 1921. Many paragraphs were lifted almost unchanged into the new manual. The last two of those given above are such examples, but they were formulated in a more concise—yet clearer—way. An important difference is the sentence: "Anyone who cancels or changes a mission assumes responsibility and has to report it." The older manual read: "... any commander who cancels or changes a mission assumes responsibility and has to report it." Thus the newer field manual allowed everyone the same freedom and responsibility that was previously reserved for commanders—an example of how decision-making was pushed down in the organization.

This German approach contrasted sharply to the French doctrine. A recurring theme in French military art during the interwar period is the

Good communications were crucial. The Germans used a variety of radio and wire communications to transmit information. Photo courtesy of Krigsarkivet, Stockholm.

"methodical battle." This meant that actions had to be carried out with precision and careful synchronization, which was given precedence over quick decision-making and local initiative. Centralized decision-making was emphasized and little room for initiative at lower command echelons was allowed.[35]

This differed starkly from the German art of war, where initiative was almost demanded at all levels. Furthermore, the German emphasis on local initiative was closely connected to the emphasis on time. Quick decision-making and issuing of orders were encouraged. Equally important was swiftness of execution, which required quick decision-making at all levels. If only the top commander made decisions, unexpected events—which were very common in war—would delay the execution. By conducting battles and other actions rapidly, the Germans intended to put the enemy units in an awkward situation, causing them to be surprised or in an unfavorable position. Thus the Germans hoped to get the upper hand despite their lack of other advantages. Most importantly, the Germans could conduct operations quicker due to the way they distributed decision-making, responsibility and initiative. This helped to compensate for the fact that German vehicles and aircraft were not generally faster than those of their opponents.

There were a few other important ideas that shaped the German art of war. One of them was the thinking around the concept of main effort. By concentrating resources to the area where the chances of success were greatest, a rapid decision could be forced. Dissipation of resources and efforts should be avoided. However, this concept was used flexibly; for example, a commander could denote a unit as main effort, thus indicating that other units should subordinate their actions to the unit designated as main effort by the commander.

The Germans sought decisive results, so attacks that only pushed the enemy back were to be avoided. Instead, they focused on the thorough defeat of the enemy to prevent them from being able to fight again. Encirclement was emphasized for this reason, preventing the enemy from retreating, as well as cutting off supply lines.

The focus on encirclement was connected to operational thinking that had been prominent in the German Army since at least the middle of the nineteenth century.[36] Different results could be achieved depending on spatial and temporal scale, not least as a consequence of cutting the enemy's supply lines. Occasionally, days or even weeks could pass before the enemy's combat capabilities were significantly impaired due to their supply lines being cut off. Many small encirclements were more difficult to conduct; sufficient depth was often required to prevent the encirclement being too loose and thereby difficult to maintain. Encirclements were accordingly more profitable if conducted at the operational level, from corps to army group level.[37]

Finally, the German Army emphasized offense. Defense was regarded as a temporary posture that could not produce decisive results. However, a wise combination of defense and attack could be the best alternative. Nevertheless, the German emphasis on offense should not be exaggerated—many of the traits fostered by offensive training were also useful in defense.

The German Army

> Six Panzer divisions (plus one *ad hoc* Panzer division "Kempf")
> Four light divisions (mechanized)
> Four motorized divisions
> Three mountain divisions
> Eighty-four infantry divisions
> One cavalry brigade

On the Verge of War

In 1939, the German armed forces had no superiority in numbers. A war against a weaker opponent, such as Poland, could be won by sheer force, but Germany could not similarly defeat major powers like France, Britain or the Soviet Union. Furthermore, the German capacity for a prolonged war was decidedly inferior. Given these limitations, a particular Blitzkrieg concept for winning wars in short campaigns would have been advantageous for the Germans, but neither their military forces nor the industrial and economical capabilities backing them up had been thus designed. Instead, they proceeded from their fundamental views on the character of war to identify the characteristics needed by armed forces to enable them to function well despite friction, hardships, the fog of war, and all the other difficulties in battle. New technology might well fit into the German concept, but it was not the starting point.

Despite the lack of superiority, Hitler had decided to proceed with his aggressive foreign policy. He ordered plans to be drawn up for a full-scale attack on Poland that was to be initiated before the fall rains. He simultaneously intensified his diplomatic efforts, believing that the western powers would not go to war over Poland. In a sense, this conclusion was reasonable as they had not resorted to arms to save Czechoslovakia. Perhaps Hitler was more concerned about what Stalin might do. In August, he sent his foreign secretary, Joachim von Ribbentrop, to Moscow for negotiations. An agreement was quickly reached that the two major powers would divide Poland between them. Other parts of Eastern Europe were also divided into a German and a Soviet sphere of interest.

While the diplomatic maneuvers proceeded, the German armed forces continued the planning and preparations for an attack on Poland. Nobody could know how a future war would end, but by the end of August, the Germans had gathered as strong a force as they dared along their eastern border.

CHAPTER 2

THE UNFINISHED CONCEPT

During the last ten days of August, the signs became ever more apparent to the Polish government. The war that had loomed was inevitable, but that was not surprising. After all, Poland had re-emerged and become independent as a result of two wars—World War I and the Russo-Polish war of 1919–20.[1] As a result of these wars, Poland was positioned between two major powers—Germany to the west and the Soviet Union in the east. Poland's exposed position was immediately evident, but as long as Germany was militarily weak following the Treaty of Versailles and the Soviet Union was exhausted from civil war, the young Polish republic was relatively secure. During the 1930s, however, the shadows of danger grew ever longer. Hitler's assumption of power meant that the danger from the west mounted quickly. In the east, the Red Army grew much stronger, but this was perhaps not fully appraised outside the Soviet Union. The Polish republic would have to walk a tightrope.[2]

During the second half of the 1930s, Hitler embarked upon a more aggressive foreign policy. Up to then, the Polish defense planning had mainly focused on the threat from the east, but with Hitler's mounting military strength, Germany appeared to be a more imminent danger. The Red Army was regarded as weak following Stalin's purges.

On August 23, news from Moscow revealed that Poland faced the most difficult situation conceivable. The Molotov-Ribbentrop pact, named after the foreign secretaries of Germany and the Soviet Union, had been signed. Officially it was a non-aggression pact, but the secret protocol divided Eastern Europe between the two signatory powers. Although the latter was kept secret, the public part of the agreement was ominous enough. No longer could the two major powers be played out against each other. Poland could only rely on remote France and Britain.

The ink on the agreement had barely dried before Hitler decided to launch the planned attack on Poland. The code-word to proceed with the attack was issued on the afternoon of August 25, revealing to the German armed forces that Poland should be attacked at dawn the following day.[3]

Overall plan for the German attack on Poland

As Poland signed a formal alliance with Britain, Hitler hesitated momentarily. At the last moment, the attack order was countermanded. However, a few attacking units were revealed to the Polish before the units received the order to abort. In particular, the Germans had prepared surprise attacks to capture the railroad bridge over the Wisła at Tczew, northern Poland, and the rail tunnel at the Jablunka Pass, southern Poland. These targets had to be captured intact, and the German troops detailed for the mission had already left the night before the attack; the countermanding order failed to reach them until just after they had entered Polish territory.[4]

The called-off attack alerted the Polish armed forces and government. Hitler did not remain indecisive for long, but when he ordered the code-word to be sent out for the second time—on August 31, 1939—the Polish armed forces had already began to position themselves for the impending German attack.

Case White

If the number of divisions or soldiers are compared, the Polish armed forces were not remarkably inferior to the invasion force assembled by the Germans, but the advantage becomes clearer when comparing equipment. In particular, the Germans had far more tanks and aircraft. However, most of the invading forces were made up of infantry divisions, which still made up around 85 percent of the German Army. The soldier's feet were expected to bring him forward, while field kitchens, baggage, much of the artillery and other supporting components relied on one of warfare's oldest creatures—the horse.[5]

Given the scarcity of mechanized formations, the Germans could be expected to concentrate them to certain sectors; indeed, one of the armies gathered was decidedly stronger than the other four. It was the 10th Army, commanded by General Walther von Reichenau, which had been given the mission to attack from central Silesia towards the Polish capital. It included no fewer than 160,000 men and reinforcements within the next few days would raise von Reichenau's manpower to over 200,000.[6]

The 10th Army comprised thirteen divisions, more than any other German army involved in the attack on Poland. Von Reichenau also had an unusually large share of the mechanized and motorized divisions—two Panzer divisions, three light divisions and two motorized infantry divisions.[7]

Further south, with the 14th Army directed to capture Krakow, the Germans committed two Panzer divisions and one light division. The remaining mobile divisions were subordinated to Army Group North. The 4th Army in Pomerania included one Panzer division and two motorized divisions. There was also one Panzer division in Pomerania, being held as an Army group reserve. Finally, there was an *ad hoc* Panzer division, the so-called *"Panzerverband Kempf,"* in East Prussia. It was made up of Army units as well as SS-units.[8]

The deployment suggests that the Germans made the strongest effort in the center, but also that they were prepared to strike powerful blows on the flanks. This is perhaps not a deployment in line with traditional notions on the Blitzkrieg, but given the weakness of the Polish defense, it mattered relatively little. The hopes of surprise had already been dashed, but the Polish Army had to defend an area that was very large compared to its resources. Inevitably, the defenses became thin and the chances to halt the Germans were slim.

At dawn on September 1, the German attack—Case White—was launched, marking the beginning of what would turn out to be the most destructive war in history. Tanks and aircraft crossed the border, but most notable were the innumerable soldiers trotting east, accompanied by horse-drawn carts, field kitchens, medical wagons and many other pieces of equipment that would not have surprised their fathers in 1914. Comparatively few German soldiers saw any tanks. Neither did they see many aircraft dropping bombs, as the Luftwaffe mainly attacked targets far away from the front line.

On the first day of the war, the Luftwaffe mainly sought to knock out the Polish Air Force by attacking it on the airfields. Conceived as a surprise attack, the aerial offensive can be regarded as a typical way to open a Blitzkrieg campaign. However, the first attacks accomplished little. As the Polish Air Force had already taken effective measures to protect its units, the Luftwaffe failed to strike vital targets. The Polish Air Force would put up a gallant defense for much of September.[9]

The other important component of posterity's perception of Blitzkrieg, the Panzer divisions, enjoyed mixed success on the first day of the war. At Mława, close to the southern border of East Prussia, Kempf's *ad hoc* division attacked. It was repelled by Polish defenders in fortified positions. At Mokra, the 4th Panzer Division attacked headlong into the Polish Wolynska cavalry brigade. The Poles did not yield and halted the German tanks in a costly battle.[10]

In the south, the 2nd Panzer Division attacked across the Carpathian Mountains, but it did not cause significant alarm in the Polish high command on the first day of the war. The 5th Panzer Division enjoyed greater success as it advanced to Pszczyna, 40 km from the border, but that area was not particularly significant to the Poles. Similarly, the 3rd Panzer Division successfully attacked through the Polish Corridor, but the Polish high command had not expected to be able to defend that area for long.[11]

Only one German Panzer division achieved something that might be termed a decisive success. Lieutenant-General Rudolf Schmidt's 1st Panzer Division exploited a gap in the Polish defenses and advanced 25 km through the main Polish defense line. On the second day of the war, the advance continued so swiftly that the Polish units could not keep pace. Schmidt's division, which belonged to Von Reichenau's army, split the Polish defense west of Wisła. Thus the Poles were trapped in a situation they could not wriggle away from.[12]

During the days that followed, the Luftwaffe continued to attack airfields and communications well behind the Polish front. No significant close support was offered to the German ground combat units. The image of the Luftwaffe as a "flying artillery" is hardly supported by the war diaries from the campaign. Neither does the image of tank armies storming forward find much support from the events as they actually took place. The German infantry divisions did most of the fighting.[13]

Two factors contributed to the less than splendid performance of the German Panzer formations. The first was insufficient training and the second was weak tanks. Former chief of general staff Ludwig Beck had warned against this. The 2nd Panzer Division fought a surprisingly uncoordinated action on September 2, and the deficiencies in this operation can only be attributed to insufficient training within the division. During the previously mentioned actions fought at Mokra and Mława, poor coordination between infantry and tanks, as well as the weak armor and armament of the German tanks themselves, were responsible for the poor performance exhibited by the 4th Panzer Division and *Panzerverband Kempf*. These were the consequences of the rapid expansion during the second half of the 1930s.[14]

The shortcomings could, of course, not be corrected during the campaign in Poland, but *Panzerverband Kempf* bypassed the Polish position at Mława after German infantry divisions had already created a gap to the east. Then the division could advance south, reaching the Narew River on September 5. It was committed to capturing the town of Różan.[15]

Tanks Against Forts at Różan

Captain Collin received the attack order just before noon on September 5. It was quite brief. His company was instructed to capture two old forts dating from World War I on the western outskirts of the small town of Różan in northern Poland. The mission was clear and did not require much elaboration. Instead, Collin could instruct his platoon commanders. In addition to Lieutenants Parow and Schnelle, who both were platoon commanders in Collin's company, two more platoons, commanded by Lieutenants Friese and Stöhr, were attached for the mission.

From positions northwest of Sielun, situated approximately 5 km from Różan, Collin's company and the battalion it formed part of would attack. The attack would unfold along the road to the west of Sielun and Różan. After crossing a creek, the battalion would advance to a point west of Różan, where Collin's company would turn left and attack two forts numbered 2 and 3 by the Germans.[16]

After instructing his subordinates, Collin mounted a tank. The regiment had been in action from the very first day of the war and had suffered losses; several tanks had either been knocked out by enemy fire or suffered breakdowns. Usually, Collin commanded from a specifically

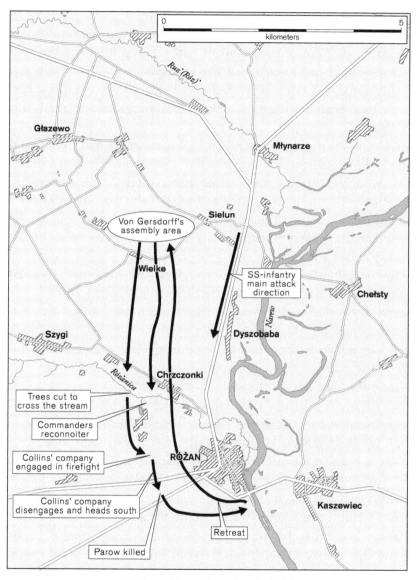

Battle at Różan September 5, 1939

designed command tank based on the Panzer I chassis. A fixed super-structure had replaced the revolving turret to accommodate a radio operator and sets for receiving and transmitting radio messages. In the original Panzer I, the interior was so crammed that only a receiving set could be accommodated. Such a limitation was, of course, wholly unacceptable to a commander, but it had sufficed for basic training and the Panzer I had been envisaged for such purposes. However, Collin's command tank had been damaged and taken to a workshop. He thus chose to lead from a Panzer II, whose vexed commander had to climb into a Panzer I.

Like Collin's normal command tank, the Panzer II had a crew of three, including the commander. The driver was positioned forward in the hull in both vehicles, but the tasks to be performed in the turret differed. In the Panzer II, the commander had to aim the gun in addition to his other duties. The radio operator doubled as loader of the 2-cm gun. This was far from ideal, but the small size of the Panzer I and Panzer II precluded better solutions.

Favorable fall weather had characterized the previous days. Except for some mist at dawn, visibility had been very good and the ground remained dry. Good weather reigned on September 5 too, when Collin's company began to move south. The commanders saw the sun ahead as they moved with their heads up through the turret hatches. They proceeded somewhat cautiously, perhaps remembering the debacle near Mława on the first day of the war.

After advancing slightly more than 1 km, Collin's company reached higher ground, where a halt was ordered. He observed the terrain closely through his field glasses. No sign of the enemy was seen, but fires were evidently raging in Różan. The church had been spared up to now, but Collin saw the flames reach it. Some of the villages closer to Collin's company were also ablaze.

While Collin considered what might lie ahead, he also glanced at the flanks. To the right, he could see tanks from Captain Hoheisel's company move forward into positions in line with his. Hoheisel's unit was also mainly equipped with Panzer Is and IIs, supplemented by a few heavier tanks. Crackling voices in the headphones interrupted Collin's thoughts. The battalion commander, Major von Gersdorff, had called for Hoheisel, but as all the company commanders used the same frequency, Collin overheard the conversation. The problem discussed was the poor

Armored cars provided firepower and mobility for the reconnaissance units of the Panzer divisions.
Photo courtesy of Krigsarkivet, Stockholm.

reconnaissance, which meant that it was not clear where the creek ahead could be crossed. After a brief conversation, von Gersdorff decided to send the heavy tanks—Panzer IIIs and IVs—forward to reconnoiter the creek, which was difficult to see due to its wooded banks.

Perhaps the Germans had hoped to reach the creek undetected, but the large dust clouds created by the tanks would almost certainly arouse the suspicion of the Poles. No fire was directed at the Germans, but the dust must have been visible from a great distance. To make matters worse, the German commander began to despair as no ford had been found, and thus the entire attack might stall.

It was too early to call off the attack. As they were not fired upon, the German commanders dismounted from their tanks and reconnoitered the creek on foot. Collin instructed Second Lieutenant Stöhr to guard the flank with his platoon while the search for a ford proceeded. Despite their efforts, the Germans could not find a suitable ford, but there was perhaps still one chance. Collin believed the creek could be crossed at a particular spot provided the muddy banks were reinforced. The tankers quickly had to stand in as lumberjacks. Armed with axes, they attacked the trees along the creek. The heat and sunshine made them sweat as the strenuous work proceeded, but after one hour they had reinforced the banks sufficiently to allow the tanks to cross the water barrier.

The men were allowed a rest before the tanks crossed, while some of the officers crossed the creek on foot and approached a haystack to observe the terrain ahead. Major von Gersdorff, Captain Hoheisel and Captain Collin could clearly see the landscape in front of them. They saw the two windmills that marked the entrance to the town on their maps, thus concluding that they were on the right track. Forts number 1 and 2 were supposed to be located close to the windmills, according to the information available to the German officers. When looking to the left, they could also see infantry from the SS-Regiment Deutschland advancing towards Różan. Artillery shells began to explode around the windmills.

Major von Gersdorff issued attack orders. Collin's company would attack on the left wing. There was still time for Collin to personally instruct his platoon commanders, except Stöhr, whose flanking mission had taken him too far away. At the haystack, Collin gave the necessary orders and pointed out the targets that could be seen from there.

Supported by the tree trunks, Collin's tanks negotiated the muddy banks and took up positions south of the creek, waiting for the final attack order. They did not have to wait for long. At around 2 p.m., the order "Forward!" was heard in the headsets. The drivers revved the engines, which roared loudly. The squeaking sound from the tracks indicated that the attack had begun. The terrain ahead was rather open, but undulating. The tankers had to navigate carefully to avoid exposing their vehicles unnecessarily.

The German formation successfully reached a position west of the forts they were to capture. They stopped here as buildings, haystacks and vegetation might have been concealing Polish defenders. There were no friendly forces ahead of the German tanks and so there was no risk of fratricide as they opened fire against suspected targets. Collin tried to observe the effectiveness of the fire, but it was difficult to judge if it had had the intended effect. Unfortunately, Collin's gun malfunctioned. Evidently dust had caused some part of the mechanism to jam.

Suddenly Collin was ordered to attack immediately. The intractable gun had not yet been attended to; armed only with a machine gun, Collin moved forward with the other tanks in his company. Very soon, a Polish antitank gun opened fire on the German left flank. Lieutenant Schelle immediately ordered his gunner to return fire. The dull and yet sharp sound from the gun revealed that a 7.5-cm shell left the barrel. The exploding shell threw up earth, stones and debris, but, as is common in war, it was difficult to know with certainty what effect the bursting shell had resulted in. Schelle remained stationary and continued to fire while the other tanks thrust forward.

Soon, von Gersdorff countermanded the attack order. Instead, Collin was to disengage and attack further south. Such a maneuver was not uncomplicated, but Collin managed to assemble his company and set it in motion southwards. The tanks crossed the northernmost of the two roads that ran west from Różan. At that moment, they took fire from Polish positions closer to the town.

Lieutenant Parow drove past Collin and took up a firing position. Collin watched as Parow fired three or four rounds before ordering his driver to continue forward. With the malfunctioning gun pointing straight forward, Collin's tank began to move, but almost immediately Collin saw a shell hit the turret of Parow's tank. Collin had hardly grasped what had happened before four men bailed out of the stricken tank and took cover. Another shell hit Parow's tank within a second. Collin drove closer to the damaged tank to identify the men who had abandoned it. He first saw the loader, then the radio operator. Slightly later, he saw Private Köhler bandaging a bleeding man who Collin recognized as Private Boehlke. At this moment, Collin realized that Parow had been killed.

The sight of Parow's damaged tank, as well as the men who had abandoned it, paralyzed Collin. Köhler, who attended the wounded Boehlke, had the presence of mind to wave Collin forward as his tank was in the line of fire of the Polish antitank weapons. Despite this, Collin remained numb until he had somehow absorbed the sight of Parow's tank and the four crewmen. Not until then could he bring himself to order the driver forward, thereby continuing the attack past the second of the two roads from Różan.

Suddenly, an NCO from the SS-Regiment Deutschland and a few of his men jumped aboard the tank. Collin warned them against this, but they took no notice of his advice; instead, the NCO asked Collin to close the hatch so he could obtain an unobstructed field of fire. "Madmen but brave," Collin and the radio operator, Guhl, said to each other.

An extended period of firing and short movements followed. Collin cursed the machine gun that malfunctioned. Guhl provided some consolation by handing Collin a lit cigarette, and the driver, Dörfle, offered him schnapps from his hip flask. Subsequently, Collin realized that the SS-NCO had disappeared. Guhl believed that he had been hit.

Collins finally passed fort 3 and approached fort 4, which meant that he and several other German tankers reached a point where they could look down into the depression where the river Narew flowed. They could see the road bridge and the open terrain on the eastern side of the river. Collin opened the turret hatch and found an SS-lieutenant on his tank. Except for four other SS-men on board a Panzer IV, no other infantry seemed to have accompanied Collin's tanks.

Collin's thoughts were abruptly interrupted by Polish fire. Despite the crammed interior of the tank, Collin ensured that the SS-officer came into the protection afforded by the thin armor of the Panzer III. The exhausted infantry officer was offered a cigarette and some schnapps. Unfortunately, he became entangled in the cable to Collin's headset and pulled it off. Collin had hardly managed to get his equipment in order before another order crackled in the headphones; his company was ordered to attack towards Rózan, northward along the river—a mission he deemed unsuitable.

It was quite late, and the sun had begun to set. It was so low that Collin was blinded when he turned his face west. Despite the poor visibility, the attack would continue. Collin's company proceeded, passing an obstacle, but then Polish antitank weapons opened up at long range. Fortunately for Collin, the Polish fire was short. He turned the turret clockwise, but suddenly he heard the SS-officer behind him moan. The officer was being squeezed by the revolving turret basket. At that same moment, the engine coughed and died. Collin was nearly overwhelmed by his rising fears, but he and his crew managed to connect the reserve fuel.

The battalion commander, Major von Gersdorff, drove along side Collin's stationary tank and shouted, "Why don't you move?" A moment later, Collin's driver started the engine and received orders from Collin to drive towards the dust cloud surrounding the other tanks. He objected as the dust made visibility very poor; at most, the driver would accept moving forward at a very slow pace. Collin urged him on and said that he would give the driver ample warning of obstacles as he could see more easily from his position in the turret. The tank resembled a drunken elephant staggering forward, but the attack was effectively aborted. Collin had to drive hard to catch up with his platoons, which headed east. Thus the German unit passed along the Polish forts, which began to fire at the flank of the tanks.

Collin finally caught up with one of his light platoons, but he had no idea where to find the rest of his company. He saw a few heavy tanks, but he did not know whether they belonged to his company or another. There was also a risk of friendly fire as the dust accumulated on the tanks to such an extent that the white crosses of the German tanks were hard to see. Collin's fears were soon realized, but not as he had anticipated; one of the heavy German tanks opened fire on German infantry, but the shell did not hit. Collin raised his fist and drove in front of the muzzle of the other tank to stop it from firing.

At this stage, Collin and his company had again reached the two roads running west from Rózan, which clearly showed that they were heading back. The dust made it impossible to see Parow's damaged tank, but

Collin could at least see the battalion commander's tank driving down into a depression and disappearing. Collin ordered one of his platoon commanders, Lieutenant Stöhr, to follow the battalion commander. One moment later, the ground shuddered as artillery shells exploded around the tanks. The tanks increased their speed in an attempt to escape north.

When Collin let his eyes drift to the right, he suddenly saw something that made him doubt the accuracy of his senses—German tanks formed up as if they were on a peacetime parade. Collin tried to make them move by using the radio, but this was met without any apparent success. The tanks finally assumed a formation better-suited to the realities of war and proceeded to the area where the creek could be forded.

As the evening became ever darker, Collin reached the creek and realized how exhausted he was after more than five hours of uninterrupted action. Gradually, he came to realize that the battalion had suffered dearly. Some of the light tanks were towed by their heavy brothers, but eleven tanks that had been hit were left behind. Additionally, some that had suffered mechanical breakdowns or had become stuck in difficult terrain remained behind. Those still capable of moving forded the creek in the light from burning houses. Some exhausted SS-infantry rode on the tanks.

After crossing the creek, the battalion created a hedgehog defense, but it soon received orders to move to the area west of Sielun, from where the attack had begun. Collin found the path to the staging area far too winding—his tank was very low on fuel—but eventually they reached it. When the arduous journey had been completed, the officers gathered and discussed the casualties and the pointlessness of the attack while the men bivouacked. Food was offered, but few of the officers and soldiers had much of an appetite after the depressing experience. The exhausted tankers were sent to some barns to sleep, while the baggage men defended the area during the night.

The Battle of Różan featured but one of the many examples of a German army that went into war without being properly prepared. At Różan, light tanks attacked fortifications, while the coordination between tanks, infantry and artillery was very poor. In this particular case, the Panzer division had been formed at very short notice by putting together components from the Army as well as the SS. This did not facilitate coordination, but Army divisions also suffered from shortcomings.

A Reconnaissance Mission

Traditionally, descriptions of Blitzkrieg have emphasized close cooperation between air power and tanks. However, the image of dive-bombers and tanks working intimately to achieve great success seems to be a reconstruction after the events, or a propaganda myth. Admittedly, the Luftwaffe often tried to support ground combat units, but the result was hardly impressive. In particular, the Luftwaffe attacked friendly ground units far too often. Ground units also sometimes shot down friendly aircraft.

These shortcomings did not mean that the Luftwaffe and the Army could not benefit at all from working with each other. There were significant advantages to be gained, but of another character. For example, as the German ground units advanced, they captured Polish air bases, thus diminishing the Polish Air Force's chances of putting up effective resistance to the Luftwaffe. This also worked in the opposite direction; for example, as the Luftwaffe dominated the skies, the Polish Army units tended to move in darkness. After a few days, this could result in increasing fatigue as the soldiers did not get enough sleep. The air attacks behind the front also strained the Polish supply situation. However, such effects were rarely immediate; time had to pass before the situation became serious. Thus, in a sense, these efforts could be regarded as a manifestation of attrition.

Obviously, the risks of fratricide were far less grave when the Luftwaffe attacked targets behind the Polish front. However, by attacking targets far behind the front, the Luftwaffe deprived itself of close cooperation with the Army. This choice was partly dictated by lack of inter-service training, which was the result of the rapid expansion earlier in the decade. The examples of successful cooperation between air and ground forces can be attributed to initiative by individual officers rather than systematic work.

However, there were other ways for the services to support each other. An often disregarded but nevertheless important component in the German successes was air reconnaissance. There are many examples of air units providing valuable information to German ground units. Reconnaissance aircraft took off early in the morning on September 1, despite the fog, to reconnoiter ahead of the attacking German 3rd Panzer Division. They initially reported that hardly any opposition could be expected, thus allowing the Panzers to attack swiftly. At around 11 a.m., the reconnaissance aircraft found Polish antitank defenses and immediately reported them to the Panzer division. One of its Panzer regiments was informed and quickly maneuvered accordingly, allowing it to knock out the Polish defense rapidly.[17]

Lieutenant Gerd Schroeder was twenty-five years old and had served with the 134th Infantry Regiment until summer 1939. In mid-July, his request to serve with a reconnaissance unit was approved. He was transferred to an air unit named "1. (H) 14 Pz," an air unit designated to cooperate with tank units. It was mainly supposed to conduct reconnaissance missions, courier flights and similar tasks. The unit included twelve reconnaissance aircraft and three liaison aircraft.[18]

On August 17, Schroeder was informed that he would, for the first time in his life, fly on the following day. His aircraft was to be flown by the experienced pilot Hannes Gaub, who was, according to Schroeder, a fine man. Unfortunately, technical problems with the aircraft caused Schroeder's first flight to be postponed. On the same day, Schroeder's unit was informed that it would be subordinated to the 2nd Panzer Division from August 19. The order provoked frantic activity. Fortunately, many of the necessary preparations had already been conducted, such as testing the gas masks, inoculation and similar procedures. Nevertheless, the equipment had to be unpacked as the unit would regroup from the Wien area to Engelswald (modern-day Mosnov) in Czechoslovakia. It soon became apparent to Schroeder and the other men that this was part of the preparations for the war they had feared.

On August 27, the unit was moved even closer to the Polish border, to Žilina. Two days later, Schroeder flew for the first time when he accompanied a reconnaissance mission along Poland's southern border. Great care was still taken not to fly over Polish territory, but soon such caution would be a thing of the past.

The penultimate day of August was remarkably tranquil. Schroeder had met a female singer and they had went for walks in the beautiful and serene environs. It seemed inconceivable that a war was imminent, but on the following day Schroeder was again reminded of the risk of war. He was sent on another reconnaissance mission. Hannes Gaub was again at the controls and Schroeder ensured that numerous photographs were taken. The other reconnaissance aircraft in the unit were also sent on similar missions on that day. A few hours later, the final instructions for the attack on September 1 were issued and liaison officers were sent to the 2nd Panzer Division.

Schroeder and his fellows were awakened at exactly 3 a.m. It seemed almost unreal that a war was about to begin. After twenty minutes, five crews had been briefed. Schroeder noted that the men looked pale despite their efforts to appear resolute and grim. They all grasped the severity of the situation. Exercises and enjoyment had come to an end. When the briefing was completed, the airmen went to their machines. Every aircraft had a crew of two, the pilot and the observer. The latter was the commander. Thus Schroeder, as a lieutenant, was higher in rank than Gaub, who was at the controls of the Henschel Hs 126. The mechanics had already ensured that the aircraft was ready for take-off. At 4.45 a.m., Schroeder and Gaub climbed on board to begin their mission, during which they would drop smoke over designated areas. They immediately received the go-ahead. Gaub increased the throttle and the small aircraft rapidly increased speed. The air rushed ever quicker against the two heads protruding from the open cabin. The ground crew saw the small aircraft dart along the runway and finally take off. Its peculiar silhouette, caused by the wing mounted above the fuselage, contrasted against the dull sky.

Gaub maneuvered the aircraft into a valley through which he and Schroeder had previously flown, but this time they did not turn before reaching the Polish border. Instead, they aimed for a mountain called Babia Góra, where Polish artillery directors were believed to have observation posts. However, neither Schroeder nor Gaub saw anything to confirm this assumption; they only saw a few wooden huts dotted across the tranquil landscape.

As Gaub and Schroeder feared Polish antiaircraft fire, they flew at quite a high altitude, but no rounds or bullets were fired at the small plane. As they were inexperienced, Gaub and Schroeder did not know the optimum altitude for the mission to which they had been assigned. After some time, Schroeder decided to proceed at lower altitude to enable him to see better. Suddenly he discovered some people moving on the ground. Instinctively, he fired a few machine-gun bursts, but then realized he had overreacted considerably. At that time Schroeder and Gaub had reached the position where they would begin to diffuse artificial fog, which hopefully would blind enemy fire directors. Schroeder activated the system and Gaub maneuvered the Henschel aircraft to cover the designated area. Schroeder thought Gaub handled the plane almost like a paintbrush, covering the ground with fog released by the unit.

After concealing the designated area in fog, Schroeder found a few people near a small building. Had the aircraft carried bombs, he could have released them, but the weight of the fog unit prevented any other payload. When all the fog had been released, Gaub and Schroeder turned to fire a few machine-gun bursts at the suspected persons near the small building, but the results were inconclusive.

When they headed back to the air base, Schroeder pondered the mission, which he thought had been quite stupid. According to him, the use of the artificial fog was nonsense. The presumed fire directors were most likely nothing more than products of imagination; the people on the ground were, perhaps, simply a family visiting a hut. His thoughts were interrupted when the aircraft hit the runway at 6.13 a.m. He was consumed by his misgivings.

The NCO Lohsack served in the same unit as Schroeder. Together with Sergeant Nieber, he went to his aircraft, a Heinkel He 46. The mechanics made their final preparations under an increasingly lighter sky. When they reached the aircraft, Lohsack and Nieber discussed their mission with the other aircrews over a map. While the mechanics fitted bombs underneath Lohsack's and Nieber's plane, the final details of the mission were discussed. Lohsack felt an eerie feeling in his stomach. This would be his first combat mission—and perhaps also his last.

As the Heinkel's engines were started, Lohsack and Nieber entered the cabin. Lohsack checked the instruments for the last time before take-off. One of the mechanics showed him the emergency lever for the bombs. Nieber checked his machine gun and then tapped Lohsack's shoulder to indicate that everything was okay. The brake blocks were removed and the aircraft began to move forward. Lohsack gave full throttle, and soon the plane became airborne. Ahead, Lohsack and Nieber could see Gaub and Schroeder's aircraft. Suddenly, Lohsack saw the smoke cloud from a bursting antiaircraft shell—unpleasantly close. Nieber and Lohsack quickly fired a recognition flare. The antiaircraft battery that had fired was German.

Clouds of smoke could be discerned beyond the horizon, giving the first indication of war. Czarny-Dunajec and Jablonka were ablaze. When they reached the forward German positions on the ground, Lohsack fired more recognition flares and then set course for Babia Góra. He saw the fog spewing out from Schroeder's aircraft before it turned back towards the air base. Lohsack continued at low altitude and flew over some wooden buildings, where Nieber dropped five bombs. From Lohsack's position, the bursts almost looked pretty. However, no enemy observers could be seen. Lohsack went down to an altitude of 800 meters to see better. A machine gun opened fire, but it did not hit the aircraft. Lohsack again signaled his identity and the German machine gun was silenced.

Somewhat later, Lohsack found he could see German tanks. A blown-up bridge had forced them to halt and Polish trenches could be seen beyond the small river, but it was impossible to see if they were occupied from an altitude of 800 meters. Lohsack and Nieber had to fly lower, and at a mere 10 meters from the ground they could see that the first line was undefended, as was the second. However, the third was clearly defended. The defenses included a machine gun, which opened fire on the small German aircraft. Lohsack turned and Nieber released the last bomb, aiming at the machine gun, but it fell several meters from the Polish trench.

After the bomb had exploded, Lohsack observed the helmets worn by the crew of the machine gun. They resembled German steel helmets.

He suddenly became uncertain. Had they bombed their own comrades? However, Nieber was positive that the soldiers were Polish and turned to fire one final machine-gun burst along the trench. He then knocked on Lohsack's head to indicate that they should return to base. Lohsack turned his head and saw that Nieber's hand was all bloody, but he just laughed and shook his head.

When they approached Žilina, Nieber and Lohsack saw how groups of local citizens had gathered below, possibly after being brusquely awakened by the thunder of the German artillery or German motor vehicles crowding the roads. At first, Lohsack and Nieber saw nobody when they arrived at the air base. However, when the landing wheels hit the ground, mechanics suddenly appeared and surrounded the Heinkel. At this moment, Lohsack realized that Nieber had injured his hand on the machine gun. It also turned out that two bullets had hit the aircraft without causing any significant damage.

After the landing, Lohsack and Nieber went to the division commander, Major Eberhardt, for debriefing. Barely concealing their pride, the two airmen reported on their observations during the mission. Other crews of the division were also debriefed and soon a report could be sent to the 2nd Panzer Division indicating that the first Polish defense line was undefended, as was the second, but resistance could be expected at Wadowka.

These were some of the first reconnaissance missions flown during the war. Many more would be conducted, not least by German aircrews. Units of the kind Schroeder, Gaub, Nieber and Lohsack served in were designed specifically to conduct reconnaissance missions for Army divisions, but there were many other reconnaissance units in the German Air Force. In fact, reconnaissance units made up about one fifth of the Luftwaffe.[19]

Further reconnaissance missions were conducted by 1. (H) 14 Pz on September 1 and the observations made were continuously reported to the 2nd Panzer Division. Thus the division could maneuver more effectively, advancing more rapidly on the ground when it knew if the terrain ahead was not defended by the enemy. Additionally, flank cover could be reduced if air units reported that no threat existed.

This is an example of the contribution made by air reconnaissance units. Important information could rapidly be transmitted by radio, or simply by dropping a canister with written messages near the staff or command posts. As the information might soon be out of date, rapid transmission was vital.

It is, of course, difficult to compare the importance of different kinds of efforts, but it is conceivable that the Germans benefitted more from air reconnaissance than close air support. Admittedly, they would go on to develop more efficient close air support as the war progressed, but the value of air reconnaissance would remain.

The examples from this unit also indicate that identification was often problematic or downright erroneous. The aircraft were fired upon by German flak and the airmen attacked ground targets without knowing with reasonable certainty whether they were friendly soldiers, enemy soldiers or even civilians. It seems that an attitude of "fire first and ask questions later" prevailed. This resulted in numerous friendly fire casualties, but also civilian casualties.

Armored Reconnaissance

The German emphasis on reconnaissance is not only evident in the Luftwaffe. The Army had also created many reconnaissance units. A regular infantry division included a reconnaissance battalion, but some of the recently raised formations still lacked such a unit. The Panzer divisions were even better equipped; not only did they have a well-equipped recon battalion, they usually had a motorcycle battalion as well. The latter was often assigned reconnaissance missions as the mobility of the vehicles suited this type of work. Armored cars were an important component of the recon battalions included in the German Panzer divisions; their mobility allowed them to find and exploit gaps in enemy defenses, and their light armor afforded protection against low-caliber enemy weapons and shrapnel from bursting artillery shells. The cars were also provided with an extra driver, who was positioned in the rear of the vehicle. He could quickly drive the car away from dangerous situations as several reverse gears were included in the gearbox.

During the first week of September, the recon units served the Germans well; the operations had immediately taken on a fluid character, which suited these units. In the north, the Germans cut off the so-called Polish Corridor in three days and established a land connection between Pomerania and East Prussia. The German attack southward from East Prussia in the area around Mława forced the Polish defenders to fall back on the Wisła and Narew rivers. In the south, German forces closed in on Krakow, and the Polish defense ahead of them crumbled.[20]

The Polish high command had not expected to halt the German attack close to the border. Instead, the western armies would retreat towards the southeastern parts of Poland; when French forces attacked western

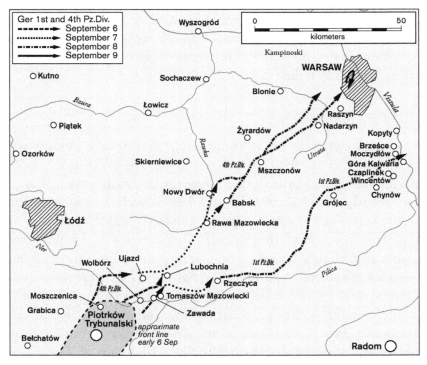

German operations in the Warsaw area September 6–9, 1939

Germany, the Poles would launch a counteroffensive. Unfortunately, the expected French offensive did not materialize. Furthermore, the German pressure caused the Polish retreat to become ever more uncoordinated, particularly in the center.[21]

The German 1st Panzer Division had already penetrated the Polish defenses near Kłobuck on the first day of the war, and then it had dashed east to cross the Warta River. As soon as bridgeheads had been established, it turned northeast, towards Warsaw. It would thereby create a situation the Polish Army could not extricate itself from.[22]

The 1st Panzer Division reached a point just south of Piotrków on the evening of September 4. It had advanced more than 110 km in four days, leaving several Polish formations behind. A Polish counterattack on the following day failed. The 1st Panzer Division defeated the Polish 19th Division and captured Piotrków on September 5.[23]

The fall of Piotrków was a severe setback for the Poles, but the Germans did not rest. The 1st Panzer Division—as well as the 4th, which had advanced alongside it—immediately continued advancing towards the Polish capital. Fierce battles raged on September 6 too, but both German divisions gained ground inexorably and captured Tomaszów, thus opening the roads to Warsaw.[24]

Both the 1st and 4th Panzer Divisions continued attacking in a north-easterly direction, with Reinhardt's 4th on the left and Schmidt's 1st on the right. They aimed for Warsaw and the Wisła. Reinhardt headed straight towards the Polish capital while Schmidt strived to establish a bridgehead on the eastern bank of the Wisła. During September 7, the 1st Panzer Division advanced from Tomaszów Trybunalski to Rzeczyca, covering approximately 25 km. On the following day, the divisional motorcycle battalion was ordered to form a vanguard and was reinforced by tanks from the divisional Panzer brigade as well as three armored cars from the reconnaissance battalion.[25]

The motorcyclists received their orders at 4 a.m. on September 8. They were very tired after a week of continuous fighting and advancing. They had also been marching on congested roads until 10 p.m. the night before. Despite the lack of sleep, it was noted in the battalion's war diary that "this [mission] was a real task for motorcyclists, which dispelled all fatigue." This cheerful mood was helpful, not least as the battalion was only allowed half an hour to prepare the attack.[26]

The hasty preparations created a throng along the road from which the motorcyclists and the attached tanks and armored cars would launch the attack. The confusion was aggravated by the debris left behind by retreating Polish units. It appeared that a Polish supply unit had previously been deployed along the road; field kitchens and damaged vehicles littered the area and partly blocked the roads. Some of the attached German tanks pushed damaged vehicles aside, thus allowing other German vehicles to get into position in time for the attack. At dawn, many Polish soldiers approached with their hands above the heads. The prisoners were quickly dispatched to German rear formations.[27]

Despite the hectic preparations, the 1st Company of the battalion was able to set out on time, joined by the tanks and armored cars attached. Lieutenant Voss commanded the armored car section detached from the reconnaissance battalion, and he was found at the tip of the attack. He recalled that no Polish defenders were seen initially. When they approached Nowo Miasto, his soldiers found a shepherd who, after a while, was willing to provide some information. He claimed that Polish cavalry had passed by around an hour earlier, but the Germans received the information with misgivings.[28]

Lieutenant Voss ordered his section to proceed into Nowo Miasto, and no Polish soldiers prevented his armored cars from entering the western parts of the village. The small German force continued into the center and reached the market square, which looked comic according to Voss. The section continued east, passed the outskirts of the village and reached the cemetery. Suddenly, shots rang out, prompting an immediate German reaction. The motorcyclists halted, dismounted and attacked the area from where the shots had been fired. Meanwhile, the tanks and Voss's armored cars opened fire.[29]

The rapid German reaction quickly scattered the defenders, and the armored cars set out to pursuit the retreating Poles, who were raked by fire from German automatic weapons. After a brief chase, Voss and his men found a bunch of Polish baggage vehicles at a distance of approximately 250 meters. They immediately shifted their fire to the new target and quickly destroyed it.

The German tanks and armored cars wasted no time, proceeding at high speed and leaving large dust clouds behind them—which were perhaps more annoying than the Polish resistance. A few small groups of enemy cavalrymen were seen by the Germans and fired upon, but except for such skirmishes, the German advance guards reached Grójec at 10 a.m. without meeting any resistance.[30]

Thus far, the Germans had advanced almost 60 km in little more than five hours, resulting in an average speed of approximately 10 km per hour. This may not appear particularly impressive at first glance considering that the motorcycles could be driven much faster. However, the pace displayed by the German formation was exceptionally high. Combat units can seldom drive forward carelessly; they have to halt frequently, searching the edges of woods and perhaps opening fire on areas where the enemy might have prepared ambushes. This was not only vital to ensure that the men survived; a vehicle hitting a mine might block an important road. Thus, mechanized units seldom advanced much faster than a brisk walker could manage in peacetime.

If the units seldom advanced more rapidly than a walking man, what was the point of mechanization? The answer lies in the time lost due to the many halts—time spent looking for signs of enemy units or minefields, issuing orders, resting, eating and so on. As so much time was lost on such activities, it was in fact even more important to move rapidly when there was an opportunity. The dash made by the motorcycle battalion of 1st Panzer Division on the morning of September 8 was more like a combination of rushes and pauses rather than a smooth and steady advance at an almost constant pace.

After capturing Grójec, the motorcycle battalion aimed for Chynów, located 16 km to the east. The village was captured by the Germans an hour later, after which only 12 km separated them from Góra Kalwaria, where the Germans believed there were bridges across the Wisła. To the west of Góra Kalwaria, at Czaplinek, the German battalion paused to change battle formation. The 1st Company was to advance north of Góra Kalwaria, through Moczydlow and Brzesce to Kopyty, where, according to German intelligence, a Polish military bridge across the Wisła was located. In addition to the tank platoon that had been attached to the 1st Company, it was also reinforced by a platoon from the divisional engineer battalion.[31]

The 1st Company began its attack at 1 p.m. and made good progress. It passed Góra Kalwaria, which was undefended. Voss saw several Jews on the streets of the town. They seemed very surprised to him, but the German unit did not waste any time and quickly pushed north along the road to Moczydlow and Brzesce. Both of these small towns were captured without much fighting. The German force swiftly proceeded towards Kopyty, which was situated approximately 10 km north of Góra Kalwaria.

The motorcyclists carefully approached the village, which was little more than a collection of houses along the riverbank. As always, tension was high before a built-up area was entered. This anxiety usually proved to be excessive, but not on this occasion. Violent fighting erupted when the Germans drove into the village. The armored cars commanded by Voss participated in the attack, being surprised by an ambush and fired on from behind. Polish defenders fought from buildings and fired from windows and cellar openings. The Germans had to clear the village, and many of the buildings caught fire in the process. The fighting was brief as these Polish defenders were stragglers and civilians who had not been able to retreat across the Wisła. The bridge at Kopyty no longer existed; only a small ferry was found, and this was used to bring a platoon across the river. However, the division commander, Lieutenant-General Rudolf Schmidt, arrived soon afterwards and decided that the platoon should pull back. The Germans had to contend with searching the abandoned Polish vehicles and carts. In addition to large quantities of ammunition, many boxes of cigarettes were found. Voss seized so many cigarettes that he could generously offer some to his comrades in the reconnaissance battalion when he returned in the evening.[32]

During the pause at Czaplinek, attack orders were not only issued to the 1st Company. The 2nd Company also received orders to attack. It was to advance through Wincentów, south of Góra Kalwaria, and capture Polish war bridges. A tank platoon was attached for the mission, as was an engineer platoon and an infantry howitzer platoon. The latter was part of the battalion's heavy company. Such *ad hoc* battle groups were commonplace in the German Army at virtually every level of the organization. It would prove to be a characteristic of the Army throughout the war.[33]

German battalions usually comprised four companies, among which the fourth might be a heavy company equipped with heavy machine guns, infantry howitzers, mortars and other heavy weapons. The motorcycle battalion of the 1st Panzer Division adhered to this pattern.[34]

The battle group, formed with the 2nd Company as its nucleus, attacked almost immediately. A quick dash brought it to the bank of the Wisła at Brzumin, approximately 10 km southeast of Góra Kalwaria. Thus far it had not been delayed by any significant opposition, but when the motorcyclists reached the river they found that the Polish bridge had already been destroyed in five places. Prepared Polish defenses could be seen on the opposite side of the river. The Germans opened fire on them and the Poles responded.[35]

Soon afterwards, the motorcyclists were subjected to an air attack. As the aircraft appeared to be German, they regarded it as yet another case of fratricide. Apparently, the Luftwaffe did not realize that German ground units had already reached the Wisła in this area, presuming that the ground units had to be Polish. A note in the motorcycle battalion's war diary read: "… probably once more were we attacked by German aircraft."[36]

The Polish fire ceased shortly after 4.30 p.m., but this mattered little to the Germans; they were unable to cross the river here anyway, but that would subsequently prove to be inconsequential. By the evening of September 8, the German 3rd Army had already reached the Bug River approximately 75 km east of Warsaw. Considering the weak defense offered by Polish forces along the Bug, the area east of Wisła was already seriously threatened. When the German XIX Corps launched an attack with two Panzer divisions and two motorized divisions further east, the Polish situation deteriorated even further. On the same day, the German 4th Panzer Division reached the outskirts of Warsaw, tearing the Polish center apart together with the 1st Panzer Division and leaving its remnants behind. In southern Poland, the Germans captured Kraków on September 6 and continued east at high speed. The Polish defense had been too disorganized to allow a coordinated resistance against the German invaders.[37]

The Riflemen

The rapid advance conducted by the German 1st and 4th Panzer Divisions on September 8 is a good example of the mobility these formations possessed. Formation for formation, the German Panzer divisions were

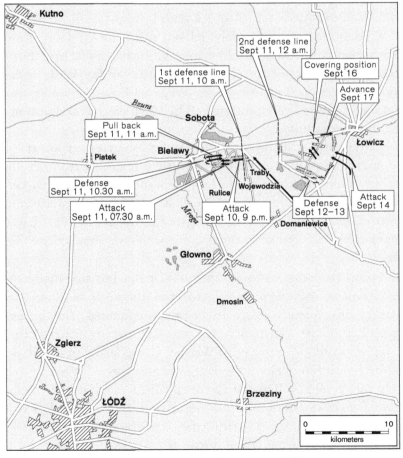

Battle at Lowicz September 11–17, 1939

undoubtedly more important than the infantry divisions during the September campaign. On the other hand, the infantry divisions were far more numerous. Overall, they carried the main burden of the fighting, and quite often they managed to match the advance rate of the Panzer divisions.

Marching was one of the most common activities for the German riflemen. Lieutenant Scharnagl commanded a platoon in the German 10th Infantry Division, which fought with the 8th Army. From the staging area in Silesia, just east of Breslau, he and the other riflemen in the division marched approximately 160 km in the first week of the war.[38]

The dawn of September 10 revealed a bright, sunny day. Lieutenant Scharnagl had spent the night in a barn near Dmosin, around 20 km northeast of Łódź. He had badly needed a good sleep after the hardships of the previous days. At 6 a.m., he and his men were suddenly alerted by the warning: "The Poles are coming!" Polish cavalry could indeed be seen, but the riders appeared to head north. The platoon nevertheless moved into a defensive position, but the Poles had soon moved so far away that they could no longer be seen. Instead, the German unit made itself ready for another day of marching. Many soldiers gathered around wells, where they washed and shaved. A few patrols returned with prisoners, which were sent to the rear.[39]

As the soldiers prepared to march, a rumor began to circulate that the day would instead be devoted to rest. If so, it would be the first day of rest since the war began. However, the soldiers' hopes were dashed when an order to march was received at 11.45 a.m. by the company Scharnagl belonged to. Intelligence indicated that Polish forces were located near Sobota and they were to be attacked by the 20th Infantry Regiment, whose III Battalion Scharnagl belonged to.[40]

Sobota was located approximately 25 km north-northwest of Dmosin. Thus Scharnagl would have to march partly backwards after arduously striding towards Warsaw. As commander of an infantry platoon, Scharnagl was not informed of the overall situation, but had he received such information, he would have known that the only major Polish counterattack in September had precipitated the German reaction Scharnagl's platoon was part of. Commanded by General Kutrzeba, the Polish Poznań Army attacked southward from the Kutno area at dusk on September 9. Despite almost being cut off from Warsaw when the Germans reached the outskirts of the capital, Kutrzeba still attacked south. Elements from the German 10th Division had already been attacked when Scharnagl's platoon received their marching orders.[41]

It is unsurprising that Scharnagl, like virtually all of the junior officers and enlisted men, was uninformed of the bigger picture. They seldom received information regarding events far beyond the missions they were given. This was partly motivated by the limited capacity of the German information systems, but the need for secrecy was the chief reason. However, the paucity of information resulted in rumors flourishing.

Scharnagl and his men did not ponder long on the broader events as they marched through Głowno. Instead, their attention was drawn to the immense number of refugees crowding the roads. During the days of September 1939, vast numbers of refugees moved along the roads, walking slowly while pulling carts loaded with precious belongings.[42]

Scharnagl and his soldiers did not have to march far. All the companies of the battalion moved to Domaniewice, where they were loaded onto trucks in the afternoon. The vehicles transported them to their new staging area. Scharnagl's platoon was among the last to be taken onboard the trucks, and he and his men ate while waiting. They would have to wait longer than expected; at 6 p.m., the trucks that were supposed to take them to Traby had still not appeared. The men were not bothered—waiting is part of the soldier's life. However, this time their wait was interrupted by an artillery shell bursting uncomfortably close to them. Another fell not far from the nearby church. Scharnagl's platoon moved to a field further away, where they were soon loaded onto the trucks bringing them to Traby.[43]

They arrived at Traby at dusk and began to dig shelters. The 9th Company, to which Scharnagl's platoon belonged, was dug in behind the 10th and 11th companies, near the battalion staff. The 10th Company had already been in action and captured the village of Wojewodza, where it had dug in for the night. Part of the village was still ablaze, and the glare illuminated the surroundings. The fighting had been costly, with one of the German platoon commanders, Lieutenant Kammermaier, being killed. The surgeon, Dr Sticht, had decided to set up his dressing station at a building in Wojewodza, very close to the front line. He had many soldiers to attend to, taking care of the wounded Polish soldiers as well as the Germans.[44]

No more fighting took place during the night, but Scharnagl and his men hardly got any rest. At midnight, they were sent to bring up ammunition for the company. It was to be delivered to Traby, but the vehicles did not arrive with the desperately needed ammunition until 2 a.m. The most arduous element of the work came after the ammunition had been unloaded, as it still had to be carried to the forward positions—a distance of almost 3 km. The soldiers panted and sweated from their heavy burdens, but they had no other option; the ammunition might be badly needed just hours later.[45]

After the ammunition had been carried forward, Scharnagl and his men received a new task. The regimental infantry howitzers had to be moved, and Scharnagl's platoon was to provide the muscle required. The howitzers were urgently needed as the battalion was to attack at 5.30 a.m. The men persuaded themselves that this was the final battle they would have to fight; then the campaign would be decided. Thereby they found the strength to overcome their fatigue.[46]

The idea was to bring the howitzers into firing positions at the western outskirts of Wojewodza, but deep sand proved impossible to overcome. The soldiers' strength proved insufficient to bring the guns—which had a caliber of 7.5 cm and a weight of 400 kg—past the sand. When the moment to begin the attack arrived, only the ammunition for the infantry howitzers had been moved forward. However, the division commander, Lieutenant-General von Cochenhausen, regarded the attack as too important to accept any delay. He believed the attack would pose a threat to Kutrzeba's flank. The German General and his staff had been awake all night, working to find different ways to handle the serious situation resulting from Kutrzeba's attack.[47]

The absence of the guns did not initially impair the German attack. The divisional artillery fired a five-minute barrage before the infantry attacked, and the first objective, hill 116, was captured without encountering any opposition. At this stage, the German fire controllers lost contact with their batteries. The attack nevertheless continued and quickly reached the village of Rulice. No Polish defenses had been encountered thus far.[48]

With the capture of Rulice, the German battalion had advanced approximately 1 kilometer. The commander ordered a brief pause to marshal his units before resuming the attack. The next objective was a stream east of Bielawy. On approach to the stream, the Germans spotted Polish soldiers. A firefight lasting around an hour ensued, after which the Germans ran low on ammunition despite the nocturnal efforts of Scharnagl and his men. At this moment, the German artillery intervened and staved off a Polish counterattack.[49]

At noon, Scharnagl saw II Battalion retreat. It had fought further north and became subjected to heavy Polish fire, forcing it to withdraw after suffering casualties. Scharnagl's battalion also sustained losses. One of the company commanders, Lieutenant Seiff—who had already been wounded during the campaign and had just returned from the hospital— was mortally wounded by a rifle bullet. One of the platoon commanders was also hit, but he was very lucky; a shell exploded close to him and a splinter tore a hole in his trousers, but it passed his leg without even touching it. The situation was dire, and at around 1.30 p.m. III Battalion had almost exhausted its ammunition.[50]

III Battalion found itself in an awkward position when the other two battalions retreated. It was engulfed in a Polish attack and fired upon from three sides, but it had insufficient ammunition to fight back. At the last moment, it received an order to pull back to Traby. The order had been issued by Lieutenant-General von Weichs, the commander of XIII Corps, to which the 10th Infantry Division was subordinated. By positioning himself at the front, he could see with his own eyes how the fighting had proceeded and issued the retreat order. There was no time to waste as significant parts of the 20th Regiment were almost surrounded, but they escaped thanks to the timely retreat.[51]

Almost inevitably, Polish fire inflicted casualties as the Germans pulled back. An NCO named Grüner ensured that the men of his squad, who still had some ammunition, covered the retreating German soldiers. He was awarded the Iron Cross for this feat, the first soldier in his company to receive the coveted distinction. However, despite his effort, the Germans suffered serious casualties. On this day, Scharnagl's battalion lost thirteen men killed in action, forty-nine wounded and eight missing—almost 10 percent of its personnel.[52]

This example is somewhat unusual as it shows German soldiers on the defensive, which was not particularly common during the September 1939 campaign. Scharnagl and the other men of the 20th Infantry Regiment became embroiled in a costly defensive battle, as were the soldiers of many other German regiments during Kutrzeba's offensive. The units of the German 30th Infantry Division were hit particularly hard.[53]

The attack conducted by General Kutrzeba's Poznań army would be known as the "Battle of the Bzura." According to the main Polish defense plan, the armed forces would gradually pull back to the eastern part of the country. The Polish ground forces mainly attempted to adhere to this intention, and Kutrzeba's attack was the sole major exception. However, at this stage of the campaign—almost two weeks into September—the Germans had fundamentally undermined the Polish plans. Far to the east, General Guderian's XIX Corps was closing in on Brest-Litovsk, where the Polish high command had been located since it abandoned Warsaw. In the south, the Germans had reached the outskirts of Lwów and a large part of the Polish Army had been surrounded along the Wisła. The campaign was effectively decided after twelve days, and Kutrzeba's offensive would result in most of his soldiers ending up as prisoners of war.[54]

Pastoral Care

Although the campaign had been decided after around ten days, Polish forces continued to fight, despite the fact that a coordinated defense was no longer possible. The fighting took on a more local character, and such actions could be very costly, resulting in much work for the field hospitals.

Another busy category of personnel was the field chaplains. The German armed forces strived to connect its units with a specific area in Germany. For example, most of the conscripts in a division were usually drafted from one specific region, although this principle could not be fully adhered to at all times. As German citizens comprised both Catholics and Protestants, units often had one chaplain for each of these two denominations of Christianity. Catholic and Protestant chaplains often worked in pairs as they could expect to meet soldiers of both faiths.

Rüdiger Alberti served as a field chaplain during the campaign in Poland. His tasks included conducting services and burials, but he also devoted much time to visiting and talking with wounded soldiers at hospitals. The wounds suffered by those who had been brought to hospital could differ greatly; some were so badly wounded that they were close to death, while others might survive as invalids. However, most of the wounded were able to return to service after a period of convalescence.[55]

The hospitals had different departments for various wounds. Alberti visited several of them. One day, he and another priest arrived at a hospital in Częstochowa, approximately 30 km east of the German border, where the badly wounded were treated. The hospital was very modern. In the large building, which had the Red Cross flag hoisted on the roof, more than 100 wounded received care and treatment. There was a column of trucks outside the building. More wounded were being unloaded and brought into the hospital, as Alberti entered.[56]

He walked along a corridor and could easily see that the staff had much to do. Wounded soldiers sat waiting on chairs in the corridors. The head of one of the men was heavily bandaged; he remained silent and did not move. A bullet had gone straight through his jaw, and his face was soaked in blood. Alberti put a hand on the wounded man's shoulder, looked into his eyes and tried to comfort him with a few well-chosen words. The wounded man could not even move his head, but Alberti sensed a streak of gratitude in his eyes.[57]

Together with the other priest, Alberti proceeded to the physician who was responsible for the reception of the wounded. Alberti was hardly able to recognize the man. He was frightfully pale; not a trace of a spark could be seen in his eyes, and his stamina seemed to be completely drained. A Red Cross nurse sat on a bench nearby and appeared similarly exhausted. During the first days of the war, the doctor and the nurse had been hale and hearty, but now they were pallid from exertion. There were no exceptions to this exhaustion; one of the surgeons had fallen asleep while eating his lunch, having worked all the previous night.[58]

The two chaplains continued into a room where soldiers who had been hit in the lungs were resting. There were eight beds, with a very pale soldier in each of them. Some already appeared to have the marks of death on their faces. Virtually all the soldiers were apathetic. One by one, the two priests walked around to talk quietly with the soldiers, to comfort and console them. It was difficult as the soldiers were very downhearted, except for a comparatively cheerful NCO. He was delighted by the visit and became even more so when the chaplains promised to return later. He strongly wished to sit up in his bed, but he could not—the damage to his lung made every movement painful.[59]

Alberti and the other priest said prayers for each of the wounded. As they visited around 2,000 wounded men, it was an extensive job. They did, however, find some consolation from the fact that the eight soldiers with wounded lungs appeared more spirited during the priests' second visit. Their eyes were more lively and their faces less pale. However, the next time Alberti came to talk to the men, he found that one of the beds was empty. A young private, the son of a widow, had been in it before. The chaplains immediately became alarmed and asked why the bed was empty. The reply was disheartening; the young soldier had died the previous evening. He had suddenly become compelled to rise from his bed and go to wash himself in cold water. After that, he had begun to talk feverishly about his mother, claiming that it was her birthday and he had to write to her. His strength then failed him and the poor widow thus lost her only child.[60]

In an adjacent room, Alberti saw a tall man near the door. He too had been shot in the lung, and he looked particularly miserable. His face was yellowish and his eyes were empty. He twisted and moaned. When Alberti and the other priest entered the room, the wounded man hid his face behind a newspaper and took no notice of the two chaplains. They left him alone. Instead, they went up to a gray-haired, heavily bandaged man. A wrinkled, dirty and bloodstained hand peeped out from a snow-white bandage. He had served as the stoker on a steam engine. A destroyed bridge had put a brutal end to his journey, but he had survived the violent crash. Many bones in his body had been broken. The two chaplains comforted the man, who was very grateful.[61]

A sign with the text *"Heim ins Reich"* hung above a bed. With a mere dozen letters, it expressed what everybody desired—to be allowed to get home, either to the family or a so-called "reserve hospital." The latter was a medial institution in the soldier's native district, where the wounded were attended to before they were declared fit. Every day, wounded soldiers lay in their beds hoping to be sent home. Alberti was often asked by individual soldiers if they would be permitted to go home soon; of course, he had no say in these matters, but he at least tried to instill a sense of hope and comfort in the men.

Lessons Learned

It would be highly misleading to regard the September 1939 campaign as a live-fire exercise in which a modern German army utilized a revolutionary concept to quickly overrun an adversary who fought in an outmoded fashion. Alberti's many visits to wounded soldiers strongly suggest that the German victory was not won without considerable bloodshed. Early reports indicated that the German casualties amounted to 8,082 killed in action, 27,278 wounded, and 5,029 missing.[62] Most of the missing would never be found, and some of the wounded would also eventually perish, meaning that subsequent reports would raise the number of dead to 15,450.[63] Compared to the overall casualties in the two world wars, this was almost insignificant, but compared to most other wars of similar duration, the German casualties in Poland were not inconsequential.

The fact that the Polish armed forces fought tenaciously is also shown by the casualties they suffered. Precise figures are hard to come by, but estimates given indicate 70,000 dead, around 130,000 wounded and, of course, a very large number of men taken prisoner.[64] The great German hauls of prisoners were, of course, partly a consequence of the Polish defeat, but the fact that approximately 200,000 Polish soldiers were killed or wounded suggest that the Poles certainly tried hard to halt the invaders. The campaign in September 1939 was no walkover.

The German equipment losses also indicate a hard-fought campaign. Losses of tanks and aircraft were particularly heavy. Initial reports showed that 819 tanks had been knocked out, with light models accounting for 703 of them.[65] Later reports did, however, show that most of the lost tanks were in fact repaired and again put into service, but 244 were irrevocably lost.[66] Aircraft losses were also significant; the Luftwaffe had to write off 285 aircraft and another 279 were badly damaged. The Polish Air Force lost 327 of its 435 aircraft, the balance mainly being evacuated to Romania.[67]

Greater resources, such as more soldiers, tanks, aircraft and guns, made the German victory almost inevitable. The price paid by the Germans suggests that they did not put a revolutionary new mode of warfare, where tanks and aircraft cooperated to win an easy victory, into practice. Most of the German mechanized Army formations were subordinated to four corps—XV, XVI, XIX, and XXII. The war diaries of these corps reveal few examples of successful inter-service cooperation, but many complaints of friendly-fire incidents.[68]

The perception of closely cooperating bombers and tanks seems to be a myth, one that was perhaps created by German propaganda. On the other hand, the propaganda did not emphasize reconnaissance missions, which is hardly surprising as their value was rather subtle compared to Stuka aircraft howling towards ground targets. A propaganda message has to be simple and yet striking to be effectively communicated. The reconnaissance missions were neither simple nor striking.

It is not only the effectiveness of the Luftwaffe's close support that can be called into question. In fact, it is doubtful that the involvement of the Luftwaffe was a major factor in the Polish defeat. Rather than dealing the enemy a decisive blow, the German Air Force may have done something akin to throwing sand into machinery. Despite German efforts, the Polish Air Force was not destroyed on the ground immediately after the outbreak of the war. Attacks on Polish ground combat units produced modest results. However, the attacks on communications and related targets caused delays and often induced Polish units to move in darkness. Gradually, this meant that the soldiers became increasingly tired and also poorly supplied. For example, the Polish General Rommel, who commanded the Łódź Army, believed that poor food supply made many soldiers dispirited and prone to panic. The Polish supply difficulties were mainly caused by a poorly organized rear zone, but attacks by German armor and air power aggravated the situation. Another example is the Luftwaffe attacks on the railroad between Mława and Ciechanów during the first day of the war, which hampered Polish efforts to furnish the artillery with badly needed ammunition.[69]

Thus the Luftwaffe seems not to have been a major factor in the downfall of Poland, but perhaps that was inevitable. With an economy dominated by agriculture and little industry, Poland offered few suitable targets for air power.[70] Neither could air attacks on the raw material supply produce the kind of rapid results the Germans strived for. As close cooperation between ground and air units had been insufficiently trained for, there were hardly any realistic alternatives for the Luftwaffe except for attacking communications and interrupting Polish mobilization. However, as most of the Polish armed forces had already mobilized by September 1, no decisive results could be attained by focusing on such targets. All that remained was to attack communications, which could hamper the Polish efforts. Actually, there was another option—attacking cities. The Luftwaffe did conduct such attacks, particularly on Warsaw, but they hardly influenced the outcome.

Poland was defeated as the German Army defeated Polish combat units and conquered territory, a procedure which appears quite conventional. It may legitimately be asked what role the Panzer divisions had in the destruction of the Polish Army. When the invasion began on September 1, one Panzer division was deployed in East Prussia, one in Pomerania, two in central Silesia, one in southern Silesia, one in the Carpathian Mountains and also one in reserve in Pomerania. During the first days, only one of them can be said to have played a decisive role—Lieutenant-General Rudolf Schmidt's 1st Panzer Division, which broke through the boundary between the Polish Łódź and Kraków armies. The 3rd and 5th Panzer Divisions also made good (but hardly decisive) progress during the first day. The other Panzer divisions did not excel during the initial days.

Since the Panzer divisions were comparatively few in the German armed forces—which committed seven Panzer divisions, four light divisions, four motorized infantry divisions, three mountain divisions and thirty-seven infantry divisions—their mixed performances during the initial phase indicate that they did not have a unique and decisive role.[71]

The German Panzer divisions can hardly be regarded as fighting in a way fundamentally different to the infantry divisions. They fought according to the same basic principles. Owing to their equipment, the Panzer divisions could generate more firepower and mobility, but it was a difference in degree. Offensive action, initiative, independence, rapid decision-making and combined arms were emphasized in both types of division.[72]

Despite the emphasis on initiative, rapid decision-making and independent action, the German Army's high command did not regard the performance of the officers and men as sufficiently good in these respects. It is possible that the German generals had very high expectations, but undoubtedly there were shortcomings that resulted from the rapid expansion and the training shortcomings that followed.[73]

There was a dark side to the German emphasis on local initiative and independent action. Atrocities had already been committed against prisoners of war and civilians during the first days of the campaign, and this was at least partly connected to the decentralized decision-making. For example, local commanders and individual soldiers decided how to treat civilians, and as saboteurs could be shot on the spot, it was often up to individual soldiers to decide whether a Polish civilian was a saboteur or not. Additionally, on a local basis, the German Army took hostages and threatened to shoot them if their decrees were not followed.[74]

Given the great latitude conferred to local initiative and the decentralized decision-making, it is not surprising that the German units treated civilians and prisoners of war quite differently. A clear-cut pattern is difficult to discern, but with a very large number of German soldiers crossing the border, being encouraged to act quickly and independently, one is hardly surprised that atrocities occurred. Such latitude for the individual has to be balanced by an emphasis on ethics, but this was not to be expected within a regime like Hitler's. Indeed, the regime depicted the Poles as inferior beings.

It would, however, be rash to conclude that decentralized decision-making results in more atrocities than centralized decision-making. Before the campaign, a number of decisions were made centrally that would result in large-scale atrocities. In particular, the SS was given the task to conduct a ruthless "Germanization" and cleanse Poland of the allegedly inferior groups of Poles and Jews.[75]

Reinhard Heydrich, the head of the secret police, was made responsible for the brutal actions that were to follow the conquest of Poland. According to the directives he received, the leading strata of Polish society would be eliminated. Ordinary people would be spared, but the nobility, the clergy and the Jews were to be exterminated. The attitude of the Army was important as the *SS-Einsatzgruppen* were operating in the rear areas of the field armies. As late as at the outbreak of the war, the commander-in-chief of the German Army, Colonel-General Walther von Brauchitsch, declared that the "army did not regard the Polish population as its enemy and that international law would be followed."[76]

Events would not turn out exactly as von Brauchitsch had intended; the German Army acted sternly against perceived or real unrest in the occupied areas. This was, however, neither a prerequisite nor a logical consequence of the way the Army fought against enemy combat units. It can also be doubted that more centralized command would have been better in this respect, considering that men like Hitler, Himmler and Heydrich were in the central positions. In mid-October, the military administration in Poland ceased and was replaced by the so-called "General Government."[77]

The German armed forces had to continue to prepare for future tasks. As France and Britain had declared war on Germany, according to their obligations to Poland, a campaign in the west was expected. Hitler had expected to have his war against Poland without anybody interfering, but now found himself in a very different situation. Poland had been conquered by a rather traditional mode of warfare that had been refined by improving the tactical capabilities of the combat units. Next time, a very different and quite unconventional operation would be conducted.

CHAPTER 3

SURPRISING THE ENEMY

Blitzkrieg is often associated with surprise. However, surprise has many meanings and can be achieved in many ways. The effects of surprise are manifold. Often, risks have to be accepted in order to achieve surprise. The German attack on Norway in 1940 fits well into this description.

Two circumstances led the Germans to attack Norway. The first was Swedish iron ore, which was very important to the German armaments industry. The second was the need for better-located naval bases, from which attacks on British Atlantic convoys could be initiated. However, during the initial phase of the war, Hitler did not intend to attack Scandinavia. As long as Norway and Sweden remained neutral, imports of iron ore continued unhindered. The second argument—the German Navy's need for better bases—did not appear particularly convincing to Hitler. He showed scant interest in maritime strategy, and it was not self-evident that Germany would fight a prolonged war against Great Britain. Had he been convinced that Norway and Sweden would not get involved in the war, he would probably have refrained from attacking either of them.[1]

The Germans began planning to attack Norway in December 1939, but only with the intention of being better prepared for something unexpected. No decision to attack Norway had yet been made, but events during the winter of 1939–40 would affect the German planning; Soviet forces attacked Finland on November 30, and few believed the small nation would be able to halt the colossus. To the astonishment of the world, the Finnish armed forces did indeed bring the Soviet advance to a halt not far beyond their border. Still, it remained to be seen for how long the defenders could hold the tide.

The French and British decided to send an expeditionary force to assist the Finns, but—unsurprisingly—it was to pass over Narvik and the Swedish iron ore fields. Churchill also advocated mining the areas through which ships transported the ore from Narvik to Germany. Hitler became aware of the attention the western powers focused on Norway and the Swedish iron ore deposits. Gradually, he became convinced that they would attempt to seize vital parts of Scandinavia.

At first, the German planning was tentative, seeking to explore opportunities, difficulties and important circumstances that might shape a future operation. It was not until General Nikolaus von Falkenhorst was appointed as commander of the future operation on February 19 that planning proceeded firmly. By early March, the German plans had developed to the point that it only remained to set the date when the operation would be initiated.[2]

In many ways, the German invasion of Norway is a milestone in the history of warfare. It was the first major operation that depended on the successful employment of ground, navy and air units. It was also an attempt to paralyze a country rather than simply defeating its armed forces, as the Germans had done in Poland. The actions fought in and around Norway would also show that air power could neutralize enemy command of the seas. Logistics are always essential to military operations, but they were perhaps particularly pertinent during the campaign in Norway. Success in the actions fought depended on the ability to transport units and supplies over the seas, in the air and on land. The importance of airfields, harbors and key roads was paramount. Consequently, the campaign was largely decided on the operational level.

For various reasons, the combatants would be forced to rely on improvisations. The Allies had to revise their plans substantially as the Germans forestalled them. The Germans themselves had to rely on improvisations for another reason—they underestimated the opposition they would meet. The plan for Operation *Weserübung*, as the attack on Norway and Denmark was called, was conceived in such a way that it must have relied on the assumption that scant or no opposition would be encountered. This assumption would prove erroneous, and the Germans would be forced to conjure up measures they had not prepared.

The key element of the German plan was the immediate capture of all major airfields and harbors. Warships with embarked Army units would sail into Narvik, Trondheim, Bergen, Egersund, Kristiansand, Arendal and Oslo, while the airfields at Oslo and Stavanger would be captured by airborne troops. The Norwegian defense would thus be paralyzed, the Germans assumed. With the airfields and harbors in German hands, the Allies would be prevented from putting ground troops on Norwegian soil.

The most vulnerable part of the operation was the sea transports to the remote harbors of Trondheim and Narvik, which lay beyond the effective range of the Luftwaffe. The two German groups of ships which were allotted these distant goals were very exposed to British sea power. A successful German attack on Narvik and Trondheim was unthinkable without the element of surprise, but the northern ports were vital, and the Germans had to try to capture them. If they did not, the British would probably take control of them and put a halt to the shipments of iron ore to Germany.[3]

An attack on Norway that would result in Allied possession of Narvik was pointless to the Germans. They had to ensure that Narvik ended up in their possession and had to move troops there, which could only be accomplished by warships. The great distance also mandated that fast warships had to be used. Their firepower would also be useful during the actual landing. Supply ships loaded with heavy equipment, fuel, ammunition and provisions were to be dispatched in advance, but they were to sail in disguise and not take part in the actual attack on the harbors.[4]

The background of the German ground combat units detailed for Operation *Weserübung* varied. The 2nd and 3rd Mountain Divisions were regular formations that had participated in the campaign in Poland, while most other units had recently been formed and lacked combat experience. For security reasons, no training for the kind of terrain anticipated was allowed, and neither were any sea-landing exercises

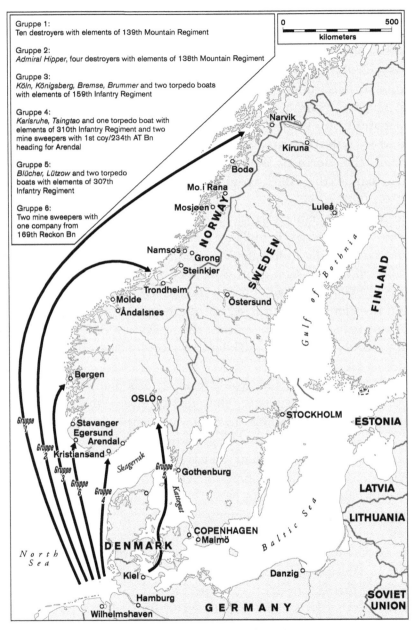

Gruppe 1:
Ten destroyers with elements of 139th Mountain Regiment

Gruppe 2:
Admiral Hipper, four destroyers with elements of 138th Mountain Regiment

Gruppe 3:
Köln, Königsberg, Bremse, Brummer and two torpedo boats
with elements of 159th Infantry Regiment

Gruppe 4:
Karlsruhe, Tsingtao and one torpedo boat with
elements of 310th Infantry Regiment and two
mine sweepers with 1st coy/234th AT Bn
heading for Arendal

Gruppe 5:
Blücher, Lützow and two torpedo
boats with elements of 307th
Infantry Regiment

Gruppe 6:
Two mine sweepers with
one company from
169th Reckon Bn

Operation Weserübung April 9, 1940

conducted. As the Germans only anticipated very weak resistance, the lack of training was not deemed a serious problem. The Norwegian resolve would be broken by rapidly occupying mobilization centers, depots, communications centers and government buildings before any mobilization took place.[5]

As the German ships were to reach the Norwegian ports undetected, favorable weather and long nights were required. On the other hand, such conditions were not suitable for air operations. There was, therefore, a contradiction within the German plan, but it was not too serious to rule out an effective compromise. The decision to attack early in April 1940 reflects the importance of weather and nights. Had the Germans waited longer, the nights would have been shorter and overcast weather less likely.

Surprise remained the pillar upon which the German plan rested. It was vital not only to paralyze the Norwegian resolve to stop the invaders, but also to prevent British naval forces from attacking the German naval units. When the German ships left their bases on the North Sea and the Baltic, the soldiers on board the ships had not been informed of what lay ahead. Neither did they know that rough seas would soon make the landlubbers seasick. In particular, the mountain troopers on board the destroyers bound for Narvik and Trondheim would suffer.

The first German warships that went to sea belonged to the group destined for Narvik. On the night before April 7, ten destroyers commanded by Commodore Friedrich Bonte headed north on the North Sea to join the battleships *Scharnhorst* and *Gneisenau*, which were commanded by Vice-Admiral Günther Lütjens. Also, the group destined for Trondheim—consisting of the heavy cruiser *Admiral Hipper* and four destroyers—attached itself to the Narvik group on the North Sea. Operation *Weserübung* had begun, but the first supply ships had already sailed three days before.[6]

Unaware of the German activities, the British had also launched an operation, named *Wilfred*, to lay mines in the sea lines off Narvik. Rear-Admiral Whitworth had gone to sea on April 5 to conduct the mine-laying mission with the battle cruiser *Renown* and five destroyers.

However, British reconnaissance aircraft observed the German warships sailing for Narvik and Trondheim on April 7. The contact was soon lost, but the British realized that the Germans were up to something. Fortunately for the Germans, the sighting could be interpreted in many ways. Nevertheless, Home Fleet, commanded by Admiral Forbes, left Scapa Flow to intercept the Germans.[7]

The British officers seemed unable to perceive that the Germans had initiated an operation as far ranging as Operation *Weserübung*. In particular, they seem to have been unable to grasp that the Germans intended to attack Trondheim and Narvik with warships. Instead, they tended to interpret the observations as stemming from a German attempt to break out onto the Atlantic to attack British shipping. Thus the Germans achieved a surprise by doing something the enemy could hardly believe they would do. The Norwegians suffered similarly, as they did not believe the Germans would attack seas dominated by the Royal Navy.

The German warships continued towards their objectives. High seas and poor visibility concealed them, but many men on board the ships suffered from seasickness as the ships heaved and rolled in the waves. They may have cursed the weather, but it certainly favored Operation *Weserübung* by enabling the Germans to reach near the Norwegian ports before being sighted. However, on April 8, the British destroyer *Glowworm* happened to encounter German warships northeast of Trondheim. She succumbed to the German gunfire after ramming the heavy cruiser *Admiral Hipper*. The *Glowworm*'s radio silenced after transmitting "engaging a superior enemy force 150 miles southwest of the Vestfjord." No further information was received by the British radio operators, which meant that they remained ignorant about German intentions.[8]

Less than a day later, the British battle cruiser *Renown* engaged the *Scharnhorst* and *Gneisenau*. This time, the Germans were intent on deceiving the British. The German battleships set a northwesterly course to create the impression that they were heading for the Atlantic and the convoy routes. Despite scoring hits on the *Gneisenau*, the British battle cruiser gradually fell behind the faster German battleships. The German commander wanted to lure the British away from the Narvik area, but the British battle cruiser subsequently turned to resume its main task, the protection of the mine-laying off Narvik.[9]

Meanwhile, Commodore Bonte had sailed into the Ofotfjord with his ten destroyers and prepared to attack Narvik. Simultaneously, the other German groups had reached far enough to begin the final—and most dangerous—phase of the operation.

April 9

Harald Zeller learned his destination in the late afternoon of April 8. He had been unaware of it since he received his task on March 28. When he was brought to Wilhelmshaven by train, he realized that the mission would include sea transport. He had been brought to the North Sea port together with hundreds of other soldiers from the 69th Infantry Division. They boarded the light cruiser *Köln*, still without knowing the purpose of the mission. At that moment, Major Linke gathered the group of soldiers Harald Zeller belonged to. He told them they were bound for Bergen. Linke showed them the location of Bergen on a map. To reach the harbor, they would have to sail through narrow waters under the guns of Norwegian coast batteries. Neither Linke nor the men around him believed the Norwegians would offer resistance; consequently, they did not regard the coast batteries as a serious threat. Linke concentrated on informing his men of their tasks. Norwegian radio transmitters would be neutralized immediately. Similarly, the French and British consulates were to be searched for radio transmitters. Zeller was included in a group that would go for the small airfield of Hartlar, located on the island Hartløya, to neutralize a radio transmitter. The attack would commence at 5.15 a.m. on April 9.[10]

It was still dark as the German naval force, commanded by Rear-Admiral Schmundt, reached the entrance to Bergen. In addition to the *Köln*, his force consisted of its sister ship *Königsberg*, the mine-laying ship *Bremse*, two torpedo boats, five motor torpedo boats and the mother ship, *Carl Peters*. Altogether, the ships carried 1,900 men from the 69th Infantry Division.[11]

From his position above the bridge, Harald Zeller had an excellent view. Together with some of his comrades, he had positioned a radio set above the bridge. Zeller saw the *Bremse*, the torpedo boat *Wolf* and an individual motor torpedo boat ahead. Lingering darkness made navigation difficult in the narrow fjord. The German force had entered the Korsfjord from the south and the channel became narrower as the distance to the batteries at Kvarven shrank. The Germans soon realized that they had been seen by Norwegian observers ashore. Signal lamps asked the ships to reveal their identity, but their questions remained unanswered.[12]

From his excellent position, Zeller could see how the German force steadily moved closer to their goal as the mountain slopes along the fjord came ever closer. In order to navigate safely and to keep noise to a minimum, the German ships sailed slowly. Suddenly, Zeller saw that a searchlight had been switched on and focused on the *Königsberg*. Only a short distance remained to Bergen, but it was the most dangerous part of the voyage. When the German ships turned east, for the final leg before they reached the harbor, their fears came true. A muzzle flash blinded Zeller, but he could nevertheless see that a shell had landed in the water before the crack reached his ears and the thunder bounced between the mountain slopes. He still doubted that the Norwegians would offer determined resistance.

The sun's rays gradually and increasingly lit up the surroundings. Zeller found the landscape enchanting, with mountains rising directly from the sea. In the bay, he saw Bergen spreading beneath the huge mountains. Several ships were anchored in the harbor. It appeared that the citizens of the Norwegian town were still asleep, or that they were just beginning to rub the tiredness from their eyes after hearing the thunder from the Norwegian batteries. However, the gunners seemed to have failed to correctly gauge the range as all the shells landed in the water, as far as Zeller could see. On the bridge, it was discussed whether the Germans should return fire or not, but Rear-Admiral Schmundt decided to hold his fire. By now, the *Köln* had got so far that she had almost escaped the Norwegian batteries' field of fire, which was restricted by the terrain.

The *Köln* reached the harbor without being hit, but before doing so she dispatched a boat loaded with riflemen who would capture the coast batteries. From his elevated position, Zeller could see how the anchor chains began to move when the cruiser had reached its intended berth. A boat with Army soldiers was launched, soon to be followed by yet another, which included General Hermann Tittel, the commander of the 69th Infantry Division. He initiated negotiations with the local authorities, and within a quarter of an hour they were concluded. Zeller could soon see the signal agreed upon to indicate that a goal had been attained—six flares resembling white stars. The same signal could also be seen from one of the Norwegian batteries.

Zeller and his comrades had put their radio into operation and immediately received a message from a party on land: "Everything in order ashore." The situation seemed to be fully controlled by the Germans.

The Germans made extensive use of bicycles in Norway, to enhance mobility and advance more rapidly through the terrain. Photo courtesy of Krigsarkivet, Stockholm.

Slowly, the *Köln* began to weigh anchor. Suddenly, a large water cascade shot up ahead of the cruiser. One of the Norwegian batteries had come round, and this time it seemed to have assessed the range more accurately than earlier in the morning. Another shell hit the water next to the German cruiser a few seconds later, this time astern. Zeller and an NCO named Möller stood next to each other and saw a third shell land in the water, close to the bridge. They thought that the next shell must hit the ship; that thought had barely crossed their minds before the cruiser shuddered, but they soon realized that it had recoiled from its own guns. A moment later, the men on board the *Köln* rejoiced. A bright light from the cliffs revealed that the first German salvo was accurate. The Norwegian battery fell silent.

Meanwhile, most of the soldiers had got ashore, but Zeller and his comrades still manned the radio station above the bridge. Zeller saw how the *Köln*'s gunnery officer walked around and shook hands with some of the crew after the successful firing. A message was soon heard from the loudspeakers: "Well done, young men!"

However, everything did not proceed according to plan for the Germans. Zeller had noted that the *Königsberg* had been hit just below the bridge, and other ships had also been hit. However, he was not allowed much time to consider the implications of the hits. His group was ordered to transfer to a launch, which took them ashore. The time was approximately 11.15 a.m. Zeller was among the last men to be brought ashore.

Once on Norwegian soil, Zeller and the other Germans were met by curious gazes from youngsters in Bergen. Zeller got the impression that the Norwegians' feelings vacillated between fear, despair, impudence, astonishment and wonder. Inside Bergen, evacuation seemed to have been initiated following instructions from Oslo, but a large number of inhabitants remained in Norway's second largest city.

A few young lads spat at the Germans, while others tried to tease them. Zeller let them have their way. Anything that might unnecessarily stir up the local population had to be avoided. Instead, his and the other German soldiers' eyes fell on young ladies, whose beauty was praised by the recently disembarked soldiers.

The Germen soldiers were not allowed much time to look around. Large quantities of weapons, baggage and other equipment had been unloaded on the quay, and it had to be taken care of. Also, a proclamation signed by General von Falkenhorst—who, as commander of Gruppe XXI, led the German ground units participating in Operation *Weserübung*—was to be posted across all of Bergen. As a British attack from the sea could not be excluded, the Germans had to take up defensive positions.

Zeller continued to work with the radio set during the day, but towards the evening he was sent to a telegraph station. German officials who had also been on board the warships had commandeered it. On the way, he could see how the Germans had taken control of the city without any fighting. However, he was reminded that a war was actually going on while he was returning from the telegraph station; at dusk, British dive-bombers attacked the harbor. However, as far as Zeller could see, the bombs fell in the water.

What Harald Zeller experienced on April 9 was far from unique. The Germans were able to occupy Bergen almost according to plan. The hits scored on the cruiser *Königsberg* by the Norwegian coast battery was, however, a setback for the Germans, as she could no longer accompany the other German warships as they sailed back towards Germany in the evening. The cruiser remained in Bergen for repairs, but after dawn on April 10 she was hit and sunk by bombs from British Skua aircraft. It was a blow to the Germans, but it did not jeopardize Operation *Weserübung*.

The element of surprise had proved to be vital; the Norwegian defenses were unprepared for the attack. However, success at one harbor was not sufficient. Success demanded that all key areas be occupied on the same day.

Trondheim

The clock struck midnight in the admiral's cabin on the heavy cruiser *Admiral Hipper*. Her commander, Captain Helmuth Heye, had assembled the company commanders of the 138th Mountain Regiment for a short briefing:

"Gentlemen," Heye said. "It is now April 9. In two hours, the German flag will be hoisted, when we sail past the Norwegian batteries. The most dangerous phase of the operation is just about to begin. If we meet any resistance when sailing through the barriers at the entrance to the Trondheimsfjord, the ship will be transformed into a volcano and we will force our way through. The army units will remain below deck, until the regiment commander gives orders to disembark. That will be all, gentlemen. Thank you."[13]

Captain Alker was one of the company commanders who had attended Heye's short briefing. He returned to his company. Like his men, he watched his surroundings tensely. Every sound was registered and interpreted to try and understand what had taken place. A rattling sound was believed to originate from the anchor chains, but the vibrations suggested that the cruiser proceeded at high speed.[14]

In the dusky night, not even those on deck could see much, but that was actually to the advantage of the Germans; Norwegian gunners would be hard-pressed to fire accurately in such poor visibility. Captain Alker was fully aware that all battle stations were manned and all weapons ready to fire. The German squadron—in addition to the heavy cruiser *Admiral Hipper*, four destroyers were also detailed for the attack on Trondheim—swiftly approached Agdenes, where coast batteries were located. Surges flushed from the funnels of the warships as the boilers were fired to provide full steam pressure for the turbines. Alker could not help noticing how the walls inside the cruiser vibrated as the engines propelled the ship.[15]

Proceeding at a speed Alker thought to be "furious," the cruiser sailed into the field of fire of the coast batteries. A Norwegian patrol boat called on the German squadron to reveal its identity, but it received no reply. Instead, the *Admiral Hipper* came abreast of the first battery. The beam from a searchlight swept the area around the cruiser. Alker believed that it was vainly searching for the German flag, attempting to ascertain the identity of the ship before opening fire. Regardless, the German force passed the field of fire before any shots were fired. Perhaps Alker's belief was partially correct, but the Norwegian battery crew had encountered other difficulties too. First of all, twelve minutes were needed to prepare the guns to fire. Then it became apparent that the electrical firing system had malfunctioned. When the crew switched to mechanical firing, the firing string snapped.[16]

The German warships continued into the Trondheimsfjord. However, the second battery had been alerted. Although some time was needed to load the guns, the battery managed to open fire on the Germans—but the shells splashed into the water. The *Admiral Hipper*'s guns immediately replied. The first salvo hit the cables providing the Norwegian battery with electrical power, and the searchlights went out. The third Norwegian battery was equally unsuccessful. On board the *Admiral Hipper*, Alker was told that the squadron had broken through the defenses and around one hour remained before it would reach the harbor of Trondheim.[17]

Meanwhile, one battalion was detached and landed from two of the destroyers. The battalion was given the mission of capturing the batteries and preparing for them to be used to repel a possible British attack. The *Admiral Hipper* and two destroyers continued towards Trondheim and reached the city without mishaps. At 5 a.m., she berthed, at full alert, approximately 1,000 meters from the quay. Her guns were trained at various targets, but fire was held. One seaplane was catapulted from the cruiser to watch over the city and its port, which appeared ever more clearly in the increasing daylight. Captain Alker and the other mountain troopers received orders to disembark and attack the city.[18]

The Army soldiers hastily collected their equipment and embarked on smaller boats that took them from the 200+-meter-long cruiser to the quay in Trondheim. The old Norwegian coronation city was practically undefended. Unhindered, the German soldiers advanced along its streets. Alker noted that the regiment commander, Colonel Weiss, was among the first to come ashore. He soon found a car, which he commandeered. Together with three companions, he went to the staff of the Norwegian 5th Division. There, he learned that the commander had already left the city. However, his second-in-command was still at his office, and he had realized that any opposition was futile. He handed over the keys to the office.[19]

The German mountain troopers took control of the city as the small ceremony took place. The German flag was soon hoisted over the old fortress. The attack had accomplished its goals. Except for the damage resulting from the *Glowworm*'s ramming of the *Admiral Hipper*, the attack on Trondheim had proceeded as smoothly as the Germans had hoped.[20]

Overall, the German attacks on the Norwegian coastal towns had met with great success. Narvik, Trondheim, Bergen, Stavanger, Kristiansand and Arendal were seized according to plan. However, the German operation did not proceed smoothly everywhere.

Oslo

The car brought Captain Werner Boese to the city of Swinemünde, where the Oder river debouched into the Baltic. Here, he and his soldiers, who were also transported by car, were to report on their progress. The journey across the flat landscape was uneventful. At 1.30 p.m. on April 5, Boese reported to the commandant, who had scant knowledge about Boese's mission. He had only heard that some kind of embarking exercise was to be conducted.[21]

Boese and his men had to wait when they reached Swinemünde. The heavy cruiser *Blücher*, which they were to embark on, had not yet arrived. Boese was told to find the local air base, where he would receive information and assistance. It turned out that the staff at the air base were very helpful. The advice to find them had evidently not only been given to Boese, because soon the commander of a coast artillery battalion and his staff also arrived.

When Boese and his men had been billeted, they began to discuss what would happen next. Among other things, Boese learned that the *Blücher* was not expected to come in to Swinemünde until the following day. The cruiser did indeed arrive on April 6, at noon. After she had been moored, Boese and the commander of the coast artillery battalion embarked and reported to Rear-Admiral Kummetz.

Kummetz explained that the soldiers would be distributed on several warships. In addition to the *Blücher*, the light cruiser *Emden* and three torpedo boats would participate in the operation. Furthermore, he informed Boese that the ground units would embark in a different manner to that which had originally been planned. Kummetz had discussed the issue with Major-General Engelbrecht, who, as commander of the 163rd Infantry Division, was Boese's superior. The Admiral wanted the assault troops to be loaded on the warships in such a way that they could disembark rapidly in the order they were to conduct their combat missions. This would result in the infantrymen and coast artillery soldiers being mixed together in their quarters, as they would be on many of the missions they conducted together. There were undoubtedly advantages with such a scheme, but it meant some additional work—not least for Boese.

The troops began to embark at dusk on April 6. Some of the units had been brought to the harbor by train. The process went smoothly, and all units were embarked in time. At 4 a.m. on April 7, the warships weighed anchor and set an easterly course. However, this was only a ruse; after sailing for approximately 50 nautical miles, the formation turned west. A brief firing exercise was conducted south of Bornholm. Kummetz's ships then continued west and anchored off Kiel at around 8 p.m., where the heavy cruiser *Lützow* joined the formation.

At 4.15 a.m. on April 8, Kummetz's unit weighed anchor and set course for the Great Belt. To sail through such a narrow channel entailed considerable risk of detection, but the distance to the Norwegian capital was short. Even if the German ships were sighted, the enemy would have less than twenty-four hours to prepare any countermeasures. Furthermore, information would probably not travel quickly from neutral Denmark to another country.

Boese suggested that life vests should be distributed to his soldiers and also that they should be instructed on how to leave the ship quickly in an emergency. His proposal was turned down as such measures were regarded as unnecessary. Neither were the soldiers given any instructions on how to operate the rafts. At this stage of the operation, the non-existent training and instruction seemed not to have resulted in any notable consternation.

Soldiers in Army uniform were to remain indoors to avoid revealing their presence on the warships. Boese borrowed a uniform from the Navy officers and was thus permitted to stay above deck. He noted that the comradeship between the Navy and Army soldiers was very good. The former did everything to make the landlubbers comfortable in the crammed compartments within the warships.

The German hopes to pass the Great Belt unnoticed at noon were unfulfilled. The radio in Oslo reported that powerful German naval forces had been observed in the Danish Belts. However, it remained to be seen what conclusions the decision-makers in the Norwegian capital would draw. Would they decide to mobilize, or would they order some other kind of increased readiness?

At 5 p.m., Boese was told that the *Blücher* had been subjected to a torpedo attack that had failed to score a hit. The warships assumed a zigzagging course to reduce the risk of being hit by submarines. By this stage, the men on board the ships had been informed about their mission. Before noon, the commander of the cruiser, Captain Heinrich Woldag, had given a short speech on the loudspeakers in which he had described the purpose of the operation.

At dusk, Kummetz's ships reached a point south of the estuary of the Oslofjord. A Norwegian coastguard ship appeared and lit a searchlight, the beam falling on the German heavy cruiser. A warning shot was fired at the *Blücher*, which repaid the favor. The small Norwegian ship was soon dealt a severe blow. While the *Blücher* continued north, the coastguard ship was rammed by another German vessel.

It was difficult for Boese to read the situation. He understood that ground troops had disembarked from the light cruiser *Emden* at around 1.30 a.m. on April 9. As far as he could see, the operation appeared to be proceeding according to plan. At Horten, he saw lights on the Norwegian mainland. Until then, the coast had been dark. Boese began to believe that the Norwegians would mount no opposition.

After passing the Norwegian naval base at Bolarne, where German troops disembarked from some of the smaller vessels, Kummetz's force continued north in the Oslofjord. At 5 a.m., his ships were just about to enter the narrowest part of the Oslofjord, near Dröback. Boese waited in a cabin below the admiral's cabin, together with Captain Prahl, Captain von Gontard and Lieutenant-Commander Kessler. The latter was a Naval officer, unlike the three Army captains.[22]

Their watches passed 5 a.m. Everything seemed to be going well. The narrow strait required careful navigation, but that came as no surprise. Suddenly, Boese heard a violent explosion. He realized that a heavy shell had hit the cruiser, not far from his position. The men in the cabin reacted immediately, quickly moving to below the armored deck. Another shell struck the *Blücher*, not far from the first hit. Boese would not understand what had happened until later; at that moment, he only thought about getting below the armored deck. Clearly, the enemy had engaged the *Blücher*.

Boese reached a compartment that was part of the system for hoisting shells to the heavy guns. It was one of the best-protected areas of the ship. A few minutes later, the lights went out and the ammunition hoist stopped. A fierce detonation shook the ship, which began to list. Suddenly, the firing seemed to cease and the emergency lights came on. No order to abandon the ship was given. However, some men gave warnings about gas. A few experienced Navy officers calmed them by explaining that they had detected the powder gasses from the ship's guns.

Half an hour later, Boese decided to leave the compartment. The list increased. As he had not received any orders, he decided to make his way upwards in the ship. The other men in the cabin followed him. Boese reached a compartment where he found several Navy officers, including one lieutenant-commander. Boese asked them if it was necessary to order everybody to abandon the ship. They replied that the list was not too serious. The answer did not reassure Boese, who took a few more steps and found Lieutenant Scholtz. At the same moment, a violent explosion shook the ship, followed by another. Boese believed two torpedoes had hit the ship.

Boese still remained below deck, but after the two explosions, orders were given that everybody should get up on deck. The list increased rapidly. It was no longer possible to walk upright, but Boese and Lieutenant Scholtz found a ladder and managed to reach the upper deck. They made an attempt to reach the admiral's staff compartment, where their baggage and weapons were located, but fires stopped them. The flames could not be extinguished, and there was a possibility that the nearby ammunition and aviation fuel would be set alight by the flames.

Once they he reached the deck, Boese saw several sailors and soldiers in life vests. He asked them where he could find more vests, but an NCO told him there were no more. This alarming answer was immediately followed by an order to abandon the ship. Boese took off his boots and went to the nearest gangway. Some sailors reached it before him, and he had to wait for his turn.

While waiting, Boese saw a small boat being lowered into the water. One man descended to the boat by using the gangway, but he found that the small craft lacked a rudder, paddles and oars. He had brought a spade and used it to maneuver the boat to the rope next to Boese. At this moment, a Naval officer appeared and ordered the sailors to allow the Army soldiers to descend first. Without any murmuring, the sailors obeyed and allowed Boese onto the gangway. He saw no signs of panic and also witnessed skilled swimmers handing their life vests to less skilled men.

Boese was the last man to find room in the small boat. Major von Necker and Lieutenant Prahl were already there. There was no time for prolonged deliberation, and nobody knew whether Norwegian units were defending the shores. There was a possibility that machine-gun fire would rake the Germans, but they had no alternative but to reach land. There were a few islets approximately 200 meters away. The distance to mainland was around 300 meters. The swimmers aimed for the closest beach. Boese and the other men in the small boat used their hands to paddle it, but they soon found that their helmets made more efficient paddles. They all exhausted themselves to reach land, whereupon Major von Necker and another man returned to the sinking *Blücher* to fetch more survivors. The temperature of the water was only a few degrees above freezing. A swimming man rapidly lost his strength in such conditions.

Boese helped the men who had swam close to the islet he had come ashore on. He threw a rope into the water to help exhausted soldiers on the last stretch before reaching safety on land. Captain Prahl lit a fire to warm the soaking soldiers who had managed to get ashore. Prahl and Boese lent their dry field blouses to two soldiers who had swam all the way to the islet.

The slowly sinking *Blücher* listed ever more, but there were still soldiers and sailors leaving her. She gradually turned to lie with her starboard side up before finally sinking. When the ship had disappeared beneath the waves, oil poured out of her and settled on the surface of the water. Soon the oil began to burn, but luckily for the Germans, the wind pulled the burning sludge away from the shores where they had sought refuge. Many who had managed to reach land began to sing the German national anthem.

The disaster that befell the *Blücher* did not only result in the death of approximately 1,000 men, it also stopped the German attempt to capture the Norwegian capital from the sea. The Germans successfully seized all of their other objectives, but the most important had escaped the German Navy's attack. The Germans did not know it, but their adversary south of Oslo was Colonel Eriksen, who commanded the coast batteries at Oscarsborg and, acting on his own initiative, had decided to halt the advancing enemy.[23]

As Kummetz's Naval force was halted at Oscarsborg, the entire German operation was in jeopardy. The Oslo region was crucial; the Norwegian government and many of the military units that were to mobilize were located in or around the city. Unless the Germans quickly seized the area, the Norwegians could organize their defenses and prevent the German occupation of the country. The German warships had not brought substantial ground units; altogether, they had brought the equivalent of an infantry division, less most of its heavy weapons. Such a force was much inferior to a fully mobilized Norwegian Army. Also, the mountainous terrain would favor the defenders.[24]

The disaster at Oscarsborg meant that Operation *Weserübung* had the potential to turn into a fiasco, but the German attack on Oslo differed from the attacks on the other objects in one very important way. Narvik, Trondheim, Bergen, Kristiansand, Arendal and Egersund were only attacked by seaborne forces. Stavanger and the nearby Sola airfield were captured exclusively from the air. Oslo was, however, attacked both from the air and from the sea. The danger to the Norwegian capital could not be averted by halting Kummetz's force. From the beach he had reached, Boese could hear the distant engine noise from aircraft high above him.[25]

The Luftwaffe had planned an extensive effort to capture Oslo. No fewer than 165 transport aircraft had been detailed to air-land the 324th Infantry Regiment, which belonged to the 163rd Infantry Division, on Fornebu. Also, I Battalion of the 1st Parachute Regiment would land on Fornebu. Thus, according to the plan, four battalions would be air-landed at Oslo on the first day of the invasion.[26]

As is usual in war, things did not work out according to plan. The aircraft bringing the paratroopers were stopped by fog and low clouds. As they were supposed to capture the airfield and thereby allow the 324th Infantry Regiment to land, the entire operation was endangered. The infantry soldiers had not received any parachute training. Their task was to land on an already captured airfield and immediately attack towards the Norwegian capital. Without the paratroopers, it appeared that the attempt to capture Oslo from the air had also failed. The first batch of aircraft transporting the 324th Infantry Regiment was already flying towards Norway, but it now received orders to turn back. Thus the entire German attempt to occupy Norway hung by a single thread. If neither the seaborne nor the airborne forces reached Oslo, the Norwegian government and military could mobilize in the comparatively densely populated Oslo region.[27]

At this stage, the German operation was saved by a combination of misunderstanding and personal initiative. Captain Wagner, who commanded one of the attacking units in the air, received the order to turn back. However, the order was issued by "*X. Fliegerkorps*," not "*Transportchef Land*," which he was subordinated to. It seems that Wagner either believed that the order was false or that it did not pertain to his unit. Either way, he decided to continue to Fornebu and land there.

When Wagner set his eyes on Fornebu from above, he concluded that it would be possible to land there. His aircraft descended, but when it had almost reached the landing strip, it was met by a hail of machine-gun fire. Wagner's aircraft was hit, and he was among those killed. However, the pilot remained unscathed, giving full throttle and managing to bring the aircraft out of range of the Norwegian defenders. The other transport aircraft circled well above Fornebu as their crews realized what would happen if they attempted to land.[28]

There were also other types of German aircraft above Fornebu. Twin-engine Messerschmitt Bf 110s waited for a chance to land; they had no other option, as they had insufficient fuel to return to the air bases in Germany. After firing on ground targets, no alternatives remained for the BF 110 crews. They had to land. One by one, they went down on Fornebu. The Norwegian machine gunners caused losses among the landing German aircraft, as well as among the transport aircraft that followed the fighters. However, when the defenders ran out of ammunition, they withdrew. A combination of luck, confusion, misunderstanding and initiative gave the Germans the Fornebu airfield.[29]

When Fornebu was captured, the road to the Norwegian political and military centers lay open to the Germans. Most of the 324th Infantry Regiment was air transported to Fornebu on the first day of the invasion. The Norwegian king and his family had to escape to Elverum and Hamar, northeast of the capital.[30]

Despite the setbacks, the Germans managed to seize all the key positions they intended to within the first twenty-four hours. This outcome can chiefly be attributed to surprise and poor Norwegian preparedness. The coast artillery was not fully manned and ammunition was insufficiently stowed. The crews had not received clear instructions on when they were permitted to fire, which caused delays. German estimates on the effects of surprise on the Norwegian defenses by and large proved correct. However, there were further dangers the Germans had to consider, particularly the Royal Navy, but surprise again aided the Germans greatly. There was a difference, though. The Norwegian defense had not yet been mobilized, thus suggesting that the Norwegians regarded a German attack as unlikely. The British, on the other hand, had mobilized their armed forces and began to put the economy on a war footing. In many respects, the British were ahead of the Germans. Hence, the Germans could not expect to confront the British unprepared for war. They had to surprise their adversary on a different level.

In war, enemy intentions and options are often difficult to surmise. Innumerable alternative scenarios exist, and the incomplete information makes it hard to realize which of them the enemy has settled for, even when an operation has been launched. Furthermore, one's own preconceptions often influence the interpretation of the observations made. Above all, the British Navy feared a German attempt to break out on the Atlantic and attack British shipping. German warships had operated on the Atlantic during the fall of 1939, which confirmed the British fears. When German warships were observed in the days before April 9, these moves were interpreted as part of a German attempt to do precisely what the British had feared.

Another circumstance that may have hampered the British was the fact that a German invasion of Norway across open sea was perceived as very unlikely. According to conventional wisdom, such an operation presupposed command of the sea, which the Germans patently did not have. At most, German Naval forces were expected to reach harbors on the Norwegian south coast, such as Arendal, Kristiansand and Oslo, before the Royal Navy intervened. Ports such as Bergen and Stavanger on the Norwegian west coast were fairly close to British Naval bases. Any German force operating against Bergen and Stavanger would very much be within striking range of the Royal Navy.

Against this background, a German attack on southern Norway seemed barely conceivable at most. However, if the Germans only seized southern Norway, they would place themselves in an awkward situation, being at war with Norway without paralyzing her defenses first. The door for British and French intervention in Scandinavia would have been wide open, and no more shipments of iron ore would have left Narvik. No matter how the British considered the problem, they arrived at the same conclusion—a German attack on Norway would be foolhardy and indeed favorable to the Allies.

Britain's line of reasoning was not divorced from reality. Indeed, the Germans seem to have underestimated the Norwegian resolve. The Norwegian mobilization was undoubtedly seriously upset by the German invasion, and mistakes aggravated the situation, but counter to German expectations, the Norwegians continued to offer resistance. British and French combat units were dispatched to assist the Norwegians in their struggle against the invaders. The Germans found themselves in a situation that did not resemble what they had anticipated when planning the invasion.

The Fighting Continues

General mobilization was ordered in Norway following the German attack. As the Germans had already captured the most important towns, seized many mobilization depots and cut communications, a smooth and complete Norwegian mobilization was impossible. The difficulties were aggravated by mistakes made by the Norwegian authorities. Communication between the government and the military was poor, which resulted in Foreign Secretary Halvdan Koht declaring on the radio that mobilization had already been ordered when, in fact, it had not, as the officers waited for permission to mobilize from the politicians. Men capable of bearing arms went to their mobilization depots only to find them locked. When they subsequently received the formal mobilization order, they were reluctant to follow it.[31]

Despite all the mistakes and difficulties, sizable Norwegian forces were mobilized and would soon be joined by British, French and Polish units. Considering the miniscule size of the German forces that had landed— approximately the equivalent of a small and lightly armed regiment in the towns attacked—the Germans could easily have found themselves seriously outnumbered. It was hazardous for them to bring reinforcements by sea, and from Stavanger and further north it was virtually impossible. It was very difficult to provide the German units in Stavanger, Bergen, Trondheim and Narvik with ammunition, and it was nigh impossible to bring in reinforcements.

However, the Germans did possess a means to turn this menacing situation into their advantage—the Luftwaffe. It can certainly be argued that the Luftwaffe was hardly essential to the German victory in Poland, but the Luftwaffe's importance for the German success in Scandinavia cannot be exaggerated. Admittedly, it was ground units that captured and controlled towns and other vital terrain, but it does not follow that that they therefore played the main role in the invasion. Neither the Germans nor the Allies committed more than a small fraction of their army units in Norway. Most of their ground forces were obviously needed elsewhere, but the size of the army forces fighting in Norway were also limited by logistical factors. This is where the Luftwaffe's contribution was essential. First of all, the Luftwaffe's transport aircraft brought substantial reinforcements and supplies to Norway. Secondly, German air attacks—or the mere threat they posed—seriously hampered the Allied efforts to bring reinforcements to Norway.

Few airfields existed in Norway, but the Germans rapidly seized them. Three airfields were of particular importance: Sola at Stavanger, Fornebu at Oslo and Vaernes at Trondheim. Also, the Germans could, after the rapid conquest of Denmark, use airfields at Aalborg. They would be essential to the German operations in Norway. The only way for the Germans to bring reinforcements and supplies to Trondheim and Narvik was by the air. As they controlled the airfields at Aalborg, Oslo and Trondheim, they possessed a chain of airfields suitable for that purpose. On April 13, a German infantry battalion was air-landed at Vaernes, near Trondheim. It was to be followed by many more.[32]

The Allies had to use the sea to transport ground units to Norway. As the Germans had already occupied all airfields and most of the main ports, the Allies faced a daunting task. They had to land their units in smaller and poorly located harbors. They were also threatened by the Luftwaffe, which attacked the ships at sea and at the harbors where the troops and supplies were disembarked.

On April 19, Hitler issued an order that harbors controlled by the British or those they claimed to control would be bombed without any regard to the civilian population.[33] In the evening, Reuters reported that British forces had landed in Namsos, approximately 130 km north-northeast of Trondheim.[34] The Luftwaffe struck the following day, causing considerable devastation. The attacks were initially made from high altitude, but when the German airmen realized there were no antiaircraft defenses in Namsos, they descended to 300 meters before releasing their deadly load. Wooden houses caught fire and most of the town burned down. Considering the scope of the attack, the number of civilians who lost their lives was smaller than anticipated, but homes and places of work were set ablaze. The strategically important damage was inflicted on the rail station, ammunition depots, storage buildings and harbor facilities.[35]

The air attack on Namsos does not only illustrate the importance of the Luftwaffe in explaining the eventual outcome of the campaign. It is also an example of how difficult it can be to distinguish terror attacks from attacks on military targets. The citizens of Namsos could certainly (and justifiably) regard the event as a terror attack. On the other hand, the Germans could argue that they attacked legitimate military targets, such as the harbor and the rail station, which were used by the British and French to bring military units to fight the Germans at Trondheim. The poor bombing precision was a major culprit, with a large number of the bombs falling far from their intended targets. In towns, this often resulted in many civilian casualties. It could thus be argued that the problem was a technological shortcoming. However, there seems to have been little or no inclination to select targets to compensate for the lack of accuracy in order to reduce civilian casualties. Rather, the civilian casualties seem to have been regarded as either inevitable or acceptable. The distinction between terror attacks and attacks on legitimate military targets may thus have been clear to those who ordered bombing missions, but it was certainly less clear to the people on the receiving end.

However, this is not the end of the story. The fact that a military target could justify a bombing mission does not exclude other motives. Occasionally, these other motivations can be found in written orders; an example can be found within the Luftwaffe's instructions for the attacks on Warsaw in September 1939.[36]

Two regions in Norway were of particular importance—the area around Trondheim and the area around Oslo. On April 10, two important events took place. The first was the Norwegian decision to abandon the defense line along the river Nitelven, which ran from north to south just east of Oslo. The decision was a misjudgment, and it offered the Germans in Oslo, who numbered no more than around a regiment, much more freedom of action. The second important event was the surrender of Oscarsborg, which opened the sea route to Oslo. These events offered the Germans a chance to initiate more far-reaching operations in southern Norway.[37]

The German ground forces that initially landed in Norway had to contend with capturing the objectives allotted to them and then establish defenses that were as strong as possible. However, as soon as the airfields mentioned and the port of Oslo had been secured, the Germans were able to initiate offensive operations. In the Trondheim area, the Germans mainly aimed at enlarging the area they controlled to make it less vulnerable to the anticipated Allied counterattack. The Oslo region, on the other hand, would become the staging area for more ambitious attacks intended to establish land communications with Bergen, Kristiansand, Stavanger, Trondheim and Arendal. Furthermore, the Norwegian units in southern Norway were to be defeated or prevented from mobilizing. The task was hard, with the difficult terrain hampering movement and favoring the defenders. Roads and railroads were few and often followed steep valleys surrounded by snow-clad mountains. The weather was also harsh as the stern winter had just begun to loosen its grip. The geography seldom offered any alternative routes of advance, and the terrain characteristics made it difficult to concentrate a strong force at the point where a breakthrough was intended. These circumstances led the Germans not to concentrate an overwhelming attack force in one sector, but to attack in different directions as reinforce gradually arrived. Altogether, substantial German forces were brought to Norway. During the two months the campaign lasted, 270 freighters and 100 trawlers brought 107,581 soldiers, 16,102 horses, 20,339 vehicles and 109,400 tons of supplies to the country. The Luftwaffe flew another 29,280 men and 2,376 tons of equipment there.[38]

Time was needed to bring these reinforcements to Norway. Although the number of soldiers may appear impressive, the reinforcement rate only equates to around 2,000–2,500 men per day. Thus von Falkenhorst did not have much strength to rely on during the first weeks of the campaign. Despite the paucity of his resources, he decided to attack almost immediately. On April 11, he issued an attack order involving almost all the troops in the Oslo area. The 196th Infantry Division, which was far from complete, was given the mission to attack the area southeast of Oslo. In fact, the division only had four battalions for this task. Similarly, the 163rd Infantry Division was instructed to clear the area west of Oslo. The latter division was also responsible for the defense of Oslo, but it was instructed to commit the bare minimum manpower for this task.[39]

This is an example of a decision imbued with offensive spirit, typical for an organization that does not focus on its own problems but instead searches for the enemy's weaknesses and tries to create difficulties for him. The Germans had to achieve this by improvisation. No suitable plans existed. The units were thrown out of order and the arrival of reinforcements was unclear. Units were sent into battle immediately upon arrival, without allowing the soldiers time for reorganization. A good example is the 362nd Infantry Regiment, which saw its first elements disembark at Oslo on the night of April 11–12. At 10 a.m., two of its battalions were sent to attack Moss and Fredrikstad. They were given mobility by the commandeering of buses, lorries, cars and other vehicles. They quickly accomplished their task and captured many prisoners.[40]

After five days, the Germans began to advance north from the Oslo area. The attacks gradually gained more momentum, and on April 21 they had reached a point slightly south of Lillehammer, approximately 120 km from Oslo. This meant that about one fourth of the distance from Oslo to Trondheim had been covered.[41]

Steinkjer

The commander of the 181st Infantry Division, Major-General Kurt Woytasch, flew to Trondheim to assume command of the German forces in the area. His division arrived gradually, allowing him to act offensively after a while. I and II Battalions (as well as two platoons from 14th Company, with six antitank guns) of the 334th Infantry Regiment arrived by air in the Trondheim area on April 24. In addition, I Battalion and around 300 men from II Battalion of the 359th Infantry Regiment had arrived.[42] Together with the units of the 3rd Mountain Division that had landed on April 9, Woytasch had approximately 3,500 men in the Trondheim area two weeks after the campaign began.

The forces on hand were not impressive, and Woytasch knew that the enemy grew stronger every day. The Germans could have chosen a defensive posture, but instead they opted to attack. On April 15, Gruppe XXI issued an order covering future operations in the Trondheim area. It was noted that the situation at Namsos was unclear and that a British landing was possible. It was estimated that Norwegian forces in the Aandalsnes area approximately amounted to the size of a regiment, but a British landing there was regarded as unlikely. The German forces in Trondheim would advance as soon as possible and capture the narrow stretch of land at Steinkjer, which would have the side effect of securing the railroad to Sweden. As soon as sufficient resources were available, the advance to Namsos and Grong would be initiated.[43]

This decision is remarkable in many ways. First of all, it meant that the threat to Trondheim was to be averted by offensive action. Secondly, this offensive action was to be attempted while the relief forces attacking from the Oslo region were still several hundred kilometers away. The solution adopted by Woytasch would prove a fine example of improvisation and initiative.

Woytasch assumed command on April 20. He immediately ordered a 375-man mountain battalion to embark on a sea voyage into the Beitstadsfjord, a northern subsidiary of the Trondheimsfjord, where the ice had weakened as the spring progressed. The battalion was to be disembarked to cut off the road between Steinkjer and Levanger, as well as to capture Steinkjer itself. Further south, two companies from the 359th Infantry Regiment would attack Verdalsøra.[44]

Under the cover of darkness, the mountain troopers embarked on the destroyer *Paul Jacobi*. Light 7.5-cm mountain howitzers were also brought on board the warship. Most of the soldiers tried to sleep below deck while the destroyer sailed north from Trondheim. She passed several narrow straits before entering the Beitstadsfjord. The soldiers who had not fallen asleep could hear the destroyer's hull chafe against the ice floes in the fjord.[45]

The weather and ice caused delays, but they seem not to have had any significant impact. At 5 a.m. on April 21, German mountain troops began to disembark at Kjerknesvaagen, 16 km southwest of Steinkjer. After a time-consuming unloading procedure, they began to move northeast. Some motor vehicles were found and used for transporting equipment. A few sledges and pulkas were also found and used for the same purpose. The deep snow on the ground forced the Germans to advance along the roads.[46]

At 9.30 a.m., the German advance guard reached Gangstad, where it encountered British forces. A brief engagement ensued in which the Germans captured one British soldier. Under interrogation, he revealed that there were three British battalions in Steinkjer. From the observations made, the German advance guard estimated that a British platoon

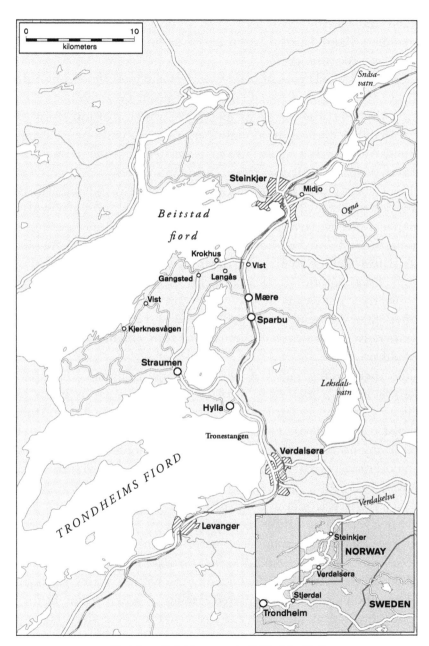

Verdalsøra-Steinkjer area, April 20–22, 1940

defended the nearby farmstead at Krokhus. The German battalion commander, Major Schratz, decided to temporarily take up defensive positions and reconnoiter.[47]

The Germans had brought heavy mortars and light field guns onto the destroyer, and these were moved into firing positions at Gangstad. Under covering fire from the heavy weapons, a German platoon stormed the farm at Krokhus and captured eighteen prisoners without suffering any casualties. Afterwards, patrols were sent out to establish enemy positions. It turned out that a British force, at an estimated strength of around 300, had taken up defensive positions at a piece of woodland at Langaas. Schratz decided to halt and resume the attack on the following day.[48]

Further south, the two companies from the 359th Infantry Regiment began their attack on Verdalsøra at 6 a.m. They faced 162 Norwegian and twenty British soldiers in prepared defenses, but despite not possessing any kind of substantial numerical superiority, the Germans quickly captured their objective. They were helped by the fact that the defenders had been informed that German forces had landed at Hylla and Tronestangen, approximately 5 km north of Verdalsøra, thus endangering the rear of the Allied position.[49]

While the fighting raged at Verdalsøra and Gangstad, the Luftwaffe attacked Steinkjer. Much of it burned down. The town itself was hardly of military importance, but it was located on a narrow isthmus. Both the main road and the railroad ran through Steinkjer. The air attack in itself did not cause any notable military losses, but it contributed to convincing the British commanders that the units south of Steinkjer had to be withdrawn. They were ordered to pull back to Sparbu and Mære in the evening.[50]

A cold night was followed by further fighting for Schratz's soldiers. Schratz first sent more patrols to establish enemy positions and gain more knowledge about the terrain. The patrols caught several prisoners, but little else came of them. At 2.30 p.m., Schratz launched a more determined attack east. At Vist, situated along the road between Steinkjer and Verdalsøra, the Germans encountered resistance. Schratz brought the light field guns into action, and their fire dislodged the defenders. His soldiers immediately continued towards Steinkjer, and at this stage they were joined by the lead elements of the companies advancing from Verdalsøra.[51]

At first, the Germans did not encounter any opposition as they advanced along the fjord towards Steinkjer, but when they had almost made it to their objective, they were fired upon from the beach on the other side of the bay to where Steinkjer is located. Once again, the light field guns proved their worth. They silenced the opposition and opened the way to Steinkjer, which was almost completely burnt down. Fires were still raging in many places.[52]

While the soldiers from the infantry regiment took up defensive positions, Schratz's men continued towards the important bridge at Midjo. It turned out to be blocked by trucks, and three Norwegian machine guns raked the area. Yet again, the Germans brought a light field gun into firing position. The fire support it provided enabled one platoon to cross the frozen Ogna River and overthrow the Norwegian position. A very important objective had thus been attained without the mountain troops suffering any casualties on April 22. One soldier had been killed the day before. The two companies from the 359th Infantry Regiment had suffered somewhat higher casualties.[53]

The German attack on Steinkjer is interesting in many ways. First of all, it is an excellent example of the German use of mobility to force the enemy to abandon a suitable defense position. No mechanized units were available in this case, but by making use of a warship, Woytasch could create a diversion that put the Allied units in a dangerous position. The Luftwaffe had similar impact. German air attacks were not directed at Allied ground combat units, but the German activities in the air affected the decision-making of the Allied commanders.

The resources available to Woytasch were numerically inferior to the Allied units in the Trondheim region.[54] He nevertheless decided to attack, despite the fact that the relief forces were closer to Oslo than Trondheim. Thereby he not only secured the vital Trondheim region, but also created favorable conditions for a continued attack north as soon as the link-up between Oslo and Trondheim had been accomplished.

The desire to resort to offensive tactics, to use maneuvers and mobility and to act rather than wait in unclear situations appears obvious in this example. The forces advancing from the Oslo region also conducted operations in the same style. To reach Trondheim they advanced along two valleys, Gudbrandsdalen and Østerdalen. On April 18, the German force attacking along Østerdalen reached Flisa, approximately 45 km north of Kongsvinger, while the group advancing in Gudbrandsdalen reached Tangen, approximately 30 km north of Eidsvoll. The distance remaining to Trondheim was approximately 360 km. Twelve days later, the German force advancing in Østerdalen linked up with their compatriots at Trondheim.[55]

Although part of the distance was covered by the Trondheim group attacking southwards, most of the distance, around 320 km, was covered by the forces advancing northwards. That was a pace comparable to the German Panzer divisions in Poland half a year before. Furthermore, the units in Norway had to advance along poor roads in narrow valleys, surrounded by mountains and in poor weather. As the roads were few, a single destroyed bridge could cause significant delays. Against this background, the German advance from Oslo to Trondheim appears even more impressive.

After a land connection between Oslo and Trondheim had been established, it only remained for the Germans in southern Norway to enforce the surrender of the remaining Norwegian units. On May 4, Gruppe XXI declared the fighting south of Trondheim to be over. However, it remained to link up with the most distant German forces, which were at Narvik. Major-General Eduard Dietl's mountain troops had captured the town on April 9, but they had subsequently been cut off save for sporadic deliveries of supplies (mainly from the air). More than 600 km separated Narvik and Trondheim, as the crow flies. Not only was the distance great, the terrain was particularly difficult, with mountains, winding valleys and very few roads. Also, Dietl's soldiers were ever harder pressed by Allied forces sent to capture Narvik and its valuable harbor.[56]

Operation Wildente

The conquest of Steinkjer provided the Germans with a suitable staging area for an offensive northward. Lieutenant-General Valentin Feurstein, the commander of the 2nd Mountain Division, was made responsible for the mission to establish a land connection with Dietl's troops. Perhaps the very difficult terrain north of Steinkjer motivated the choice of Feurstein to lead the advance. Mountain troops were required, as well as a commander acquainted with the kind of terrain that lay ahead. For these reasons, the 2nd Mountain Division had received orders on April 23 to prepare for transfer to Norway.[57] The sea voyage was not completed without loss; British submarines torpedoed transport ships and caused casualties amounting to fifty dead and sixty-four wounded. It was not known at the time, but those losses would constitute approximately half of the casualties suffered by the 2nd Mountain Division during the campaign.[58] As many of the bridges and roads north of Oslo had been damaged, substantial elements of the division were air transported from Oslo to Trondheim, as was part of the supplies.[59]

When Feurstein began his operation on May 4, he only had small forces available. His attack force was formed of one battalion each from the 137th and 138th Mountain Regiments, as well as a company from the 136th Mountain Regiment, supported by three mountain artillery batteries and an engineer platoon. It was not a strong force, but Feurstein believed that the defenses were weak and accordingly attacked with what he had on hand.[60]

Reconnaissance conducted by air units and patrols on the ground on May 3 showed that Allied units were retreating. On the following day, Feurstein struck. The German attack proceeded without major drama. On May 5, Feurstein reported that the Namsos–Grong line had been reached and that many prisoners had been captured.[61]

In the evening of May 5, Feurstein's troops were already hurrying north from Grong towards Mosjøen, moving at very high pace. Within twenty-four hours they had reached Fossmoforsen, 60 km north of Grong, where a destroyed bridge halted them temporarily. They soon overcame the obstacle, and two days later Feurstein's men reached Fellingsfors, where they brushed off Norwegian defenders.[62]

However, Mosjøen was only an intermediate goal. Gruppe Feurstein would immediately continue northeast, but the terrain proved extremely difficult, particularly between Elfsfjord and Korgen. A daring plan was quickly conceived. On May 7, the Germans commandeered the passenger ship *Nord-Norge*. A reinforced mountain company commanded by Captain Holzinger embarked on the evening of May 8, whereupon the ship weighed anchor. It set course for Hemnesberget, located between Mosjøen and Mo. The operation was called *Wildente*.[63]

Soon after departing, the *Nord-Norge* was discovered by a British submarine. As the operation risked being revealed, the Germans turned back, but at 10.30 p.m. the following evening, the *Nord-Norge* set sail again. This time, there were no signs of the enemy. She continued towards her destination, which required her to cover around 380 km.[64]

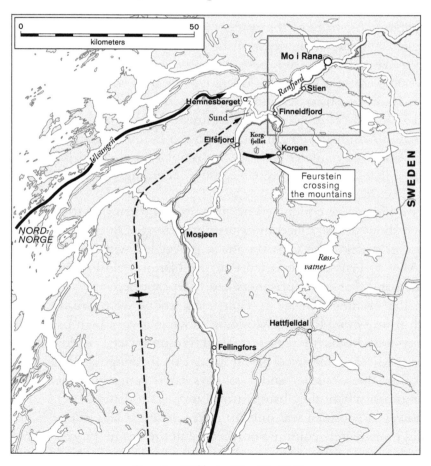

Operation Wildente, May 10, 1940

Norwegian coastguards, who reported to the Allied forces at Harstad, had, in fact, observed the *Nord-Norge*. The Germans did not know this and continued towards their objective. After sailing for forty hours, the crew on the *Nord-Norge* could see Hemnesberget ahead. They steered towards the quay, but when only 40 meters remained, rifle shots cracked through the air. The Germans immediately brought a heavy machine gun into a firing position on the deck and riddled the suspected enemy positions with bullets. They also opened fire with a 2-cm flak gun positioned on the *Nord-Norge's* deck.[65]

The fire from land inflicted casualties among the German soldiers on the *Nord-Norge*. The noise from the firing blended with the moaning from the wounded as the ship gradually drew closer to the quay. A sailor jumped off the ship with a hawser and moored her. A rifle squad immediately stormed ashore, rapidly followed by two more. Another two platoons disembarked soon afterwards. Bitter close combat ensued as the Germans worked their way into the village. The battle raged from house to house. A mortar squad brought ashore by the Germans proved very valuable in the hard fighting. Building after building was set ablaze and the number of wounded rose. Two German platoon commanders were hit and the entire force ashore had to be led by the one who remained.[66]

Suddenly, a nasty surprise hit the Germans. A British destroyer appeared on the scene and opened fire on the *Nord-Norge*, which sank quickly. The Germans were thereby deprived of their baggage and a large amount of ammunition. Even worse, many wounded had been brought on board, and they now sank to the bottom of the fjord together with the ship. However, the Germans had already brought their heavy weapons ashore, and they were now turned to fire on the destroyer, which sailed away and passed out of sight.[67]

By midnight, the noise of fighting began to fade away. As the night was not pitch dark, the Germans could again discern the destroyer on the surface of the fjord, but its guns remained silent. Instead, boats were launched, making the Germans believe that reinforcements were coming ashore, but in fact the remains of the troops that had defended Hemnesberget were evacuated instead.[68]

Hemnesberget is located at the tip of a peninsula, and the route followed by Gruppe Feurstein passed Finneid, at the base of the peninsula. It was very important to link up between Hemnesberget and Finneid. Prisoner interrogations revealed that there were also German units at Sund, around 1 km south of Hemnesberget. A platoon was dispatched while mortars and light guns were prepared to support the advance. Suddenly, a grenade exploded near the advancing platoon and wounded four soldiers. The heavy German weapons immediately replied and silenced the enemy.[69]

The platoon resumed the advance towards Sund. No further resistance hampered the German platoon. When it reached Sund, fellow German soldiers were indeed found. Around seventy men from the 7th Company, 138th Mountain Regiment, had been flown there by seven seaplanes. Led by Lieutenant Rudolf and supported by three Stuka dive-bombers, they had fought a night battle akin to the one experienced by Holzinger's men, securing a bridgehead. These actions had secured the Germans a foothold on the Hemnes peninsula. Holzinger's company had lost nine killed, ten wounded and three missing, while Rudolf's unit only suffered one killed and one wounded.[70]

While Holzinger's and Rudolf's men fought at Hemnesberget and Sund, Gruppe Feurstein proceeded north. On May 11, it captured Mosjøen. Thus approximately 50 km remained to be covered to establish contact with the units landed as part of Operation *Wildente*. As the terrain was very difficult, the distance could not be covered quickly, but contact was finally established on May 16. Meanwhile, Holzinger was supplied from the air, allowing him to attack towards Finneid, which was captured on May 15. When this goal was reached, Holzinger sent patrols to reconnoiter both northwards, towards Mo i Rana, and to Korgen, in the south. The information gained by these patrols facilitated Gruppe Feurstein's subsequent advance.[71]

Operation *Wildente* is of interest in more ways than one. It can almost be regarded as a miniature version of Operation *Weserübung*, when ground, sea and air units cooperated. However, at Hemnesberget, the cooperation took place at the tactical level. In addition to the air transport and fire support from Stuka dive-bombers, air reconnaissance was also very valuable to the two German companies.[72]

The attack on Hemnesberget also illustrates the German penchant for circumventing the enemy, as well as their habit of making use of mobility and high tempo. In this case, there were no mechanized units available. Instead, a solution had to be improvised at short notice. Outflanking maneuvers had frequently been used to upset the enemy during the advance from Oslo to Trondheim. It would again be used to great effect in a battle fought shortly after Operation *Wildente*.

The Battle of Stien

Air reconnaissance informed Lieutenant-Colonel Sorko that British units had established strong defensive positions at Stien, halfway between Finneid and Mo i Rana. The information was correct. Two companies from the Scots Guards had taken up positions along the river Dalselven at Stien, where the bridges over the river had been blown up. Another Scots Guards company and an independent company were in reserve slightly north of Dalselven, along the road to Mo i Rana. Also, four 25-pounder howitzers were in firing positions with the reserve. The British soldiers were responsible for the sector closest to the fjord. Further east, two Norwegian ski platoons covered the area around Bjerkmoen and Lille Ackersjøn against German outflanking maneuvers. The Norwegians had also told the British that they should hold the so-called Kobbernaglen hills north of the Dalselven, but the warning had been ignored.[73]

Lieutenant-Colonel Sorko commanded a mixed force to attack the enemy position at Stien. Most of the soldiers belonged to his battalion (II Battalion, 137th Mountain regiment), but one of its companies had been detached to defend Mosjøen. He had also received two companies from the 136th Mountain Regiment and a ski platoon named "Karolus." Fire support was provided by one platoon from the 112th Mountain Artillery Regiment. Sorko realized that the terrain would make a frontal attack costly and unlikely to succeed. The road from Finneid to Stien followed the shore of the fjord. To the east, ravines, cliffs and other obstacles would

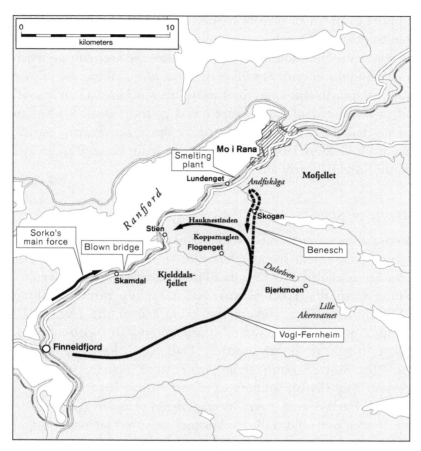

Battle at Stien May 16–18, 1940

hamper any advance. Sorko opted for a more wide-ranging outflanking move. All units available to him would be used in the attack. Captain Holzinger, with the forces that had participated in Operation *Wildente*, was made responsible for the defense of the Finneid area.[74]

At 10 a.m. on May 16, Sorko gave the necessary instruction to Captain Vogl-Fernheim. As commander of the 6th Company, he would conduct an outflanking move deep inland. He received, in addition to his own company, the ski platoon Karolus, which consisted of specially selected mountaineers. Vogl-Fernheim would first lead his men east from Finneid. After having advanced in this direction for 10 km, he would turn north. He would cross the river Dalselven at Flogenget, approximately 5 km upstream from the estuary. After overcoming the water obstacle, Vogl-Fernheim's main force would turn west and advance along the southern slope of Koppernaglen. The platoon Karolus, commanded by Second Lieutenant Benesch, would continue north and advance towards a smelting plant at Lundenget, southeast of Mo i Rana.[75]

Vogl-Fernheim's men prepared for the mission during the afternoon. Skis were tested and adjusted. Other equipment items were carefully checked, and at 11 p.m. Vogl-Fernheim's men were ready to embark on their mission. They set out, skiing up the slope east of Finneid in darkness. The vegetation soon concealed them from the remainder of Sorko's force.[76]

As Sorko's main force would not have to move as far through difficult terrain, it was allowed to rest during the night of May 16–17. In the morning, the first elements—a small bicycle force—set out to establish whether the road was blocked somewhere between Finneid and Stien.[77]

Sorko's lead company, reinforced by a mortar platoon and an engineer platoon, set out at noon. An obstacle was encountered at Skamdal where a section of the road had been blown up. This was not an insurmountable obstacle to Sorko's men, who continued along the road and reached the bay where the Dalselven debouched into the sea. They could see the blown bridges over the river.[78]

Suddenly, British artillery shells exploded around them. The commander of the lead German platoon, Second Lieutenant Lampertz, was seriously wounded and would subsequently die. The British artillery had opened fire at a moment when the Germans were vulnerable, as there was little cover for them to find. Machine guns also began to fire at the exposed Germans.[79]

Sorko surged forward when he heard the noise. When he arrived, he saw a scene that did not appeal to him at all. The British held commanding positions on the slopes north of Dalselven. They had made good use of the terrain and camouflaged their positions well. They had excellent fields of fire and could riddle the entire southern slope along the river and the bay. Sorko immediately realized how difficult his situation was and ordered the heavy weapons—the mortars, the light infantry howitzers and the platoon from the mountain artillery regiment—to be brought into firing positions.[80]

It was a difficult and arduous task. If the heavy weapons were positioned on the road, they would either be exposed to British fire or only have very limited fields of fire themselves. The only realistic alternative was to pull the heavy weapons up the rocky slope to find better firing positions. The German soldiers had to strain every muscle to move the guns and mortars, but by 4 p.m. all the light infantry howitzers and one mountain artillery piece were ready to fire.[81]

At 4.15 p.m., Sorko ordered the lead company to advance to the terrain above the road while the heavy weapons provided fire support. A machine-gun platoon had also positioned itself on the slope north of the Kjelddalsfjell, from where it could fire upon the British positions. The soldiers of the company moved eastwards through the forest on the slope and took up firing positions, from where an attack on the Dalselven and the area north of it could be initiated.[82]

The British did not rest silently. The German movements in the forest were noted and mortar fire was directed towards the area. As the other British units held their fire, the Germans could not establish their positions with sufficient accuracy, but at 5.30 p.m. they were helped by the Luftwaffe—albeit in an unusual way. A German reconnaissance aircraft appeared above the British soldiers. The latter opened fire on the aircraft, thus enabling Sorko's men to detect many positions and better understand how the British had organized their defense.[83]

Sorko had no information on the whereabouts of Vogl-Fernheim at this stage. A German Army reconnaissance aircraft had reconnoitered the area where Vogl-Fernheim's men were supposed to advance, but it could only report that it had not found them.[84]

Meanwhile, Vogl-Fernheim was just as ill-informed about what had happened close to the estuary, where Sorko's main force maneuvered slowly. Vogl-Fernheim's men had continued forward in darkness and not encountered any enemy until 2 a.m., when a British recon aircraft appeared. As the Germans had reached the bare mountain region above the tree line, the men had to keep still between rocks to avoid detection. After some time, the British aircraft disappeared and the march could be resumed. After a few hours, a break was taken to allow the men an hour of rest before they continued on at 6 a.m.[85]

After the break, Vogl-Fernheim's men proceeded north. They soon encountered a Norwegian ski patrol. This was a bad sign, as the vital element of surprise might have been lost. Ski tracks from other patrols could also be seen in the snow, but nothing else was seen of the enemy. Despite his worries, Vogl-Fernheim decided to continue according to plan. He and his men had reached so far north that they were about to descend into the valley where the Dalselven flowed. At this stage, Vogl-Fernheim ordered Benesch to take his twenty-three-man platoon north. As they would have to cover a greater distance, they had to move more quickly. Benesch chose a more easterly route than Vogl-Fernheim's company.[86]

Both German units had to get down the slope to cross the Dalselven. The slope was very difficult to negotiate as it was steep and rocky. Vogl-Fernheim's men had to carry their skis and proceed on foot. Benesch's men were more fortunate as they found a narrow and yet useful depression after searching the terrain for a while. They could ski down the slope and cross the Dalselven without much difficulty. Vogl-Fernheim was not as lucky. When his company reached the river, it turned out that the ice was cracking, making it impossible to cross the river. The men reconnoitered upstream and finally found a stretch of ice that was strong enough to support them. They had lost time due to their search, however, and the company did not reach the northern shore until 2 p.m. Despite being behind schedule, there was, in fact, no alternative but to continue; the thin ice sheet had cracked when the company crossed it.[87]

The terrain to the north of the river proved very difficult. Cliffs and snowdrifts made the advance time-consuming and arduous. Vogl-Fernheim realized that he would not be able to launch the attack on time, but he nevertheless continued in the direction planned. He hoped that by continuing he could at least could facilitate Sorko's attack.[88]

At around 4 p.m., Vogl-Fernheim and his men heard the noise of battle from the west. They presumed it originated from the Stien area. Despite being exhausted from the grueling march in deep snow and difficult terrain, the sound of the battle urged them to continue. Meanwhile, Benesch had continued towards the smelting plant. At 5 p.m., he and his men reached Skogan. From there, they could attack presumed Allied positions along the Andfiskaaga stream.[89]

Sorko only vaguely guessed where the outflanking units might be. He occasionally heard firing in the Mo i Rana direction, but it hardly made the situation clearer. After careful consideration, Sorko decided to wait and see, but as a precaution, he ordered two of his companies to move east without being observed by the enemy, cross the Dalselven and then attack the flank of the enemy position.[90]

These maneuvers did not end the noise of the Battle of Stein. Artillery and mortars continued to fire, but after a while, the Germans had to conserve ammunition. They had very little available except for what they had pulled along on sledges. A few half-hearted attempts to cross the river on the severely damaged bridges failed. It only remained for Sorko to wait for the outflanking movements to pay off.[91]

The daylight gradually faded away, but as it was the second half of May, the nights did not become pitch-dark at this latitude. Sorko still had no information on Vogl-Fernheim's whereabouts, but at 11 p.m. he suddenly heard machine guns in the area near the enemy's east flank. The noise was easily recognized; the very high rate of fire produced by the German MG 34 machine gun resulted in a characteristic sound that was quite different from the machine guns used by other armies. Red and white flares confirmed that the flanking force had appeared.[92]

This became the attack signal for Sorko's men. The heavy weapons intensified their fire while the mountain troopers stealthily moved towards the British positions. When the defenders began to fire with small arms, the Germans could see them and direct mortar and howitzer fire accurately at the British positions. At the same time, the German mountaineers attacked the enemy flank and gradually rolled it up.[93]

A fierce battle ensued as the British soldiers offered dogged resistance, but the outflanking moves had given the Germans the edge. As German forces attacked it from the east, the British position was rendered untenable; by 3 a.m., the engagement was over. The British withdrew across the ridge north of the Dalselven as the Germans continued to fire at them.[94]

As the fighting raged at Stien, Benesch's platoon attacked the smelting plant. At Skogan, there was a bridge spanning the Andfiskaaga, which the Germans captured intact. The Norwegian picket at the bridge was surprised and did not even get a chance to open fire. Had this coup failed, Benesch would probably not have been able to continue—the water barrier could hardly have been crossed anywhere else.[95]

Benesch and his men hurried towards the smelting plant at the shore, but before they reached the target, a force consisting of thirty-eight Swedish volunteers led by Captain Björkman was encountered. The Swedes opened machine-gun fire from a distance beyond the range of the submachine guns Benesch's men were equipped with. The Germans found good cover in the terrain, but to Benesch it appeared that he was about to be outflanked. He decided to pull back, which his men successfully did, except that contact with a group of eight men was lost. The German soldiers again crossed the Andfiskaaga on the bridge and hid in a nearby farm. They used the pause to snatch some rest.[96]

Benesch and his soldiers remained in the Skogan area until dusk on May 18. At that stage, after having observed the Allied forces nearby, Benesch decided to return to Finneid. His platoon conducted a seventeen-hour march before reaching Finneid. It is unclear to what extent Benesch's mission contributed to the German success at Stien, but perhaps his foray caused alarm in the British and Norwegian units that defended the area southwest of Mo i Rana.[97]

The night fighting had exhausted Sorko's men, but at 8 a.m. on May 18 they began to pursue the retreating enemy. The Germans reached the smelting plant at Lundenget at around 11 a.m., after which fighting took place for a few hours before the Germans broke the resistance. Sorko sent out patrols that returned at 8 p.m. and reported that the enemy had abandoned Mo i Rana.[98]

Over the course of May 17 and 18, Sorko's battle group suffered casualties amounting to fourteen killed and twenty-six wounded. The British lost over seventy killed and wounded, to which losses in the Norwegian and Swedish units can be added. Without any notable numerical superiority, Sorko had maneuvered successfully to oust an enemy from a strong defensive position while enduring only half as many casualties as the enemy.[99]

Narvik

While Sorko fought at Stien, the situation at Narvik grew ever more ominous. Lieutenant-General Dietl's soldiers still held a rather large area, but they were being pressed hard by far larger Allied forces. Approximately 300 km still separated Dietl's men from Feurstein's. When Dietl and his mountain troops landed on April 9, they rapidly captured Narvik and soon established control over a relatively wide perimeter. However, the ten destroyers that had transported his men could not return to Germany as the tankers failed to show up. Without fuel, they had no alternative but to remain at Narvik. British Navy forces subsequently attacked and sunk the German destroyers, whose crews would be employed as ground soldiers. Only one of the supply ships arrived, the *Jan Wellem*, but she was sunk in the harbor before her cargo could be unloaded. The Germans managed to salvage some valuable goods from the wreck, but Dietl's supply situation remained precarious and left him with few options.[100]

As on so many other occasions during the campaign in Norway, the Luftwaffe was instrumental in bringing supplies to the far-flung areas where Army units fought. For a brief period, transport aircraft were able to land on the frozen Hartvigsjøn lake, and float planes also landed next to Narvik's quays to bring supplies. However, even if supplies were brought to Narvik, it still remained to haul them to the positions defended—a strenuous task in the meter-deep snow.[101]

The difficult terrain, deep snow and scarcity of roads were not only disadvantageous to Dietl. His adversaries also suffered from the harsh environment, and as they were intent on dislodging the Germans, they faced the problem of bringing all their combat units forward in the prevailing conditions. This fact goes a long way to explain why Dietl did not have to face a determined attack until May. Vacillation amongst the Allied commanders also afforded the Germans some respite.[102]

In May 1940, the Allied buildup in the area close to Narvik had reached such an extent that Dietl's men were in grave danger. The situation became especially critical when Allied forces landed at Bjerkvik, north of Narvik. As the area Dietl had to defend was large and the enemy's numerical superiority was almost overwhelming, reinforcements were urgently needed. The Germans tried many alternatives as it was unclear whether Gruppe Feurstein would reach Dietl before it was too late.[103]

Air power was vital for bringing reinforcements to Narvik, but the Luftwaffe could also contribute in other ways. The German parachute formations belonged to the Luftwaffe, and some of them could be sent to Narvik. I Battalion of the 1st Parachute Regiment had participated in battles in the Netherlands in May and was then sent to Stendal in northern Germany, where it arrived on May 19. Two days later, it received orders to transfer immediately to Norway for an imminent air landing at Narvik.[104]

Sergeant Fritz Scheuering served in the parachute battalion. Like his comrades, he began to pack equipment, weapons and everything else that was needed for a combat mission. This time, they were also instructed to bring mountain boots and snow smocks. As the newspapers had already written several articles on the battles fought by Dietl's mountain troops, the paratroopers could already guess their mission by the time they climbed aboard the train that would take them northwest.[105]

At Flensburg, Scheuering made his morning toilet on German soil for the last time for several weeks. The train then continued into Denmark, towards Aalborg. When the train arrived, trucks waited to bring the parachutists to the airfield outside the town, where the men boarded Ju 52 transport aircraft. They were to fly them to Norway, and no time was to be wasted. The pilots revved the engines as soon as everything had been taken aboard. The parachutists were offered life vests, but they just laughed and said that nothing would happen during the flight. They could soon see the bluish-green waves of the Skagerrak below the aircraft.

Scheuering absent-mindedly noted how the Danish mainland gradually fell behind the aircraft. The humming noise from the engines made him drowsy, but after a while he was woken by the yell, "Norway ahead!" He moved forward to a window and saw the coast. Somewhat later, his eyes fell on valleys bathing in sunshine, wooded peaks and rapid watercourses. The beauty of the Norwegian landscape impressed him greatly. A few people next to some houses waved at the German aircraft.

The landscape was more barren further north. The transport aircraft had to fly at higher altitude and encountered clouds. Scheuering could hear the radio operator tune in to the frequency used by the control center on the ground and call it. Soon, he shouted, "Only a few minutes remain before we reach our destination!" The pilot gently descended. It turned out that the navigation had been almost perfect; the crowded air base not far from Trondheim appeared ahead of the heavily laden Junkers, but despite the frantic activity on the ground, the landing was conducted without any problems. However, one transport aircraft was shot down not far from Rena, between Oslo and Trondheim. All on board were killed. It was probably a case of fratricide, as there were no Allied units in the area at this time in May.[106]

Scheuering, however, managed to safely disembark from the Junkers that had flown him to Trondheim. He found the small air base astonishingly well organized. Bombers, fighters, transport aircraft and dive-bombers had all been allotted separate sectors. Trucks brought bombs and ammunition to the aircraft readied for various missions. Canisters with supplies for the troops at Narvik were secured at Heinkel He 111 and Junkers Ju 88 aircraft. A transport aircraft took off with a deafening noise and left a huge cloud of dust behind, which partly obstructed Scheuering's vision. A sudden alarm signal interrupted his reflections. The sound was caused by another aircraft about to land, carrying more men from his battalion.

The parachutists were soon shown their station, a large wooden building inside which straw mattresses had been prepared for them. The rest of the day was spent chatting, but towards the evening, when his watch showed 10 p.m., it struck Scheuering that it was still fairly light outside. As he had never been so far north, he asked a few soldiers who had already spent some time at Trondheim, "When does the night begin here?"

"There is no night here," laughed one of the soldiers.

The parachutists realized that they had better try to get some sleep despite the brightness of the night. As they were experienced soldiers, they knew that they might have to wait for a long time until the next moment of rest came. However, it was difficult to sleep near the airfield. As the night never became pitch-black, aircraft could land and take off all night. The noise from aircraft disturbed the soldiers as they tried to sleep. The soldiers who had managed to fall asleep were awakened at 2 a.m. as they had to prepare their parachutes and other equipment. Soon thereafter, Scheuering and the other men marched to the Junkers aircraft that were waiting for them. An old World War I pilot waited next to the aircraft that was to bring Scheuering to Narvik. He greeted the parachutists with the words, "Well then, lads. Time to enter the case."

However, it was not easy to enter the aircraft. The Junkers had been modified to enable it to cover the distance to Narvik and back. Extra fuel had been stowed on board, and there were few suitable places remaining for the soldiers themselves. Nevertheless, the aircraft was soon ready for take-off. The pilot revved the engine; the Junkers increased speed along the runway and soon moved rapidly enough to lift off with its heavy load.

Parachuting Over Narvik

Scheuering had been assigned a place near the hatch they would jump out from when the target area had been reached. From his position, he had an excellent outlook of the terrain below. The sun blazed on mountains, mires, cliffs, snowfields and ice-covered lakes. The Junkers flew at rather low altitude as the pilot made use of the terrain to avoid detection. It had been reported that British fighters operated in the area. Scheuering stood next to the radio operator and could not conceal his admiration for the pilot. The radio operator said that he had flown with the pilot for more than a decade, beginning when they both worked for Lufthansa.

The hours passed as the Junkers flew north. Scheuering observed that the landscape was more barren in the north. He saw nothing but mountains, cliffs, snow and ice. No roads could be seen. He tried to imagine what it looked like at Narvik, where, he presumed, battles were raging. He realized that he might soon be engaged in vicious fighting. Suddenly, a shout brusquely interrupted his thoughts—"Ready!"

Scheuering secured the cord that would release the parachute soon after he had jumped out of the aircraft. Remarkably, he could see a large swastika flag, with the red colour contrasting sharply against the surroundings, which were composed of a small green patch in a desert of cliffs and snow. His eyes also found a few small buildings and something that appeared to be a railroad.

Someone behind Scheuering shouted, "Ready to jump!" He grabbed the handles at the opening and stepped forward. The icy wind caused his eyes to fill with tears. He still waited for the signal to jump; it seemed like an eternity before he finally heard it. He reacted almost instinctively and threw himself into the air. He swirled down towards the ground

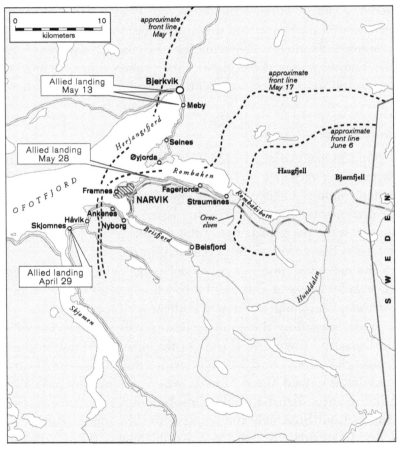

Narvik area April–June 1940

like a leaf in the fall wind before his parachute unfolded and slowed him down. After a textbook landing, Scheuering immediately undid his harness. Two Messerschmitt Bf 110s circled above him, but he only deigned to give them a brief look before searching for his comrades. It turned out that only one of them had been injured in the landing; all the others had landed safely.

The unit Scheuering belonged to gathered in the wooded huts that he had seen from the aircraft just before jumping. Some soldiers who had fought at Narvik for a long time soon found them. They were very glad to see that reinforcements were arriving. However, the pleasant atmosphere soon gave way to the harsh realities of war. Scheuering and his comrades had landed close to the railroad and climbed aboard a car to be brought closer to the front line. During the rail journey, Scheuering was captivated by the surrounding landscape. They had to proceed cautiously when they reached the Rombaksfjord in case British destroyers appeared and opened fire. Finally, they reached a point beyond which it was imprudent to proceed by rail. The parachutists had to make the last part of the journey on foot, and a considerable distance remained. Hour after hour the soldiers walked along the railroad. They occasionally saw British destroyers; Scheuering expected to see muzzle flashes from them, but nothing happened.

The arduous march continued. Rain made the situation even more deplorable, and after a while the group of men left the railroad and ascended the slope south of it to find combat positions in the mountains. Finally, Scheuering saw a few grey figures. Were they enemies or Germans? The distance was too great to determine their nationality. Scheuering and a few other parachutists slowly stole closer. As a precaution, Scheuering placed a machine gun in a firing position to provide covering fire if the soldiers continuing forward needed it. The distance to the grey figures shrank, and at last Scheuering could see that they wore German parachute uniforms. The men belonged to the same battalion, but they had landed earlier.

Scheuering asked where he could find the battalion commanders' post and was told that he would have to walk for twenty minutes to reach it. He immediately set out in the direction shown and shed his caution as the grey figures had turned out to be friendly. He quickly walked towards a crest to reach the command post. Suddenly, as he reached the crest, bullets whizzed past him. Scheuering immediately threw himself into cover, firmly resolved not to expose himself to any undue risk again.

At last, Scheuering and his men reached their destination. They were utterly exhausted, but there was no time for sleep. They were sent to man defensive positions. Dressed in their soaking-wet uniforms, they crouched in the dugouts while an ice-cold wind swept over the mountain. Nothing else remained to do except wait and watch the surrounding terrain. The hours passed slowly. On one occasion, the men were ordered to regroup to a nearby position. They rose laboriously, cursing the exertion, but it helped little.

A rest in some buildings near the Orne River was more heartening. The men also received warm food, a luxury for frozen and hungry soldiers. They could also hang their wet clothes to dry. After eating and taking care of his uniform, Scheuering fell asleep. He continued to sleep despite the rolling thunder from artillery fire. Meanwhile, the situation deteriorated for the Germans in the Narvik area. After he had slept—Scheuering had no idea how long he had been asleep—he and his men were sent to defend positions closer to the Rombaksbotn.

The new positions were subjected to heavy fire, with British destroyers joining in. Scheuering wished that at least one German gun had replied, but the only thing he and the other parachutists could do was to crouch down. Powerless, he saw comrades being hit and wounded. Medical orderlies worked to bring the wounded into safety, but it was a difficult and dangerous task. One of the wounded waited more than three hours to be evacuated as the shelling made evacuation impossible. He eventually died, and the Scheuering thought the corpse resembled a wax doll.

The Allied fire cut the telephone lines at times. It also made it difficult for the Germans to bring ammunition forward. Individual soldiers were detailed to carry ammunition and food to the dugouts, but it was a very dangerous task. Scheuering saw several of them suddenly fall down after being hit in the head by snipers.

The weather had been forbidding ever since Scheuering landed at Narvik, but at this stage the sky actually cleared. Sunshine was definitely preferable as it allowed the soldiers' clothes to dry. Scheuering was also delighted by another sight: bombers from the Luftwaffe attacking Allied positions, thus providing some relief to the hard-pressed parachutists. Scheuering and his comrades waved their hands, but the aircrews probably failed to see them. Nevertheless, he noted that the Allied fire eased after the air attack. A few hours later, he also witnessed an attack by German dive-bombers.

Neither Scheuering nor anybody else on the German side knew it, but the Allies had already decided to evacuate Narvik on May 25. Despite the fact that Dietl was heavily outnumbered (reinforcements notwithstanding), the Allied forces would content themselves with wreaking as much damage as possible to the harbor and the railroad. Meanwhile, they exerted as much pressure as possible on Dietl's men, not least to conceal the impending evacuation.[107]

Further south, Gruppe Feurstein captured Bodø early on June 1. Dietl's situation reports indicated that his forces, which hung onto an area east of Narvik, near the Swedish border, were on the brink of the abyss. Several German schemes were conceived to reinforce Dietl, but none of them materialized except Operation *Büffel*. The latter was conducted by very skilled mountaineers who crossed the extremely difficult mountainous terrain between Bodø and Narvik, where no roads existed. However, the distance was considerable and they did not reach Dietl until the Allies had evacuated Narvik. It only remained to accept the surrender of the Norwegian forces in northern Norway.[108]

A Unique Operation

At first glance, Operation *Weserübung* may appear to be an anomaly in the German Blitzkrieg. Tanks were used in Norway, but they were quite few and their contribution was not significant. Even less important was the alleged combination of dive-bombers and tanks. If it were presumed that the Blitzkrieg first and foremost was a concept based on technological development—such as tanks and combat aircraft—the campaign in Norway indeed would appear to be an impasse in the development of Blitzkrieg. If, however, the Blitzkrieg is regarded as a continuous development of the German art of war, the campaign in Norway does not appear anomalous. The efforts to attain conclusive results rapidly by relying on surprise, maneuver, initiative, mobility and speed characterized the plan for Operation *Weserübung* as well as its conduct.

Small German armor units were committed in Norway, particularly in the advances along the Gudbrandsdalen and Østerdalen. They contributed to the German success, but clearly they were far less important compared to the other campaigns discussed in this book. However, if the contribution of the armored force was far from substantial, the same can certainly not be said of the Luftwaffe's successful contribution to the campaign. The German Air Force contributed in almost every way, but perhaps the least important was the direct fire support to ground combat units. Despite the shortage of artillery, the German Army units fighting in Norway only occasionally received fire support from the air. Gruppe XXI described the tactical cooperation between ground and air units as "black sheep." There were many cases of fratricide, as well as air attacks on positions not held by the enemy. The difficult terrain, which put an emphasis on skilled navigation, was part of the explanation for this, and the communication lines between ground and air units were also too long, which was particularly disadvantageous in fluid actions.[109]

However, there was a more fundamental explanation, and this was emphasized in the report written by the 3rd Mountain Division. It stressed that close cooperation between air and ground units had hardly been practiced at all in peacetime. Many of the problems associated with close air support were thus not revealed until operations had been initiated. One such example is the fact that the airmen were often issued maps of unsuitable scale.[110]

The problematic and often ineffective close air support should not, however, obscure the overall contribution by the Luftwaffe. By rendering Allied sea transport to Norway very dangerous, the Luftwaffe severely curtailed Allied freedom of action. Conversely, the Luftwaffe's capacity to transport men, equipment and supplies increased the number of alternatives the Germans could choose from. These two aspects alone sufficed to make the Luftwaffe crucial to the German success, but the value of German air power was even greater. For example, Sorko was aided by reconnaissance aircraft in the action at Stien, and this was far from an isolated example. During Operation *Wildente*, the Luftwaffe air-landed troops and provided fire support. The attacks against Allied artillery observed by Scheuering at Narvik not only reduced the number of shells fired at the parachutists, but also boosted German morale—and probably had the opposite effect on their opponents.[111]

Many Luftwaffe officers had previously served in the Army, which probably facilitated inter-service cooperation. The shortcomings that were nevertheless evident can probably be attributed to the rapid expansion in the second half of the 1930s. It has been claimed that the German campaign in Norway 1940 was the first major example of an operation where success depended on the efforts of three services acting jointly. The observation appears correct. This cooperation was mainly achieved by individual cooperation at all levels rather than a clear doctrine shaping their actions.[112]

The Army combat units were also dependent on initiative at low levels in battle. Sorko was on his own at Stein, and he did not hesitate to allow a junior officer to independently conduct a wide-ranging and vital flanking move without having any kind of means to communicate. This could also be observed at Steinkjer and during Operation *Wildente*. Furthermore, these actions were fought after very brief preparations.

A study on how the German ground combat units fought in Norway shows many similarities with what is regarded as typical of the armored units. In fact, the German ground units advanced rapidly in Norway too. For example, the Germans covered 130 km in a week when they advanced from Aasmarka to Otta in the Gudbrandsdal.[113] Perhaps even more impressive was Feurstein's advance from Grong to Mosjøen, when 160 km were covered in six days.[114] These performances relied on repeated outflanking and other kinds of maneuvers conducted by the infantry and mountain troops. This behavior is evident at all levels in the organization and is testimony to the initiative fostered in the German ground forces. The frequent employment of hastily formed battle groups, big and small, was also common in Norway.

The battles fought in Norway did not result in major casualties. The Germans reported 1,317 killed in action, 1,604 wounded and 2,375 missing or lost at sea.[115] Neither did the Allies pay a high price in blood. The British lost 1,869 killed, wounded and missing during the ground fighting in Norway and around 2,500 lost at sea.[116] The combined Polish and French casualties amounted to 530.[117] Around 860 men in the Norwegian armed forces appear to have lost their lives, and their number of wounded seems to have been similar.[118]

Equipment losses seem to have had greater consequences for future operations. Luftwaffe losses included 242 aircraft of all types.[119] Worse for the Germans, one heavy cruiser, two light cruisers, ten destroyers, one torpedo boat and six submarines were lost and four cruisers and six destroyers were damaged.[120] The warship losses meant that the German Navy had little use for the bases that had been captured. Therefore, one of the reasons an attack on Norway was deemed worthwhile would not be realized until later. Similarly, the damage inflicted on the harbor at Narvik meant that iron ore would not be shipped until many months later. However, as the ice melted in the Baltic, the iron ore could be transported by rail to Luleå and shipped to Germany from there. Meanwhile, the Germans could repair the harbor at Narvik during the summer and fall of 1940.

The German victory in Norway depended on the element of surprise during the initial phase of the operation and subsequently on the performance of the units in Norway. However, there was another important reason for the outcome; Norway was not the only arena to consider. Further south, huge ground forces had gathered and were ready for battle. The expected operations in Western Europe had a profound influence on the ability to devote military resources to Scandinavia.

CHAPTER 4

TO SURPRISE ONESELF

After the victorious campaign in Poland, Hitler found himself in a situation he had feared but not expected. He had presumed that the western powers would allow him to take his bite of Poland without hearing much more than a grumble. The British and French declaration of war on September 3 was a grave disappointment to the German dictator. He had counted on the western powers lacking the resolve to declare war.

The events that followed during the fall of 1939 did, however, show that Hitler was not entirely wrong in his assumptions. Neither France nor Britain made any earnest attempts to help Poland. When the Polish government was forced to flee to Romania as Stalin attacked from the east, the fate of Poland was already decided. The French and British had already settled for a prolonged war with Germany, a war in which the supply of raw materials were envisaged as one of the deciding factors.

Hitler was well aware that Germany lacked the raw materials for a prolonged war. Such a war did not favor him. Furthermore, he could not count on Stalin to remain reasonably friendly. It was probably considerations such as these that led the Führer to decide to attack westwards as soon as the fall of 1939.

The German armed forces argued against such a scheme and emphasized the unfavorable weather expected. However, there was also another cause for concern. The campaign in Poland had revealed many shortcomings, not least in training standards. The Army high command was very anxious to correct them before embarking on another major operation, but Hitler differed. Judging from events that would occur later in the war, Hitler had a tendency to exaggerate the importance of ideological commitment and enthusiasm and downgrade the value of training and education. He also seems to have believed that Britain and France lacked enthusiasm and conviction at the time.

In any case, it turned out that Hitler would repeatedly settle for a date for the beginning of the offensive in the west only to be forced to postpone as the weather proved unsuitable. Nevertheless, Hitler persisted until January 1940, when a German courier plane mistakenly landed near Mechelen, Belgium. A German staff officer was on board the aircraft, and he was carrying secret documents in his briefcase. As the plans were thus presumed to have been revealed to the enemy, the Germans decided to postpone the offensive for several months.[1]

It seems that the forced landing at Mechelen was a blessing to the Germans. Possibly the most important advantage was the time that could now be devoted to the lessons learned from the campaign in Poland. An ambitious program was created to reveal and attend to the shortcomings through extensive training and exercises. The German Army undertook this process thoroughly, and with a degree of frankness and self-criticism that was unusual for a victorious army.[2]

The extensive training and exercise program allowed the Germans to reach a high level of proficiency that had not been attainable during the rapid expansion before the war. The lessons learned in Poland allowed the Germans to focus their exercises on matters that were crucial to combat and operations. The campaign in Poland had also showed that some commanders were not up to the task. These less capable commanders could be weeded out by making the exercises very demanding. It is likely that these measures made the German Army of 1940 notably more proficient than it had been when the attack on Poland was launched.[3]

The Germans also changed the composition of some of their units. Four light divisions had fought in 1939, but these were converted to Panzer divisions before the offensive in the west was launched. The fact that the light divisions were disbanded has been seen as an indication that they had been a failure during the campaign in Poland, but that is not quite true. Hermann Hoth commanded XV Corps, which consisted of two light divisions. The corps successfully accomplished its missions and the light divisions performed creditably. This is also evident from the reports Hoth wrote after the campaign. One of these reports began with the sentence: "The success attained by the light divisions has exceeded high expectations." Another report, slightly burnt at the edges after a fire caused by a British bombing attack in 1942, stated that "the light divisions, whose infantry attacking power combined with armor and artillery support allowed them to advance deeply, have proven themselves."[4]

It is quite clear that the light divisions could be compared to the Panzer divisions. In the south, the 4th Light Division fought alongside the 2nd Panzer Division for three weeks. The two divisions seem to have enjoyed an equal share of success. The light divisions in Hoth's corps also acquitted themselves well. These observations may be interpreted as showing that the German mechanized formations outmaneuvered their Polish adversaries rather than defeating them by overwhelming firepower—the light divisions were as mobile as the Panzer divisions, but had fewer tanks.[5]

Why, then, were the light divisions converted to Panzer divisions? Another report, again from Hoth's XV Corps, provides a clue. It emphasizes that a central tenet from the years before the war broke out had been confirmed—tanks should be employed in large formations. Attacks by individual platoons led to failures and unnecessarily high losses. Interestingly, the report compared the German experience with French doctrine, with the latter advocating the commitment of smaller units over larger sectors of the front.[6]

As Poland's border was quite long relative to the size of her armed forces, her defenses had had comparatively low density. Under such circumstances, the risk of failure when attacking with tanks was reduced, although such incidents did nevertheless occur. An attack in Western Europe would be very different. The British, French, Belgian and Dutch forces were numerically far stronger than the Polish armed forces had been in 1939. Furthermore, the front line was actually shorter in the west. The Germans had to expect a much denser defense. Additionally, the units of the western powers were better equipped than the Polish because the former had a much larger economy to rely on. These circumstances suggested that many tanks were needed per division—more than the light divisions, with their single armored battalions. In particular, when the units had been reduced due to losses, the light divisions might be even worse off.

Except for abolishing the light divisions, the Germans avoided significant changes to their combat units. The emphasis was on strengthening the combat power of the existing units by training and exercises that were often conducted in larger formations. This extensive German effort contrasts against the Allied preparations. They did not spend much time at all on exercises. However, given their different views on the fundamental characteristics of war, it is doubtful whether they would have benefitted as much as the Germans did from an extensive training program.[7]

The Germans continued working on their plans during the winter and the spring of 1940. The campaign in Norway and Denmark did not cause any significant interruption as separate staffs and units were detailed for Operation *Weserübung*. The early plans, which superficially resembled the Schlieffen Plan of 1914, were discarded. Instead, a completely different concept was chosen. This originated from Lieutenant-General Erich von Manstein, chief of staff of one of the three Army groups that were to participate in the offensive.[8]

The original plan placed the center of gravity on the northern wing, which was made up of Army Group B, commanded by Colonel-General Fedor von Bock. It would attack through the Netherlands and Belgium while Army Group A, commanded by Colonel-General Gerd von Rundstedt, would advance through southern Belgium and Luxembourg and, like a door moving on its hinges, follow the southern flank of Army Group B. In the south, Army Group C, commanded by Colonel-General Wilhelm von Leeb, would assume a rather passive role—to defend along the border, opposite the so-called French "Maginot Line."[9]

Erich von Manstein's proposal was radically different. First, the center of gravity would be moved from Army Group B to Army Group A. Second, the entire purpose of the first stage of the campaign was altered. The Germans would surprise the enemy by moving strong mobile forces belonging to Army Group A through the Ardennes. After crossing the Meuse River at Sedan, the German main force would proceed west at high speed—towards the English Channel—and cut off the Allied forces in the north from their supplies. Army Group B was allotted a more limited role—to attract and engage Allied forces.[10]

The plan would become known as the "*Sichelschnitt-Plan*" (Sickle-cut-Plan), but not until the operation had been completed. Also, its originator would be transferred from the western front at the end of January to assume command of the XXXVIII Corps. The radical thought that had guided von Manstein was not fully shared by those who worked with the plan during the winter and the spring of 1940. This did not result in the original concept being diluted, but expectations became more modest.[11]

In many ways, the attack in the west heralded a new epoch; this operation saw the assembly of what must be regarded as the first Panzer army in history. Seven Panzer divisions were included in Army Group A. Three of them were found in Guderian's XIX Corps and two in Reinhardt's XXXXI Corps. Together with Gustav von Wietersheim's XIV Corps, with two motorized infantry divisions, they formed *Panzergruppe von Kleist*, which would have a crucial role during the operations in May, when it would attack across the Meuse at Sedan and Monthermé. Next to von Kleist's northern flank, Hermann Hoth's XV Corps, with two Panzer divisions, would attack. It was a concentration of armor the likes of which had never been seen.[12]

Parachute units figured prominently in the German invasion of Norway, and the planning for the attack in the west also included a spectacular effort by airborne units. However, in the latter operation, they would actually serve mainly as a diversion to ensure that the Allied commanders had their eyes riveted on the events in the north rather than the Ardennes. The Belgian fortress Eben-Emael, commanding

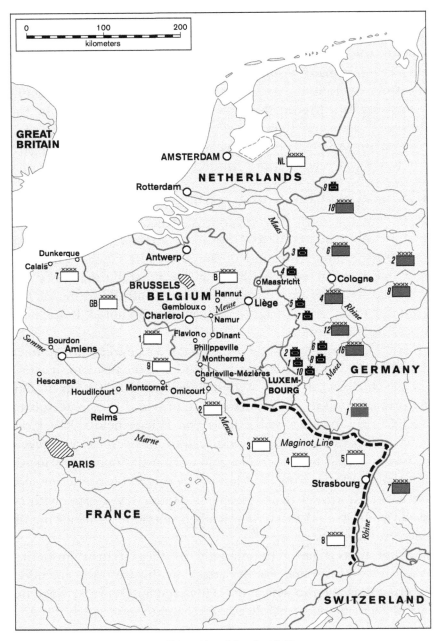

Dispositions May 9, 1940

important river crossings south of Maastricht, was regarded as one of the most modern fixed defense works in existence. A daring assault by stormtroopers landing by gliders on the fortress roof would knock the fortress out at the beginning of the offensive.[13]

Airborne troops would be used extensively in the Netherlands, where numerous canals and rivers threatened to halt units advancing on the ground. A quick victory in the north would free German units for employment elsewhere. The water barriers could delay units advancing on the ground, but air landings offered a chance to capture vital bridges before the Dutch defenders destroyed them.

In fact, it was not self-evident that the Netherlands would be attacked at all. She was not included in all the various plans drafted by the Germans. They presumed that they could send some of their ground forces through the southernmost parts of the Netherlands without being bothered by anything more serious than diplomatic protests. Thus an invasion of the Netherlands was not strictly necessary from the perspective of ground operations, but in the final plan it was nevertheless included, something the Luftwaffe had advocated since 1938.[14]

The Allied commanders had settled for the so-called "Plan D," which called for British and French forces to rush into Belgium once the Germans launched their attack. They intended to take up defensive positions in central Belgium, east of the two main Belgian cities—Antwerp and Brussels—and prevent the Belgian Army from being defeated by the Germans. In the other sectors, particularly the northeastern border of France, the Allies would remain static. They did not expect the Germans to make their main effort in the Ardennes.

In many ways, the Allied plans served to fit the German intentions perfectly. As Plan D was conceived, it tended to focus on events that took place in northern Belgium. The Allies seem to have believed that the Germans would place their center of gravity in this area, as they had done in 1914. The airborne operations planned by the Germans would reinforce the Allied beliefs in a main German effort in the north. By sending their best units into Belgium—in a maneuver akin to a left hook—the Allies acted in a manner that fitted the German plans almost perfectly. The best Allied units would be caught in the cauldron created if the German armored spearheads reached the Channel. However, neither Hitler nor most of the senior German officers seem to have expected such a success.[15]

As we are sitting comfortably decades after the events, aided by hindsight, we often find it difficult to see things as the decision-makers did in the reality that we know as history. Given the circumstances at the time, there was little reason to expect anything other than a long, drawn-out struggle. The British and French had more and often better tanks than the Germans. They were also better supplied with artillery. They had more aircraft, and the German models hardly had the technical qualities to compensate. Finally, the Allies were also producing weapons at a higher rate than the Germans, which, of course, meant that Hitler's chances of winning a protracted war were slim.[16]

The force ratios spoke against an immediate German victory, and the arms production figures as well as the raw materials situation spoke against a German victory in the long run. Hitler had maneuvered himself into a very awkward situation as he launched the attack

Table 1: Force Ratios, May 10, 1940

	France	Belgium	Netherlands	Great Britain	Germany	Ratio All:Ger
Personnel (Army)						
Total	5,500,000	640,000	400,000	1,600,000	4,200,000	1.9:1
On WF*	2,240,000	640,000	400,000	500,000	3,000,000	1.3:1
Tanks						
Total	4,111	270	40	?	?	?
On WF	3,254	270	40	640	2,773	1.5:1
Artillery						
Total	10,700	1,338	656	1,280	7,378	1.9:1
Air (bombers and fighters)						
Total	3,097	140	82	1,150	3,578	1.2:1
On WF**	879	118	72	384	2,589	1:1.8

*On the Western Front
**Includes only combat-ready aircraft
(Source: K-H Frieser, *Blitzkrieg-Legende*, 42–59)

on Poland, which had provoked the British and French into declaring war on Germany. The agreement with Stalin gave him a neighbor in the east who was not hostile—for the time being, at least. However, time was not on Hitler's side, and little suggested that he was about to win an overwhelming victory in the west. Not only did the force ratios favor the Allies, the French were also protected by the strong Maginot Line, the most formidable defense system created thus far. In northern and western Belgium, roads were abundant and of good quality, but the many urban areas were a potential hindrance to an advancing army, as were the numerous rivers and canals. The Ardennes, a hilly area with dense woods and few roads, dominated southeastern Belgium and Luxembourg. As the Allies had declared war in September 1939, they had had ample time to mobilize and prepare their defenses. It appeared that the Germans had little chance of achieving a surprise.

A German victory in the west would require a series of favorable circumstances. One of them had already been achieved at the planning stage—considering the intentions of the Allies, the German strategy was almost perfectly designed. However, this was not known at the time, and by itself it was not sufficient to result in a German victory. The German troops had to perform better on the battlefield for the Germans to turn the scales in their favor.

Case Yellow

The German armed forces completed their preparations for the attack on the evening of May 9. Sergeant Hilpert later recalled that the day had been warm and beautiful as he and the other soldiers of the 3rd Company, 35th Panzer Regiment of the 4th Panzer Division checked and maintained their vehicles and other equipment. The tanks, which required a great deal of maintenance, were checked particularly carefully, as was customary for the experienced men of the Panzer regiment. They worked hard, but they looked forward to the Whitsun, which would occur unusually early this year. Late in the afternoon, at around 5 p.m., there was suddenly lively activity in a nearby office. The telephone began to ring constantly as orders were issued for the main attack to be initiated on the following day. The soldiers had expected to be granted a few days' leave for Whitsun, but they were still unsurprised that an entirely different task had been given to them. The soldiers realized what the order could result in, and many of them took the chance to write a few lines for their parents, beloveds or other relatives. It was not too early; the company set out for Aachen after dusk.[17]

On the German side of the border, similar scenes could be witnessed from north to south as more than 100 divisions marched to their staging areas for the operation that had been given the codename "Case Yellow." When the first soldiers crossed the border before dawn on May 10, they initially met with no significant opposition. To many of the German Army soldiers, the first sign of war was Luftwaffe aircraft above them, flying east after completing their missions. Sergeant Hilpert saw many bombers flying east, returning to their air bases, as his company crossed the border and headed towards Maastricht. At the Dutch town, all bridges across the Maas River—which was known as the Meuse further south—had been destroyed. The 3rd Company would have to wait until the following day before it could cross the river on a bridge created by the engineers.[18]

Not far away from Maastricht lay the fortress of Eben-Emael, which, together with nearby bridges, was the target for "Assault Battalion Koch." By approaching silently with gliders, the parachute engineers attacked the fortress, regarded as one of the strongest in the world, and knocked it out quickly.[19]

The fall of Eben-Emael was a spectacular event that attracted much attention. Further north, more German airborne operations were also conducted. Several important bridges in the Netherlands were captured daringly and immediately put to use by the quickly advancing 9th Panzer Division. The seat of the Dutch government, The Hague, was attacked by German airborne units. The German offensive was conducted with resolve and at a high tempo. The Dutch forces surrendered as soon as May 15.[20]

Episodes like these caused the eyes of the world to fall on the northern sector. In accordance with the established plans, British and French formations marched into Belgium to take up their predetermined defense positions. Considering the German actions in the north, this decision appeared justified; the main German effort appeared to be directed against the Netherlands and northern Belgium. However, the appearances were deceptive. In the Eifel area, the hilly and wooded area of Germany closest to the Ardennes, German units began to move west. Among them was Panzer Group von Kleist, whose 41,140 motor vehicles, including 1,222 tanks, crowded the sparse roads.[21]

Kleist's two Panzer corps advanced abreast. On the southern wing, Guderian directed his three Panzer divisions towards Sedan, while Reinhardt's two Panzer divisions would cross the Meuse at Monthermé. Guderian's units advanced in the southern Ardennes, where the road network was better. Reinhardt had received the thankless task of moving through the central parts of the Ardennes, where the terrain was most difficult.

Monthermé

Werner Kempf commanded the German 6th Panzer Division, which was part of Reinhardt's XXXXI Corps. As the roads were too few to allow both Panzer divisions to advance abreast, Reinhardt had given Kempf the lead. He would be responsible for establishing a bridgehead across the Meuse and expanding it as rapidly as possible.[22]

Problems occurred almost immediately. The 2nd Panzer Division, one of Guderian's units, was supposed to have abandoned the area next to the border, which 6th Panzer Division would pass through. However, traffic jams had delayed the 2nd Panzer Division, and the consequences propagated through Kempf's division, which did not reach its intended goal for May 10. Hopes of making up for lost time on May 11 and 12 were dashed by fuel supply problems. Thus the 6th Panzer Division did not cross the border to France until dusk on May 12, after driving over 100 km through Luxembourg and Belgium. Kempf's men had thus far been troubled more by traffic jams and the narrow, winding roads than enemy combat units. However, the distance from the border between France and Belgium to Monthermé was hardly 10 km as the crow flies. Soon, French defenders would offer strong resistance.[23]

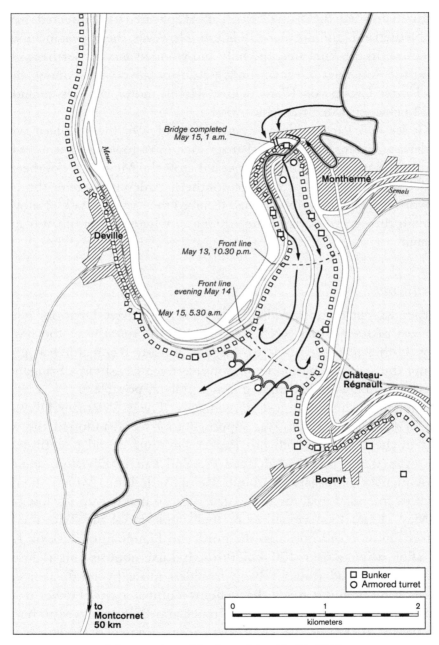

Meuse crossing at Montherme May 13–15, 1940

On the night of May 12–13, the 6th Panzer Division conducted reconnaissance in the area between the Meuse and the Franco-Belgian border. It soon became clear that the area was undefended. Only a drunken French soldier was encountered, and he was promptly captured. The French defenders were obviously waiting on the western bank of the Meuse. The Germans could not establish the strength of the defense at this time.[24]

Kempf decided to attack across the Meuse at 4 p.m. on May 13. He informed the corps commander of his decision by radio and asked for air support for the impending attack. As only some parts of his division had yet reached the Meuse, Kempf regarded air support as very desirable, but he would be bitterly disappointed in this respect. Most of the Luftwaffe was committed to other sectors, and only a few aircraft could be spared for Monthermé. Even worse, the aircraft that appeared attacked the wrong targets. Instead of releasing their bombs over the French defenders, some of the aircraft attacked 6th Panzer Division artillery batteries, killing twenty men and wounding another twenty-six.[25]

Kempf's division had relatively small resources available for the river crossing at Monthermé. The main attack force was made up of one infantry battalion supported by one tank battalion and one artillery battalion. As the French had blown up the bridge spanning the Meuse, there was no alternative but to attack with infantry. The tanks could provide fire support, but almost all of them were light vehicles that Germany had captured when she annexed Czechoslovakia. They were armed with 3.7-cm guns whose shells were not particularly powerful.[26]

Kempf could hardly claim to be enjoying ideal circumstances, and when he and the officers directly involved in the imminent attack studied the terrain, they could immediately see that the attack would be very difficult. The river was not remarkably wide, but the banks were steep and craggy. Barbed-wire obstacles had been created by the French along the western bank. Also, much of XXXXI Corps was stuck in traffic jams further east.[27]

Despite the difficulties, preparations for the attack continued. A few kilometers east of Monthermé, engineers inflated rafts. Tanks laboriously found firing positions that allowed them to cover important sectors of the west bank. The weather was stifling on this afternoon, Whit Monday, and the soldiers sweated as they struggled to move infantry howitzers into position. The time chosen for the attack also meant that the Germans would probably risk being blinded by the sun as they attacked.[28]

The Germans intended to attack Monthermé and the surrounding area, where the reaches of the river resembled a loop. If the riflemen managed to cross the river, they would find themselves surrounded by water on three sides, and the loop was less than a kilometer wide. Even if a bridgehead were captured, it would be difficult to expand as the German axis of advance would be obvious to the French defenders. They could easily concentrate their fire at the narrow river loop, but the late German start on the day might be an advantage. The attack could possibly be continued into the night, allowing the Germans to capture the loop under the cover of darkness. The terrain beyond was wooded, but at least it allowed more room to maneuver.[29]

The attack was to be conducted by III Battalion of the 4th Motorized Infantry Regiment. It consisted of four companies. As was customary in German regiments, the companies were consecutively numbered, giving I Battalion companies numbered 1–4, II Battalion companies 5–8 and III Battalion companies 9–12. There were also often companies in the regiments with higher numbers, but those were specialized, such as engineer, heavy infantry howitzer, antitank and antiaircraft companies.[30]

One of the companies to attack was the 11th Company. The company commander's adjutant kept the war diary and described the action in unusually great detail. Early in the afternoon, he sat on a lorry that brought him and other soldiers to a mountain crest, where they unloaded and sought cover to avoid artillery fire. Tanks and an infantry howitzer platoon simultaneously took up firing positions nearby. The riflemen lay hidden for as long as possible. Suddenly, an infernal noise drowned out all the other sounds as tanks, infantry howitzers and artillery opened fire on targets on the west bank of the river. Moments later, the riflemen stormed over the crest and down the slope towards the bank. The drive succeeded as only scattered French fire was directed at the slope.[31]

With their hearts in their mouths, the riflemen reached the built-up area at Monthermé, where they found shelter. The tanks escorted them to the river to fire at targets on the west bank. A moment of confusion

In the early campaigns, the German 3.7-cm antitank gun was not overtaxed, but would prove ineffective against the heavier enemy tanks encountered in the west in 1940 and in the Soviet Union in 1941. Photo courtesy of Krigsarkivet, Stockholm.

occurred as several soldiers were hit by French fire. One of them, Private Köster, was killed. The company commander, Lieutenant Strotheicher, did, however, notice that the French fire had eased and yelled, "Hurry! Into the rafts, the fire has ceased."[32]

The boats were brought forward as rapidly as possible and the first groups hurried across the river. The soldiers used rifle butts and even helmets as paddles. Meeting only weak fire, the Germans reached the western bank without suffering more than minor blemishes. However, when they arrived on the other side of the river, they found that they were not the first Germans across. Corporal Hackländer, who was known throughout the entire company as a reckless good-for-nothing, had found a rowing boat and crossed the river all on his own.[33]

The platoons gathered on the western bank, but Lieutenant Strotheicher had been wounded in one of his legs and had to hand over command to Lieutenant von Ellerts. The German attack proceeded and the 11th Company confronted the French fixed defenses, which consisted of barbed-wire obstacles, bunkers, armored gun turrets and machine-gun positions. The men of the 11th Company had no clear picture of what took place on the flanks, where French fire held up much of III Battalion. At this stage, the German tanks provided valuable support. Major Stephan, commander of I Battalion of the Armor Regiment, ordered one of his platoons to move forward to the abutment of the blown-up bridge. From there, they could effectively fire at the French positions. Thus the French fire abated notably, which was probably the reason why Strotheicher was able to urge his men into the boats.[34]

As the Germans continued their attack on the western bank of the Meuse, a series of small skirmishes occurred when platoons and squads fought independently as they encountered French defensive positions. The German emphasis on individual initiative paid off. NCO Wiechering gathered a number of German soldiers who had become separated from their units and led them, together with Second Lieutenant Ingenerf, in a renewed attack. They cleared the meadow south of Monthermé and paved the way forward, allowing half the river loop to be captured by 10.35 p.m.[35]

French artillery shelled the forward German positions during the night, but also the area behind them to prevent ammunition and other supplies reaching the attackers. A few machine-gun bursts were also heard, but they inflicted no casualties among the Germans, who thought the fire was being directed at random.

The French had blown the bridge at Monthermé, but it was not completely destroyed. German engineers made temporary repairs, allowing light vehicles to cross it. I Battalion of the 4th Motorized Infantry Regiment used the bridge and reinforced III Battalion. As May 14 dawned, both I and III Battalion stood ready to expand the bridgehead. Fire controllers from the artillery of the 6th Panzer Division had also crossed the river to enable effective artillery support. However, the wooded terrain and the attendant short firing ranges did not facilitate their work.[36]

The French defenders—colonial soldiers from the 102nd Fortress Division—offered tenacious resistance until noon, but subsequently they began to be slowly pushed back, not least because they ran low on ammunition. However, on this day, the Germans could not advance past a bunker line at the base of the river loop. So far, the 6th Panzer Division had lost around 150 men, of which 10 percent had been killed in action. No heavy weapons had been brought to the western bank of the Meuse and the soldiers of both battalions were exhausted. However, the 4th Motorized Infantry Regiment still had one uncommitted battalion.[37]

On the evening of May 14, the commander of II Battalion was instructed to relieve III Battalion during the night. The company commanders went forward to learn about the terrain and the positions held by III Battalion. Increasing darkness and strong enemy fire made it difficult to establish the enemy's situation. Despite these difficulties, II Battalion drove towards Monthermé. With their headlights switched off, the vehicles reached the river half an hour before midnight. The soldiers jumped off and the equipment was unloaded, whereupon the drivers took their vehicles a few kilometers back. The river could still not be crossed. In the glare of the burning buildings, the men who unloaded the vehicles could see how the engineers worked hard to create a pontoon bridge in the northern part of Monthermé. Exploding shells from the French artillery informed them that the enemy was not asleep.[38]

The engineers finished their work by midnight and II Battalion immediately marched on the pontoon bridge to reach the western bank, soon to be followed by some of the German tanks. In the meantime, the German artillery fired to harass the French defenders. The French gunners seemed to aim for the pontoon bridge, but it was not hit. The soldiers of II Battalion continued towards their nocturnal goal while the French artillery continued shelling. However, the German riflemen were not seriously hampered, and the fact that many of the French shells turned out to be duds contributed to the Germans reaching their destination unscathed.

At 4 a.m., II Battalion relieved III Battalion. The soldiers had struggled to bring the heavy weapons forward during the night—it was an exacting task in the rough terrain. The sweaty faces of the men clearly showed how hard they had worked during the night. They were tired, but ready to attack. Little time for rest remained—the bunkers would be attacked at 4.30 a.m. According to the plan, the men of II Battalion were supposed to halt soon after capturing or destroying the bunkers as a Stuka attack was to be conducted at 7.30 a.m.

The Germans lacked precise information on the French defenses as fog and darkness had reduced visibility. It was believed that four concrete bunkers lay ahead, as well as other kinds of field works. The infantry had brought the battalion's heavy machine guns into firing positions, and fifteen minutes before the attack a few tanks moved forward to support it. The roar from the tank engines and the squeak from the tracks must have been encouraging sounds to the German riflemen hiding before the attack. The soldiers from the 5th Company lay near the road, while the 7th Company would attack on the sector closest to the river.

Through the Bunker Line

The French defenders expected a German attack at any moment, but they could not know exactly when. At 4.25 a.m., their uncertainty disappeared as the first salvo from the German artillery crashed onto the French positions. For five minutes, the ground shook from the force of the explosions. The German artillery then lifted its fire 500 meters. The moment had come for the German infantry.

Corporal Lillotte served in the assault group led by Lieutenant Oeckel. He and a few other soldiers toiled with the Bangalore torpedoes they brought for blowing up wire obstacles. They had to work swiftly, or else the defenders would regain their composure. In the corner of his eye, Lillotte glanced a tank behind him, ready to open fire. Its support might prove very useful.

The men hastily brought a charge forward and pushed it onto the ground beneath the wire obstacle. As soon as it had been properly positioned, Lillotte and his comrades took cover and detonated it. The explosion tore the obstacle apart and opened a path to a bunker. Oeckel and his men immediately drove forward while the tank behind them provided covering fire, preventing the bunker crew from acting. Oeckel led a group of soldiers straight forward while Lillotte and a few others advanced slightly to the left. Lillotte encountered a roadblock, and as he suspected the area around it was mined, he threw a few hand grenades to see if any mines exploded. Nothing of the sort occurred. Instead, four German tanks moved forward. Tree trunks broke under the weight of the steel colossi. A flamethrower troop detached from the engineer battalion was ready to attack the bunker to the left of the road, near the roadblock. However, before the assault engineers attacked the bunker, its crew came out with their hands held high. Shrapnel had wounded one of them. Lillotte believed the tank fire had broken their resolution to fight. The French soldiers were brought to the rear as prisoners of war.

The first French defense line had thus been penetrated. Lillotte observed that the terrain was flatter beyond the bunker line. He still struggled with the Bangalore torpedoes, but they might prove useful further on. Although terrain was less hilly, it remained wooded and could conceal extensive fieldworks. The Bangalore torpedoes could soon prove very useful, but the soldiers carrying them became ever more tired. Approximately 100 meters further west, Lillotte encountered two roadblocks and large quantities of ammunition piled up next to the road, but no defenders remained in the area. The tanks that followed close behind the infantry left the road to move around the roadblocks.

A few hundred meters further ahead, mines had been laid at a bend in the road. Barbed-wire obstacles were also to be found in the nearby woods. Lillete saw that a five-meter-wide clearing had been cut in the woods, evidently to provide a good field of fire. The Germans proceeded cautiously. The ground showed clear signs of the German shelling, but there were still defenders remaining in their positions. Suddenly, a machine gun opened fire on the approaching Germans, who immediately threw themselves into cover. Together with two other soldiers, Lillotte managed to sneak around the machine gun and throw hand grenades into the French position. The effort produced the result sought for. Four French soldiers surrendered, while two lay dead in their defensive position.

Lillotte's action caused the roadblock to be undefended, but the mines remained a hindrance to the tanks. The Bangalore torpedo Lillotte had brought along now came in handy. It was positioned over the mines and detonated, causing four mines to explode, but some still remained.

German infantry cleared twelve mines. It was usually regarded as a dangerous work, but this time the Germans were lucky; they found that the French had not armed the mines.

As the Bangalore torpedo had been used, Lillotte no longer had any heavy load to carry. He found a bicycle in a ditch and did not hesitate before confiscating it. While he and his men had been busy clearing the mines, the parts of the company that attacked through the woods to the right of the road had advanced further. The bicycle allowed him to quickly cover the few hundred meters that separated him from the company commander. Upon arrival, Lillotte reported to Lieutenant Oeckel on the actions along the road.

Lillotte had hardly completed his report when two French trucks approached on the road. One of the German machine gunners quickly pulled the trigger. The French drivers quickly stopped and threw themselves into shrubbery to avoid the bullets. The Germans waited a few moments to allow the tanks to close up. They soon arrived. The nearest tank halted around 50 meters behind and opened fire on bunkers further up the slope, and the two trucks were also set ablaze.

The French defenders had not been silenced. Suddenly, Lillotte and the other German soldiers were subjected to a hail of fire. They threw themselves into the ditches along the road and took cover there, unable to move. Lillotte waited until there was a pause in the fire and used the opportunity to plunge into a cleft further down the slope. He reached it unscathed, but the French fire followed him. The bullets knocked lumps of earth from the ground next to him. Suddenly, a sharp bang was heard and Lillotte's head was flung to the side. He was temporarily stunned and blinded, but he soon became aware of blood trickling down his face; he then felt a burning pain below his left eye and in his neck. The wounds were not severe and he was able to bandage himself up, but that was obviously only a temporary measure. Lillotte had barely managed to attend to his wounds when Lieutenant Oeckel showed up at the cleft. He had also been wounded, receiving blows to his face and one of his hands. Fortunately for the two men, the tanks fired at the French defenders, allowing Oeckel and Lillotte a chance to move back and reach a dressing station for treatment.

It was now 7 a.m., and the 5th Company had reached its first objective, as had the 7th Company on the right wing. At this stage, II Battalion had to stop, as the Stuka dive-bombers would attack the French second defense line at 7.30 a.m. The characteristic silhouettes of the Stukas appeared right on time above the lead elements of the 4th Motorized Infantry Regiment. They dived towards their targets from a clear-blue sky, and this time they got their aim right. The most important effect of the bombing was that the minefields protecting the French positions were ripped up. The German infantry soldiers attacked as soon as the last bomb had landed, gaining ground rapidly. II Battalion managed to capture twelve officers and 364 enlisted men before 10 a.m. One of the prisoners was Colonel de Pisnin, the commander of the 42nd Regiment, which had been the main enemy encountered by the German 4th Motorized Infantry Regiment. The Germans also captured the commander of the French artillery, who said that the German artillery fire had demoralized the French soldiers. The great haul of prisoners contrasted sharply with the German casualties; on this day, II Battalion lost three killed in action and eighteen wounded. The road west, to Montcornet, was wide open for the 6th Panzer Division.[39]

General Reinhardt, the commander of the XXXXI Panzer Corps, arrived at the scene and observed that the success attained by the 4th Motorized Infantry Regiment had to be exploited quickly. A battle group was hastily assembled. It was to be led by Colonel von Esebeck, the commander of the 6th Rifle Brigade. It was composed of the motorcycle battalion, two artillery batteries, one engineer company, an antitank company, two antiaircraft batteries and the recon battalion.

During World War II, it was very common within the German Army to rapidly create battle groups as the situation changed. They were quickly assembled and sent into action. Less than three hours were available to von Esebeck, but despite having little time for preparations, his battle group was very successful. The distance to Montcornet was approximately 60 km as the crow flies, but his men captured the town by evening. The French defense fell apart, which was also evident from the great number of prisoners taken. Before the day came to an end, the 6th Panzer Division reported over 2,000 prisoners captured.[40]

While the 6th Panzer Division fought at Monthermé, a remarkable sequence of events took place higher up in the German command structure. There were many German generals who doubted that the Panzer divisions could punch through the French defense and advance deeply. As Reinhardt's corps was delayed by traffic jams and tenacious French defense at Monthermé, the misgivings seemed to have been justified. The XIX Corps, led by General Guderian, had already successfully crossed the Meuse at Sedan on May 13. Army Group A, to which von Kleist's Panzer group belonged, decided that Reinhardt's corps should be withdrawn and inserted behind Guderian's corps. The river crossing at Monthermé would be allotted to infantry divisions.[41]

Von Kleist's reaction when he received the order was remarkable, but not unusual for the Germans in the spring campaign of 1940. It also forms an important part of the explanation for its unexpected success. Von Kleist regarded the order he received as unsuitable and bluntly ignored it. Instead of instructing Reinhardt to withdraw, he ordered him to break through as quickly as possible and then immediately advance west at breakneck pace. As we have seen, this did indeed happen, and by the evening of May 15, the 6th Panzer Division had reached further west than any other German unit. The outcome silenced any criticism of von Kleist's behavior.[42]

The infantry component of the 6th Panzer Division was the most important in the fighting that led to the eventual success at Monthermé. The legacy from the stormtroop tactics developed during World War I is evident. Although tanks supported the infantry admirably on May 15— and the air support also worked as it should—the German actions were centered on the infantry, with the other components supporting. In this case, the terrain hardly allowed the Germans any alternative. However, further north, battles were fought in an area better suited to tanks.

Gembloux

Rivers figured prominently in the Allied planning before the campaign in the west. From Antwerp and southwards, the defenses would follow the Dyle River. From Namur, the Meuse would constitute a barrier until the defense lines connected to the Maginot Line. As the Dyle was rather short, there was an area north of Namur unprotected by a river. It was known as the "Gembloux Gap," named after the small town of Gembloux between Namur and Brussels.

The terrain was rather flat in the Gembloux Gap, making it a suitable attack corridor for the Germans. The Allies deemed the area vital for a successful defense along the line they foresaw. Some of the best French units were directed to the Gembloux Gap, forming part of the 1st French Army, which was commanded by General Blanchard.[43]

From the east, the German XVI Corps, commanded by General Hoepner, approached Gembloux. The corps consisted of the 3rd and 4th Panzer Divisions as well as the 20th Motorized Infantry Division and the 35th Infantry Division. These divisions had crossed the Meuse at Liége. From the west, a French corps commanded by General Prioux hurried towards Gembloux. Prioux had two mechanized divisions at his disposal and was instructed to delay the Germans long enough to allow other divisions to take up defensive positions at Gembloux. The clash between these two corps would result in some of the fiercest battles fought in May 1940.[44]

Sergeant Hilpert, in 3rd Panzer company, 4th Panzer Division's 35th Panzer Regiment, recalled May 11 as a tranquil day. The company drove across the Meuse at Maastricht and advanced unhurriedly in a south-westerly direction. Early on May 12, the company resumed the march, this time towards Hannut, located approximately 50 km west-southwest of Maastricht. Hilpert did not get embroiled in any fighting on this day, but some of his comrades engaged French tanks. Rumors about the fighting quickly spread through the company.[45]

The 3rd Company was initially given the mission of clearing the village of Jandrenouille. Rumors said that enemy tanks would offer resistance. There were indeed French tanks in the vicinity, but Hilpert and the other soldiers in the 3rd Company did not encounter them. Four guns and some tanks were captured at Jandrenouille, as were a handful of French soldiers.[46]

After gorging themselves on a Belgian lunch, the soldiers of the company set out for Perwez, further west. The march was soon interrupted. Other elements of the 4th Panzer Division, as well as the 3rd Panzer Division on the northern flank, became embroiled in fierce combat

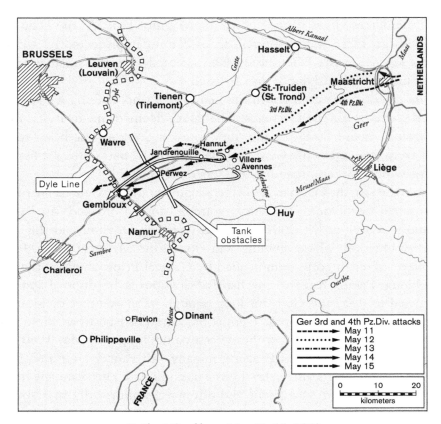

Battle at Gembloux, May 11–15, 1940

with two French mechanized divisions. These clashes would later be recognized as the beginning of the Battle of Gembloux. At the end of the day, both the 3rd and 4th Panzer Divisions summed up the day in a satisfactory manner. However, the war diaries also expressed concerns about the performance of the German tanks and antitank guns. It was also noted that the infantry component of the Panzer divisions was too weak. General Hoepner was optimistic, however, as he believed the opposition encountered was little more than a weak advance guard.[47]

When the attack was resumed on the morning of May 15, the Germans felt optimistic. They did not expect to meet a determined French defense. However, by noon, the Germans clearly had to revise their expectations. The French were not inclined to give up the position at Gembloux.

The Germans were also delayed when two infantry divisions became entangled in traffic jams. An all-out attack against the French defenses had to wait until the next day.[48]

Stukas heralded the German attack on May 15 as they hurled themselves against the French positions. The artillery opened fire after the last bomb had landed, soon to be followed by the infantry as well as fire controllers. The Germans initially made fairly good progress, but the attack petered out at noon. Strong artillery fire and well-positioned anti-tank guns halted the Germans, who suffered considerable tank losses.[49]

General Hoepner informed the two Panzer division commanders that an air strike was scheduled for 1 p.m. and that the tanks should attack immediately after the Luftwaffe's effort. The aircraft duly attacked, and the tanks immediately assaulted the enemy position, but they did not manage to crack it. Despite earnest efforts, the Germans only succeeded in denting the enemy defenses. Hoepner called off the attack at around 4 p.m., but he intended to resume it on the following day.[50]

The fighting on May 15 had cost the Germans dearly. The 4th Panzer Division reported 105 killed, 413 wounded and 29 missing. It would later become clear that no other day of the campaign was as costly to the 4th Panzer Division. Tank losses were heavy too; the 4th Panzer Division reported thirty-four knocked-out tanks on May 15, although some were eventually repaired.[51]

Sergeant Hilpert was unscathed, which could partly be explained by the fact that he was, as he put it, busy being mommy to the company. He furnished the fighting soldiers with food, beverages, tobacco and other much-desired comforts. These tasks did not make him involved in the fighting, but he nevertheless formed a picture of it. It was particularly clear to him how well aimed the French artillery fire was. He saw fallen comrades and others who had been wounded. Corporal Meyer had suffered a complex fracture below the knee. Corporal Dresel had suffered worse, and his leg would probably have to be amputated. Such sights provoked many thoughts as the sun set below the horizon.[52]

The Battle of Gembloux clearly showed the shortcomings of the German tanks. They were poorly armed and carried weak armor. Luftwaffe air strikes did not impress the French defenders. The combination of air power and tanks was effectively halted by artillery, antitank guns and infantry in this battle. It should also be noted that the limited success attained by the Germans has to be attributed to their infantry and artillery.[53]

In fact, the German tanks were as weakly armed as they were poorly armored. The lack of firepower and protection was starkly evident when one battalion from the 35th Panzer Regiment became engaged by French antitank guns south of Gembloux. After several tanks had been knocked out, the German tankers dismounted and instead tried successfully to capture the French guns in close combat. The fact that the German tankers succeeded by fighting outside their vehicles is an almost absurd illustration of the limitations of the German tanks against a determined defense.[54]

However, the German setback at Gembloux was not crucial. Hoepner's XVI Corps had only a secondary role. The main events took place further south, where Panzer Group von Kleist attacked.

Breakthrough

When the 6th Panzer Division reached Montcornet on the evening of May 15, the 9th French Army was in disarray. Not only had Reinhardt broken through, but slightly further north, Hermann Hoth's XV Corps, comprising the 5th and 7th Panzer Divisions, had also blasted a hole in the 9th French Army. Its commander, General Georges Corap, lacked the mobile units required to restore the situation. The 1st French Armored Division, commanded by Major-General Bruneau, had been diverted to Corap, but it fared no better as it met and clashed with German Panzer formations.[55]

On the evening of May 14, the French armored division had advanced towards the bridgehead at Dinant captured by Major-General Rommel's 7th Panzer Division. As the tanks had to be refueled, Bruneau ordered his division to halt in the Flavion area. He did not know that Rommel's most advanced elements were only a few kilometers away. However, Rommel was just as ignorant about the presence of the French division.[56]

In the engagement that followed on May 15, two different philosophies were pitted against each other. The French emphasized deliberate,

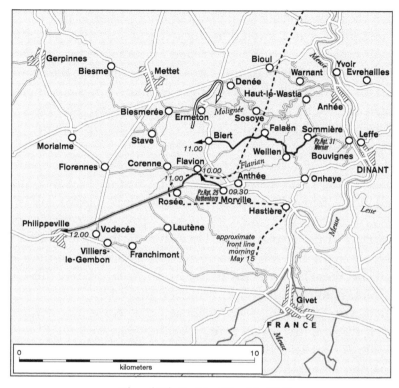

5th and 7th Pz.Div. May 15, 1940

well-planned and systematic action, but speed was not given priority. The German philosophy stressed mobility, combined arms and rapid decision-making and conduct.

On the morning of May 15, the German 25th Panzer Regiment, which was part of Rommel's 7th Panzer Division, encountered French tanks at Flavion. A violent battle ensued for a few hours before Rommel decided to break off the action and send the 25th Panzer Regiment on an outflanking move towards Philippeville. At the same time, the German 5th Panzer Division, commanded by Major-General Max von Hartlieb, approached from the east and engaged Bruneau's division.[57]

NCO Nökel commanded a Panzer III that belonged to the 31st Panzer Regiment, one of the two Panzer regiments in the 5th Panzer

Division. He moved near Flavion on the morning of May 15. The terrain was undulating and covered by thick vegetation. Abandoned French equipment littered the nearby woods and, in some places, also the road. Nökel proceeded calmly, but just east of Flavion he was interrupted by voices in his headset telling him that the lead tanks in the company had encountered French tanks at a range of 1,200 meters. The voice of the company commander immediately followed, ordering his tanks to take up firing positions.[58]

While Nökel and the other tank commanders in the company maneuvered their tanks into firing positions, further French tanks were observed at the fringe of a wood. The range was approximately 1,400 meters. The enemy tanks had one gun in a revolving turret and also one mounted in the chassis front. They were of the type Char B1bis, a heavy French tank that was better armed and armored than the German models. The French crews did not seem to have spotted the German tanks, which held the advantage of higher ground.[59]

Captain von Schönburg-Waldenburg, the company commander, ordered I Platoon to advance to a gentle crest around 300 meters away while II and III Platoons provided cover. Unfortunately for the Germans, the French saw the advancing tanks of I Platoon and opened fire. Nökel ordered his driver to take the tank to the crest as quickly as possible, as did the other tanks in the platoon. The Germans reached the crest unharmed, where they sought cover in copses. Nökel's driver maneuvered the tank into a suitable firing position while the loader and gunner ensured that they could open fire. As soon as the tank had reached the intended position, Nökel ordered his crew to fire. The shell left the muzzle and could, due to the tracer, be followed during the good second it took to reach its target. To his dismay, Nökel saw the 3.7-cm shell bounce off the enemy tank as if it were a pea. The other tanks in the platoon were just as unsuccessful.[60]

The Germans found themselves in a deteriorating situation. More French tanks appeared on the scene. They gradually reduced the distance to the German tanks, which awaited permission to fire. As the German guns had proved themselves wholly ineffective at longer range, there was no point in wasting ammunition. Nökel saw the silhouettes of the French tanks loom ever larger. He had not seen such large tanks before and had not even heard of them during training—not even during the session devoted to recognizing enemy vehicles. The tense situation made his pulse jump.[61]

The company commander issued clear instructions on the radio, allocating targets for the platoons. When the range had shrunk to 250 meters, von Schönburg-Waldenburg ordered his tanks to open fire. Three French tanks were instantly hit and came to a halt. The crews bailed out and fled the scene. Other French tanks continued forward and exposed their sides. The Germans fired on the side armor, which proved to have a weak spot where a hatch for the radiator was located. This allowed the Germans to knock out some of the heavy enemy tanks. Over the radio, they informed the other German tanks about the weakness they had found in the enemy's armor.[62]

The excellent communications equipment allowed Nökel and the other soldiers in the German company to cooperate efficiently and compensate for the poor armament and weak armor of their tanks. The Germans were also aided by further advantages. Their tank turrets comprised a crew of three men—the commander, the gunner and the loader. This allowed the commander to focus on the terrain and the enemy and make suitable decisions. French commanders also had to aim and load the 4.7-cm gun mounted in the turret. Neither did they have the kind of turret hatch fitted to the German tanks, which allowed the commander to peek out and get a full view of the surrounding terrain. All this resulted in the French commanders being overburdened in battle, and they also suffered from inferior communication and means of observation.

In a way, the poor French radio communications are puzzling. As the French Army practiced a more centralized mode of decision-making, it was actually more dependent on good communication than the German Army, particularly in mobile operations. Considering their different doctrines, it would make more sense for the French to have devoted efforts to create robust communications. In fact, it was the Germans who possessed more and better means of communication. Additionally, the German emphasis on decentralized decision-making made them less prone to complete breakdown when communications failed.[63]

The French 1st Armored Division suffered something that might be termed a breakdown near Flavion on May 15. Despite the fact that important elements of von Hartlieb's division did not reach Flavion on that date, Bruneau's division was outmaneuvered in a succession of small actions contributed to by German tanks and other arms of the 5th Panzer Division. At the end of the day, Bruneau ordered his men to retreat, but less than a quarter of his tanks remained operational. The 1st French Armored Division had ceased to be an effective formation.[64]

Although the German losses were far smaller, they were not negligible. Nökel was one of the unlucky ones; his radio malfunctioned and he became separated from the company. He was also running dangerously low on ammunition. He caught sight of a few tanks from the company and ordered his driver to steer towards them. At this stage, Nökel was so disoriented that he did not know which direction he was driving in. Black smoke from burning vehicles obscured the sun to such an extent that it was of no help for orientation. Suddenly, Nökel's tank was fired upon from the right. The driver immediately steered towards a building and managed to reach it before being hit. Nökel saw two enemy tanks firing on him. His gunner revolved the turret as rapidly as possible and fired a shell against one of the French tanks. The range was only 200 meters, and the first shot was a hit.[65]

At the same time, another French tank fired upon Nökel's Panzer III. The first shot landed in front of the target and the second behind. Nökel ordered his driver to reverse. At that moment, he saw a third muzzle flash. As the driver shifted to reverse gear, Nökel heard some kind of noise coming from the gearbox. It was the last sound he heard before a multicolored flame flashed before his eyes. The tank shuddered and sulfuric vapor reached his nose. He would never forget the smell. He could not remember how he managed to escape the tank, but once he was outside he realized that he had lost his hearing. He managed to find the crew, except for the driver, behind the tank. Still deaf, Nökel decided to check if the driver was still alive. He placed his fingers on the tank and could feel that the engine was still running.[66]

When he reached the front of the tank, Nökel saw that the enemy shell had hit above and behind the driver's position. The driver was still alive and halfway out through the hatch above his seat. He was laid on top of the tank's rear together with the wounded gunner. Nökel crept into the tank, sat down on the driver's bloody seat and turned the vehicle around. He drove to an asphalt road and turned left on it, hoping to find a dressing station.[67]

Nökel drove as fast as he could down the road, but after 500 meters he could already see French vehicles in a nearby wood. They turned out to be horse-drawn baggage carts. Nökel promptly drove past them. A few minutes later, the German tank came near a small village where a bridge spanned a stream. It soon became clear that there were French soldiers in the village. However, their backs faced Nökel's approaching tank. Without any deliberation, he gave full throttle and stormed across the bridge. Once on the other side of the river, Nökel again saw soldiers, but they wore German helmets.[68]

Nökel and his crew had reached their goal. They received the medical treatment they needed and Nökel would slowly regain his hearing. However, almost four weeks would elapse before he could serve again.[69]

Three Panzer corps comprised the spearhead of the German attack. After defeating the 1st French Armored Division, Hoth's XV Corps advanced deep into the enemy territory. Similarly, Reinhardt's XXXXI Corps headed west at high speed. Perhaps the most important attack was conducted by Guderian's XIX Corps, which operated on the most southerly axis of the three Panzer corps in von Rundstedt's Army group.

Sedan

Unlike the two Panzer corps attacking further north, Guderian's XIX corps enjoyed powerful air support. The majority of the available Stuka dive-bombers were detailed to support Guderian's attack across the Meuse at Sedan. How this air support was to be employed was subject to disagreement. Hugo Sperrle, the commander of the air fleet cooperating with von Rundstedt's Army group, as well as von Kleist, presupposed that one massive bombardment would take place. On the other hand,

Guderian and Lörzer (the latter commanded the air corps responsible for the air attacks in the Sedan area) intended to employ fewer aircraft at a time. Their intention was to keep Luftwaffe aircraft above Sedan continuously, and this had been planned in advance. Subsequently, von Kleist and Sperrle had agreed upon their alternative and issued orders to that effect. Guderian and Lörzer were dismayed when they learned about the decision taken by their superior commanders. Lörzer decided not to obey the order and claimed that it had been received "too late." Lörzer's decision was most likely the correct one. The direct effects of the air attacks were unremarkable; hardly any of the many bunkers were knocked out and the French casualties seem to have numbered under sixty, despite the fact that about 1,200 airstrikes were conducted against the area. However, the psychological effects were significant, and most of the phone lines were interrupted. The latter effect was very important as most of the French communications relied on wires.[70]

Sometimes, events that do not take place can be as important as those that do. On the night of May 13–14, German engineers created a bridge across the Meuse at Sedan. It was, of course, vital to Guderian's efforts to expand the bridgehead. For example, around 600 tanks drove across the river on this single bridge on May 14. Unsurprisingly, it was regarded as a very important target for the Allied air forces. On this day, 152 British and French aircraft were committed to destroying the bridge, but they were too late; the Germans had already positioned strong antiaircraft units and also detailed fighters to protect it. The Allied air crews certainly did not lack the courage needed, but their self-sacrificing efforts were to no avail as German vehicles continued to drive across the bridge. However, the Allied airmen paid a terrible price. For example, no fewer than forty-seven of the 109 attacking British bombers were shot down.[71]

The breakthrough at Sedan was mainly accomplished by two infantry units—the 1st Motorized Infantry Regiment and the Infantry Regiment *Grossdeutschland*—and a few platoons from the 43rd Combat Engineer Battalion. The way these units were led is illuminating. The senior commanders did not influence the actions fought by these units. Decisions were made by commanders at company level and below, usually without consulting their superiors. The overall mission was clear, and everybody acted individually to accomplish the aim. The infantry had to rely on its own heavy weapons to provide fire support, and the German infantry was quite lavishly equipped with such weapons. The entire action was fought according to the concept of "*Auftragstaktik*." There were no prescribed attack routes; instead, companies worked on their own to find weak points in the enemy defenses. It was an action molded on the stormtroop tactics from World War I. In eight hours (4 p.m. to midnight)

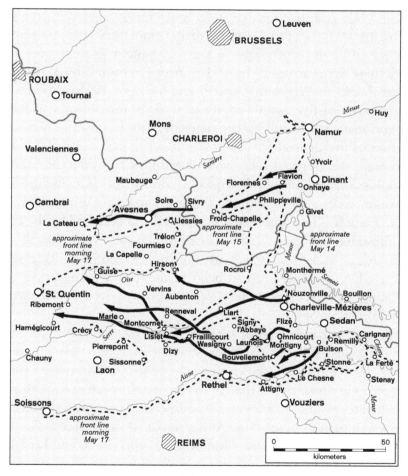

German armored thrust May 14–17, 1940

the Germans advanced more than 5 km through the French fortified defense and effectively created a breakthrough.[72]

The conclusion that the infantry was chiefly responsible for breaking the French defense at Sedan is also clear when studying the attack by Major-General Schaal's 10th Panzer Division just east of Sedan. As Guderian had placed his center of gravity on the sector of the 1st Panzer Division, little air support was devoted to the sector where the 10th Panzer Division attacked. Neither did Schaal's division receive much artillery support, as he had been ordered to support the 1st Panzer Division. Only twenty-four light field howitzers remained for the attack made by the 10th Panzer Division. Furthermore, as Schaal's division had been delayed, it did not arrive in time to benefit from the air attack. Despite these disadvantages, the 10th Panzer Division forced the Meuse, not least thanks to Sergeant Rubarth and his men. Rubarth led a small unit consisting of five assault engineers and six infantrymen. They got across and managed to roll up the defenses, thus paving the way for the remainder of the division.[73]

Above all, the German success was a result of the different command philosophies that permeated the two opposing armies. During the battles at Sedan, as well as elsewhere, the Germans acted with much less delay than the French. The counterattacks planned and prepared by the French amply illustrate this; they were launched too late and were thus ill-suited to the current situation, which usually differed significantly from the situation when the decision had been made. This is reminiscent of the battles fought in Norway, where the Germans strived to act far more rapidly than their opponents.[74]

German commanders were keen to spend as much time as possible with their units. One of the most striking examples was Lieutenant-Colonel Hermann Balck, the commander of the 1st Motorized Infantry Regiment. He remained at the tip of the attack conducted by his regiment when it crossed the Meuse and advanced all the way to Omnicourt, where a bridgehead across the Ardennes canal was captured early on May 14. He thus achieved two important results. First, the bridgehead across the Meuse at Sedan was secured. Second, a springboard for the continuation of the offensive was created. Balck's success was, however, far from assured. The soldiers of his regiment had fought very hard to gain the bridgehead across the Meuse, and they were exhausted after the battle. Balck realized that there was a window of opportunity during the dark hours, but he could not convince the weary men to continue. Finally, he loudly told them that he would attack all on his own if they did not have the stamina. He set out towards Chéhery on his own, boisterously stating that "if nobody else wanted to attack [then] he would capture Chéhery himself." After this show, his men no longer hesitated. They followed Balck and the attack was crowned with success. Balck was not the only officer to show such leadership, but he was probably one of the clearest exponents.[75]

General Lafontaine commanded the 55th French Infantry Division, which was responsible for the defense at Sedan. He was thus in many ways Balck's counterpart. According to the centralized French command philosophy, Lafontaine remained at his command post, located in a bunker at Bulson, almost 10 km south of the point where the German 1st Motorized Infantry Regiment crossed the Meuse. During the evening of May 13, a sequence of misunderstandings occurred that caused significant parts of the 55th Division to flee in panic. As the French commanders were tied to their fixed command posts, something partly attributed to the fact that most communication relied on telephone lines and not radio, they were poorly placed to stop the panic in time. The result was a French division, which had a key role in the force, being rendered unable to accomplish its task.[76]

The German command philosophy exhibited another characteristic, which was expressed as follows in the field manual:

> From the mission and the situation, the decision is derived. If the mission is insufficient as basis for decision, or if the situation has changed, a decision must reflect these circumstances. Anyone who cancels or changes a mission assumes responsibility and has to report it.[77]

This section shows that the situation was of greater importance than the orders received. The days following the breakthrough at Sedan would feature many incidents that showed these were not mere words. Guderian's behavior is particularly illuminating. At first, he fully followed the paragraph above. His first major decision was made on May 14, when he could either consolidate the bridgehead his corps had established until the morning or send most of his forces west. An attack to the west would capitalize on the disorder of the French defenses and promised a chance to reach the Channel.

Guderian did not hesitate. He ordered the 1st and 2nd Panzer Divisions to attack west. He had not yet received any orders supporting such a move. Indeed, he had been instructed to establish a bridgehead at Sedan and nothing more. However, the situation at Sedan differed from what had been anticipated, and Guderian did not wait for new instructions from his superiors. In any case, Guderian would not have had to wait long, as von Kleist reached the same conclusion. Neither had von Kleist consulted his superiors when he ordered Guderian to do what had actually already been initiated.[78]

The 1st and 2nd Panzer Divisions advanced swiftly, but after a while a new order from von Kleist was received. He told Guderian to halt along the Montigny–Bouvellemont line, which was only around 15 km west of the Ardennes canal, which Balck had crossed early in the morning. Guderian reacted rancorously and said that the order would throw away the victory at Sedan. He argued fiercely and managed to get his own way. The order was reiterated on May 15, but again Guderian obtained a free rein for a day. He immediately ordered his units to advance forward recklessly, without any consideration to flank threats. On the morning of May 17, the 1st Panzer Division had captured a bridgehead across the Oise, 120 km west of Sedan. The 2nd Panzer Division, which operated slightly to the north, had advanced almost as far.[79]

The implications of the thrust conducted by the XIX Corps until the morning of May 17 were absolutely clear to Guderian. Little more than 100 km remained to the Channel coast. Should his units reach it, the Allied supply lines to Belgium would be cut. Guderian's corps was also not the only one that headed west. Reinhardt's and Hoth's corps had reached almost as far as Guderian's. At this moment, an order from von Kleist arrived that instructed Guderian to halt.[80]

Guderian and von Kleist met at a military airfield near Montcornet. A heated discussion ensued and Guderian demanded that he be relieved of his command unless he was allowed to continue west. Von Kleist saw no other alternative than to accept Guderian's resignation, and the commander of the 2nd Panzer Division, Lieutenant-General Veiel, was chosen to lead the XIX Corps. However, this was not the end of the story. General von Kleist's superior—Colonel-General List, the commander of the 12th Army—flew to Guderian and persuaded him to remain as commander of the XIX Corps. In mutual agreement with Colonel-General von Rundstedt, the commander of Army Group A, List, suggested a compromise; Guderian would be permitted to conduct reconnaissance in force provided he did not move his staff west. It seems that the order to halt Guderian emanated from Hitler himself. Guderian believed von Kleist obstructed him, but von Kleist appears to have assessed the situation similarly to Guderian and, in fact, tried to give him as free a rein as possible.

Guderian immediately seized the opportunity, which he took to the limit. He at once ordered his Panzer divisions to attack west at maximum pace. However, they were not permitted to use any long-range radio system that could be monitored by the higher command echelons. They would have to use telephone lines to communicate with the corps staff instead. Guderian moved his command post forward, but he did not make any radio transmissions from it. Instead, he established a transmitter well to the rear and relayed outgoing messages to it by wire. Thus Guderian ensured that he would be allowed freedom of action. In the evening of May 20, the XIX Corps lead elements reached the Channel coast at Abbeville. The Allied forces in the north had been trapped.[81]

Dunkirk

When Guderian's Panzer divisions reached the Channel, they cut off the supply lines for the Allied units in Belgium and northern France. The British Expeditionary Force suffered similarly because it did not use nearby ports such as Calais, Dunkirk and Antwerp, which were regarded as too exposed to German air attacks. Instead, ammunition, provisions, spare parts, fuel and all other items required for operations were unloaded in ports located further west. The supplies were brought to the front by trucks and trains.

The German thrust had not only cut off the Allied supply lines. The cut-off units in the north fought with their front facing northeast; now they faced being threatened from yet another direction, should the *Panzergruppe von Kleist* turn north. However, it was not self-evident that the Germans would turn north. They could also choose to turn south, towards Paris, and the Allies had no way of knowing what the Germans intended to do. The defense the French could field between the German spearheads and the capital was very weak.

Clearly, the Allies had no way of knowing the intentions of the Germans, but it seems that the Germans had not yet firmly decided which course of action they would pursue either. Neither Hitler nor the senior commanders had envisaged the spectacular success attained by the Panzer divisions. In fact, the success had been won largely by local commanders disregarding the instructions they received from above. Guderian is perhaps the most obvious example, but he was certainly not the only one. We have seen how von Kleist put his given orders aside when he instructed the XXXXI Corps to attack at Monthermé. He also tried to shield Guderian from the senor commander's interference after Sedan had been captured. Another example is Major-General Rommel, who commanded the 7th Panzer Division. The halt order of May 16 did not only include Guderian, but also the other two Panzer corps in Army Group A. Rommel was explicitly ordered not to break through the French defenses ahead of him, but he ignored the order. He attacked in the night and broke through the French defense at Soire-le-Château, advancing more than 40 km before dawn on May 17. His lead elements reached Le Cateau. Rommel had thus completely shattered the French attempts to create a defensive line from the remnants of the Meuse Line. This was accomplished by Rommel making decisions on his own, not by following the instructions from superior command echelons.[82]

The stunning German success was thus not the result of explicit planning and firm leadership at the highest echelons of command. To the contrary, the senior officers—as well as Hitler—appear to have been surprised by the events of May 10–20. Perhaps they were just as surprised as the Allied commanders, but it is, of course, very difficult to judge. Many of those in important positions on both sides were undoubtedly astonished. However, it still remained to be seen how the Germans would exploit the success of the first ten days of the campaign.

When discussing these events in retrospect, the background of the decision-makers at the time must not be forgotten. The French Army was regarded as one of the strongest in the world—perhaps even the strongest. Another important fact is that rapid victories over major powers were (and remain) quite uncommon, something that had been amply illustrated by World War I. Almost every war plan presumed that wars would be protracted and eventually decided by the availability of resources. The German war planning in the 1930s did not deviate significantly from this pattern. Admittedly, the Germans placed greater emphasis on mobile operations, but what took place in May 1940 was beyond the wildest dreams of most German officers.

The German art of war focused on defeating enemy military units. Consequently, the alternative they settled for, to turn north after reaching the Channel coast, appeared to be in line with the general pattern. The Germans created a defensive line along the rivers Somme and Aisne by pushing infantry divisions forward on the heels of the advancing Panzer divisions. As soon as they had been relieved, the latter could turn north to complete the defeat of the Allied forces there.

The Allied forces in the north faced disaster. All Dutch forces had laid down arms on May 15. The remaining forces comprised the Belgian Army, the British Expeditionary Force, the 1st French Army and elements of the French 7th Army. In addition to the threat from the German units, the open right flank and the severed supply lines, the Allies suffered from an ambiguous command situation caused by three different nationalities fighting together.

However, the fact that armies from different countries had to cooperate in a very difficult situation was just one of several disadvantages. A more fundamental problem was the lack of understanding of the importance of time. The French commander-in-chief, General Maurice Gamelin, was relieved on May 19 and replaced by General Maxime Weygand. The latter spent three days learning about the situation, and those days could not be made up. Had the Allies reacted rapidly, a dangerous threat to the Germans might have been created. A gap had developed between the German armored spearheads and the infantry marching to catch up. The Germans had too few motorized infantry divisions to cover the distance. Had the Allies taken advantage of this opportunity, they could have placed the Germans in an awkward position. Instead, the moment of opportunity was spent on several meetings. Only one notable attack was made, at Arras on May 21, where British armor attacked Rommel's flank. Slow but heavy infantry tanks participated in the attack, and their armor was impervious to the German antitank shells. Nevertheless, Rommel managed to halt the British attack, partly by using the 8.8-cm antiaircraft guns. They had been envisaged for use against armor and fortifications in addition to their primary role, and they were furnished with armor-piercing shells. The battle was hard-fought and the casualties suffered by the 7th Panzer Division testify to the intensity of combat— eighty-nine killed in action, 116 wounded and 173 missing. Although ninety of those reported missing would eventually show up again alive, these were the heaviest losses on a single day for the 7th Panzer Division during the campaign in the west.[83]

Tactically, the British attack had little consequence. The motley British force had to pull back as the Germans advanced against its flanks. It would, however, influence a much-discussed decision. Guderian's Panzer corps had already surrounded Calais and Boulogne by May 24, and only 15 km remained until he reached Dunkirk. In the north, the Germans had already captured Brussels and Antwerp. Gent had also fallen to the advancing German forces. Three harbors remained in Allied hands— Dunkirk, Oostende and Nieuport. If these were lost, approximately 1 million Allied soldiers would be lost. Remarkably, they would be assisted by an unexpected German decision. Guderian and the chief of the German general staff, Colonel-General Franz Halder, realized the importance of the Channel ports, but a sequence of events resulted in yet another halt order. The decision may have been influenced by the British attack at Arras; unlike the commanders of the Panzer divisions, many senior German commanders were quite nervous. On May 22, an order had already been issued calling for a halt to the advance. It seems that the order emanated from von Rundstedt.[84]

The order was soon revoked, but it was then given again. Unlike the halt orders given around May 17, Hitler appeared not to have been the instigator this time. He did, however, soon get involved, making the order impossible to revoke without his permission. A series of discussions followed, and the Panzer units were not released again until May 26. By then, the cut-off Allied forces in the north had managed to consolidate, although they remained in a very precarious situation. On May 28, the Belgian armed forces surrendered and left a gap in the line, but the evacuation at Dunkirk had already begun by that time. Between then and June 4, approximately 370,000 men were evacuated from France, of whom 338,000 escaped from the beaches at Dunkirk. Around two thirds were British and one third French. The Allies were surprised to find that so many had escaped, but all their equipment had been left behind. The Germans did not believe that anything near those numbers had managed to cross the Channel to Britain.[85]

The Germans Turn South

As the Dutch and Belgian armies had surrendered, most of the British Army had fled the continent and the best French units had been destroyed in the north, the Germans had turned the force ratios to their advantage. When they had attacked on May 10, the Germans had inferior resources at their disposal, but less than four weeks later, they could rely on superiority of force as they prepared to attack south. As most of the French mechanized formations had been destroyed in the north, the Germans also had more tanks than their opponents in early June.

The German offensive did not open on the same day along the entire front. Army Group B was positioned near the Channel with its three armies, and it began attacking on June 5. One of the most successful German units was Erwin Rommel's 7th Panzer Division. On June 4, his combat units had entered the positions they would launch the attack from. One of the elements that would lead the attack was II Battalion of the 25th Panzer Regiment. In the afternoon, its tanks sneaked into gardens and other terrain that offered concealment against aerial reconnaissance.[86]

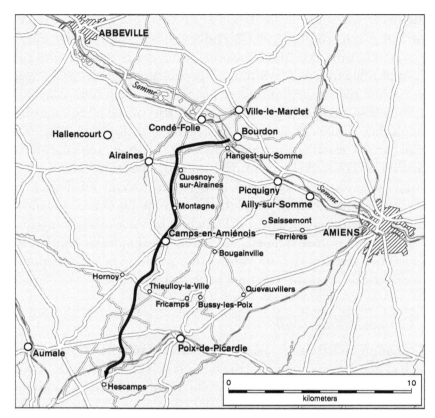

25th Panzer Regiment June 5–6, 1940

The soldiers tried to sleep as much as they could overnight, but they were woken early. At 2.30 a.m., II Battalion set out for the River Somme. The drivers strived to use roads not exposed to aerial reconnaissance to avoid detection before they reached the area near Bourdon, north of the Somme. They reached it without any drama. Now, one of the most common tasks in war began—waiting. A bridgehead had been held near Bourdon by infantry since before this advance, but the tanks had to wait a few hours before crossing the river.

At around 7.30 a.m., II Battalion received orders to cross the Somme. A railroad bridge had been captured intact and was now used by the tanks to reach the southern bank. After crossing the river, the battalion assembled in a depression and prepared to attack. It turned out that the infantry could not manage to extend the bridgehead as they were held back by strong French fire. The tanks of II Battalion were ordered to attack at 11.30 a.m.

The tanks carefully ascended from the depression and approached the positions held by the infantry. Fire from French positions in pockets of woodland near the bridgehead had held back the German infantry, but when the tanks drove past they did not encounter much opposition. The Panzer battalion continued south, but after covering around 2 km it was met by heavy fire from a wooded area. The Germans found it difficult to precisely locate the defenders, but the volume of fire from the tanks silenced the French.

By advancing south for around 2 km, the Panzer battalion had fulfilled its first mission—to support the infantry's attempt to enlarge the bridgehead. However, the encounter at the woods had resulted in German losses. The commander of the Panzer battalion, Captain Stoeckl, had been wounded, as had the commander of the 6th Company, Second Lieutenant Fortun. Lieutenant Lohrer, who commanded the 6th Company, had been killed. Several NCOs and privates had also been killed or wounded. Four tanks had been damaged severely enough to be regarded as unrecoverable. As he was the senior remaining officer, Lieutenant Maultzsch assumed command. He ordered the battalion to assume a defensive position. The killed were buried and the wounded received first aid before being moved to the rear for more thorough treatment. Remarkably, the infantry did not capitalize on the advance made by the tanks. Instead, it remained in the positions the tanks had driven past earlier.

Hour after hour elapsed without anything remarkable occurring, but after three hours the French artillery suddenly woke up. Shells began to rain down in the area between II Battalion and the other elements of the 7th Panzer Division that had crossed the Somme. This time, the Germans responded by attacking with the entire Panzer regiment. The powerful attack quickly gained ground. Despite strong French fire, the German tanks inexorably pushed forward. Soon they had captured Quesnoy and continued further south. They managed to penetrate to Montagne before dusk, approximately 10 km south of the railroad bridge they had used to cross the Somme.

As the sun set behind the horizon, the German tanks settled down for the night and awaited the infantry support they had been promised. However, the night passed without any infantry showing up. Fortunately for the German tankers of II Battalion, the French remained passive, and in the morning a few tanks were sent back to establish contact with the infantry. It turned out that the other elements of the Panzer regiment had been better supported by the other components of the division, including the infantry.

Despite various troubles, the 7th Panzer Division had achieved an important success on June 5. A solid bridgehead across the Somme had been established, from where the attack could continue. However, the price had not been insignificant. The war diary of the division recorded sixty-eight killed in action and 154 wounded, a clear indication that significant resistance had been offered by the French defenders, despite the fact that Rommel's division had captured approximately 1,000 prisoners on this day. Notably, the Luftwaffe had provided air support, but the Stuka dive-bombers had supported the infantry fighting near the river crossing despite the fact that the lead tanks were already 10 km further southwest.

Despite the somewhat unorthodox course of events, the 7th Panzer Division had created the necessary conditions for continuing the offensive. The division attacked from the bridgehead at 10 a.m. on June 6, and this time the entire 25th Panzer Regiment attacked from the very beginning, with the recon battalion on one flank and the motorcycle battalion on the other. Hard fighting ensued, with French tanks participating, but the Germans managed to advance all the way to Hescamps, approximately 30 km south of the Somme. This time, the Germans suffered fewer casualties. The 7th Panzer Division reported twenty-one killed and fifty-six wounded, but II Battalion of the 25th Panzer Regiment had lost so many tanks that the remaining were distributed amongst the other two battalions.

The success achieved by the 7th Panzer Division on June 5 and 6 cracked the western part of the defensive line that General Weygand had tried to create from the shambles of the defeat in the north. It was not only Rommel's 7th Panzer Division that had broken through; Max von Hartlieb's 5th Panzer Division had also penetrated the French defense slightly westwards. There no longer remained any possibility for the French Army to defend its home country. Further east, more German Panzer units were also poised to attack. The French situation would deteriorate even more.

Houdilcourt

Army Group A launched its offensive on June 9, four days later than the units near the English Channel. Guderian now had two Panzer corps at his disposal, both of which had been positioned in the Reims area. His grouping was the easternmost of the German mechanized formations and included four Panzer divisions and two infantry divisions. They were to be committed when infantry divisions had secured bridgeheads across the Aisne.

On June 9, Guderian's units remained in reserve. One of them was the 2nd Panzer Division, which was cautiously moved forward. Although the main offensive had been launched, it remained important not to reveal the Panzer divisions and thereby disclose the overall intensions of the Germans. The commander of the division, Lieutenant-General Rudolf Veiel, continuously received information on how the attack progressed. He issued instructions accordingly to the battle groups formed in his division. They gradually moved south, troubled by traffic jams but not unduly hindered.[87]

Early in the afternoon, alarming reports from the fighting infantry division were received. They indicated that French resistance was stiff. Heavy French tanks had also been observed, and so Lieutenant-General Veiel was requested to send tanks in support. He resisted, as he believed his tanks were inferior to the heavy enemy tanks and he did not want to reveal the presence of his division yet.[88]

The 2nd Panzer Division's preparations proceeded virtually according to plan, and early on June 10 it was ready to attack south. Veiel's division had two Panzer regiments, the 3rd and 4th, with two battalions each. They belonged to the 2nd Panzer Brigade, which was commanded by Major-General Heinrich von Prittwitz und Gaffron. He had elected to advance with the 4th Panzer Regiment in the lead. It had taken longer than expected to cross the Aisne during the night, but at 6.30 a.m., the

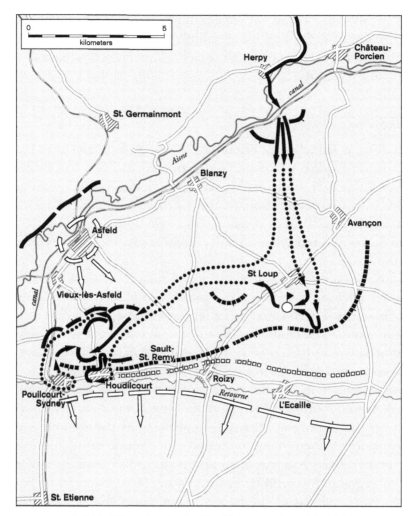

2nd Pz.Div. actions in the Houdilcourt area June 10, 1940

4th Panzer Regiment attacked. An hour later, the 3rd Panzer Regiment joined in.[89]

Beautiful summer weather accompanied the tanks of the 4th Panzer Regiment as they set out. The tanks made good progress across the billowy fields, but soon fire from a wooded area was aimed at the German tanks. The tankers asked for infantry to clear the woods. The request was first made on the radio, and then by a liaison officer. However, nothing had happened after fifteen minutes. The commander of the Panzer regiment did not wait any longer. The German tanks continued south and were soon able to report that the defenders had been defeated.

High tempo was vital to the German success. Accordingly, the 4th Panzer Regiment continued attacking, and soon after 7.30 a.m. it neared the village of St. Loup. The tanks had thus advanced approximately 5 km south of the Aisne. To maintain the tempo of the attack, one Panzer battalion from the 3rd Panzer Regiment was directed to outflank St. Loup to the east while the 4th Panzer Division attacked into the village as well as outflanking it to the west.

At this moment, the Germans observed French tanks moving north. The German tankers immediately opened fire and could soon see the French tanks turning south. Further west, the Germans found a French battery, which was also rapidly taken under fire. The French gunners tried to evade the attackers with their equipment, but the German Panzer IIIs and IVs continued to shell them. Only remnants of the battery managed to escape. St. Loup was captured without much trouble.

After this objective had been attained, the commander of the Panzer regiment ordered the advance to continue towards Houdilcourt, located approximately 8 km west-southwest of St. Loup. As was customary in the German Army, the brigade commander issued his orders orally by visiting his subordinates at their command posts. They did not find the brigade commander's instructions surprising given the overall mission. The exact direction was, of course, not self-evident, but the brigade commander indicated it clearly.

From the St. Loup area, German tanks drove towards the slopes northwest of the village, but some of them remained at the village until the infantry arrived. Most of the 4th Panzer Regiment did, however, begin to move, initially without encountering any significant opposition. The 5th Company advanced on the left flank and the tank commanders raised their heads above the turret hatch to search for the enemy. They suddenly saw muzzle flashes from antitank guns north of Sault-Saint-Remy. One of the German platoons immediately opened fire and knocked out the French battery before any tanks were knocked out.

The battle grew fiercer as the German tanks approached Houdilcourt. The village was located along an east–westerly stretch of woodland. The German maneuver brought them alongside the woods. Concealed French antitank guns, fire controllers for the artillery and heavy infantry weapons lurked beneath the branches. After the command was given, they opened fire on the German tanks, which lacked supporting infantry at this stage. Neither were the German tanks accompanied by fire controllers for the artillery.

Despite their disadvantages, the 4th Panzer Regiment continued the attack and tried to envelop the French position by advancing west, which would allow it to roll up the defense. However, the attempt failed as the French flank extended further to the west than anticipated by the Germans. The 6th Company did manage to break into Houdilcourt and clear the village, but the strongest French defenses were located in the woods east and west of Houdilcourt. The French were also protected by minefields and the bridges across the Retourne river—the swampy banks of which extended westwards through the woods—had been barricaded.

The regiment commander regarded artillery support as necessary for successfully attacking the French position. Over the radio, he requested fire support from the divisional howitzers, but this could not be provided immediately. It was not until 12.20 p.m. that the tankers received any information suggesting that artillery support could be expected soon. The tanks in Houdilcourt were ordered to move out of the village to avoid being subjected to the artillery fire. The howitzers would commence firing at 12.45 p.m.

The German tank crews anxiously waited for the shells to hit the French positions, but despite straining all their senses, they could not see any artillery fire when their watches passed 12.45. Neither did they receive any information on the radio, leaving them with no option but to wait—they could not risk being hit by their own artillery.

A sort of stalemate resulted from the poor communication between the German tanks and artillery. Finally, tanks from the 5th and 6th Companies began to move in order to find firing positions on a slope, but they drew fire from French antitank guns. Several German tanks were knocked out by the well-concealed French guns, which the Germans were unable to locate. At this moment, the German tankers decided not to wait any longer, despite the uncertainty of the artillery fire. II Battalion of the 3rd Panzer Regiment attacked east of the French position, thus rolling it up from the flank. Around 200 prisoners were captured, as well as five antitank guns.

Shortly thereafter, the Panzer regiment was able to establish a connection with the neighboring division, which detailed two of its artillery battalions to support the tanks. The latter could thus continue its attack and dislodge the defenders from their positions. The tanks could not pursue south in force until the minefields and other obstacles had been removed. However, the tanks and the temporarily subordinated artillery from the neighboring division fired upon the retreating French defenders.

Later in the evening, the 3rd Panzer Regiment took up defensive positions south of Houdilcourt, near the northern outskirts of St Etienne sur Suippes. The French line of defense had been broken, but at a cost. No fewer than twenty-one of the tanks in the 3rd Panzer Regiment had been knocked out, although it was possible to repair many of them. The 2nd Panzer Division recorded twenty-five killed in action, seventy-one wounded and three missing. Of these, three of those killed, twenty-one of those wounded and one of those missing belonged to the 3rd Panzer Regiment. Casualties within the 4th Panzer Regiment were far smaller: two killed in action, nine wounded and one missing.[90]

In the evening of June 10, two pieces of news were received by the 2nd Panzer Division. The Allies had evacuated Narvik, and thus the campaign in Norway had come to an end. Also, Italy had declared war on Britain and France. This information was enthusiastically received, but the 2nd Panzer Division had no time to rest on its laurels. During the night, the bridges across the Retourne were cleared of mines and obstacles. Another river, the Suippes, flowed across the German axis of advance further south, and the retreating French blew up the bridges spanning it. Nevertheless, the 2nd Panzer Division advanced on a broad front east of Reims on June 11.[91]

The battles northeast of Reims had shown that the spirit of the French Army was not yet broken. However, once the Germans had broken through the prepared defenses, they could not be stopped. The losses suffered previously in the north had left France bereft of any significant reserves, and when the fighting became more fluid, the Germans held all the trump cards. No significant opposition would bother Guderian's divisions after June 11.

When the Germans broke through Weygand's defensive line, the last hope for France was shattered. The few British units that remained on French soil hurried towards the Channel coast for evacuation. In some cases, they were not fortunate enough to get there. A large portion of the 51st British Infantry Division was captured at St. Valery-en-Caux. However, the British attempts to evacuate from Cherbourg were more successful.

The French Army could only offer scattered resistance as the German spearheads rapidly drove deeper into France. Usually, the defenders were unable even to retreat as quickly as the attackers advanced. Paris was not a primary goal for the Germans; rather, Army Group B mainly attacked west of the French capital and Army Group A attacked east of it. Nevertheless, the Germans remorselessly closed in on Paris, forcing the French government to escape to Tours. Paris was declared an open city, and on June 14 German soldiers marched through the undefended French capital. By then, the Germans had already advanced across the Seine and almost surrounded Paris.

The Italian dictator Benito Mussolini saw his chance to grab some of the spoils of the French and British defeat and declared war on the western powers on June 10. However, his armed forces were poorly prepared. Despite repeated attempts to attack southeast France, the Italians had no success. Mussolini's declaration of war had almost no impact on the course of events during the first three weeks of June 1940.

Opinions were divided within the French government. Some ministers advocated negotiations with the Germans, while others wanted to continue fighting. The latter, of course, realized that the Battle of France had been lost and it only remained to wage war from the colonies. It was no longer possible to prevent the Germans from occupying *la Patrie*.

The French Prime Minister, Paul Reynaud, resigned on June 17 and was replaced by the elderly Marshal Pétain. He immediately initiated negotiations with the Germans, and a ceasefire was signed on June 22. According to the agreement, the Germans occupied northern France as well as the Atlantic coast all the way to the Pyrenees. Southern France would be ruled by the so-called "Vichy Government," under the control of Pétain. French forces in the colonies would only fight if attacked. The agreement marked the end of France as a fighting power in the war. Hitler had won his greatest victory and used the opportunity to take revenge for the defeat in World War I. The agreement was signed in the very same railroad car where German delegates had been forced to sign the ceasefire agreement of 1918.

The German victory in the west was an overwhelming success in almost every sense. The French Army had been regarded as one of the strongest and best in the world, and the Maginot Line was an impressive defensive line. Few believed the Germans would defeat France, Belgium and the Netherlands and force the British to evacuate their forces from the continent. However, not only did the Germans achieve all this, they did it in a remarkably short time and with surprisingly few losses. The Germans marched into Paris in little more than a month. Seldom has a major power been defeated so swiftly.

Many German officers were just as surprised. What had been an unattainable objective for the Kaiser's armies in 1914–18 had been accomplished in six weeks this time. Indeed, it could be argued that it had all been decided in the first two weeks. A victory as stunning and surprising as this called for an explanation, but in the frame of mind prevalent in the summer of 1940, it was not easy to form an accurate analysis.

The French commander-in-chief, General Gamelin, explained the defeat by "inferiority in numbers, inferiority in equipment, inferior tactics."[92] His choice of explanation is hardly surprising, but it is clear that the Allies did not suffer from inferiority in numbers or equipment. However, Gamelin was not the only person who believed that the Germans were numerically superior. As soon as 1941, a book was released in Britain that was written by the Czech Lieutenant-Colonel Ferdinand Otto Miksche,

who had fled his home country. He tried to explain the German successes of 1939–40 and discussed the German tactics in great detail. He
also emphasized that the Germans possessed a numerical superiority in
equipment in 1940. He claimed that without this advantage, the German
tactics would not have produced the spectacular results they did.[93]

Interestingly, Miksche's book provides a very misleading analysis of the
German art of war. Of course, it is hardly surprising that it contains numerous factual errors, which was almost inevitable given the sources available
at the time. More importantly, he provides a very schematic picture of
German warfare and thus misses the point completely. His emphasis is on
equipment, organization, meticulous planning and the alleged schematic
conduct of the Germans. He could hardly have been further from the
truth, but subsequent authors have repeated his explanations.

Another peculiar explanation given by Miksche—and one that was
subsequently given by many others—is the role of so-called "fifth columnists." The term had been coined in the Spanish Civil War, during the
battles in Madrid in 1936. In that conflict, Franco's supporters claimed
that in addition to the four columns advancing towards Madrid, they also
had a fifth column operating inside the city. "Fifth columnists" would
subsequently become a generic term for saboteurs and collaborators
behind the front lines. It has been claimed that such activity paved the
way for the Germans, but that claim appears grossly exaggerated. This
was probably caused by exaggerating the influence of collaborators such
as Vidkun Quisling. Another possible explanation might be the trials
conducted by the Vichy Government at Riom after the Fall of France.
There, politicians and intellectuals were accused of having caused the
French defeat by undermining the will to defend.[94]

These accusations lacked substance, and the Riom Trials were a sham
rather than a serious administration of justice. The French defeat was caused
purely by military factors with roots that can be traced at least back to World
War I. The decisive phase of the fighting in May 1940 was the German
breakthrough at Sedan, Monthermé and Dinant along the Meuse. These
breakthroughs were admittedly achieved by Panzer divisions, but it was
mainly the infantry, engineers, and artillery within the Panzer divisions who

produced the decisive breakthrough. The methods employed by these arms were based on the infiltration tactics of World War I.

The tanks were more important from May 15 onwards, when the Germans strived to capitalize on the breakthrough at the Meuse. At this stage, the German spearheads encountered only weak resistance, and the poor armor and armament of the German tanks mattered little. Their mobility and excellent communications equipment were more important assets.

The value of decentralized decision-making was high during the entire campaign, but perhaps this was particularly emphasized when the highest commanders attempted to harness the Panzer divisions on May 17. They were effectively overruled by their subordinates, who not only ignored the decisions made at the top but also deliberately deceived the higher echelons of command. Such an explanation was, of course, difficult to see for those who tried to explain the German victory in the 1940s. Instead, the field lay open for various myths to flourish.

One of the myths that spread concerns the dive-bombers. To the Allied commanders, the image of diving aircraft, descending on their prey while howling horrifyingly, proved difficult to avoid when developing aircraft and doctrines. For reasons that can better be described as psychological and emotional rather than scientific, the Allies were captivated by the thought of aircraft attacking pinpoint targets and effectively supporting mobile forces in a way that artillery was unable to replicate. However, the dive-bombers were mainly effective against poorly trained and poorly equipped soldiers, who were susceptible to the morale-lowering effects of the Stukas. Only rarely did the dive-bombers knock out a bunker or a tank. Despite the local air supremacy achieved over Sedan, the Luftwaffe failed to isolate the battlefield and prevent French reinforcements from moving to it. It should be noted that these conclusions apply to the Sedan area, where the Luftwaffe made its main effort. At Dinant and Monthermé, further north, the Luftwaffe influenced the battle even less. Still, the XV and XXXXI Corps achieved results comparable to those attained by Guderian's XIX Corps.[95]

Despite the limited success, Luftwaffe losses were high. No fewer than 1,236 aircraft were destroyed and 323 damaged. Considering the number of aircraft committed and the relatively short duration of the campaign, these losses were substantial. Allied aircraft losses were even greater, amounting to 1,029 British aircraft and 892 French.[96]

The German Army recorded 777 destroyed tanks—619 in May and 158 in June. The light Panzer I and II models accounted for 419 of the losses. These losses were far from marginal, but as many of the lost tanks were of the light types, the consequences were not alarming. The Panzer I would soon be phased out of the combat units anyway as it had been designed for training purposes rather than battle.[97]

The German casualties were initially reported as 27,074 killed in action, 111,034 wounded and 18,384 missing.[98] However, a significant share of the missing would never be found alive and some of the wounded also perished, bringing the number of dead to 46,059.[99] However, such losses were very modest compared to World War I. The German casualties were also much lower than the French, which amounted to 92,000 dead, 250,000 wounded and around 1.5 million taken prisoner. Interestingly, the German daily casualties appear to have been higher during June than in May, suggesting that the French soldiers did not lose their resolve until the situation was patently hopeless.[100]

Like the dive-bomber, the tank would be the subject of various myths. Many observers concluded that the campaign of 1940 had demonstrated the great importance of the tank. This conclusion partly emanated from some actors on the French side who wanted to explain the sudden French collapse, but also from the German propaganda, which strived to depict the German Army as invincible. Although the important role of the tanks must be recognized, their contribution would have been far smaller had the German infantry not performed remarkably well. In fact, the battles at Sedan were won more thanks to the infantry than to the tanks.[101]

The tanks could have a psychological impact far beyond their fire-power. The most extreme example of this took place in the 55th French Division south of Sedan on May 13. A rumor claiming that German

tanks were approaching caused panic in the artillery and other rear elements of the division, which subsequently fled. However, the rumor was
utterly false as no German tanks had yet crossed the Meuse.[102]

It seems that the tendency to suffer from panic is related to poor
training. German units almost never suffered from such panic, although
there are a few examples of it from the early days of the campaign in
Poland in 1939.[103] The French preference for leading "at a distance"
appears to have aggravated the problem.

Bearing this in mind, it is hardly surprising that there were officers
in Germany who remained doubtful of the potential of the tank. After
all, it was hardly realistic to assume that the enemy would be defeated
by rumors. Despite being one of the most ardent advocates of the tank,
even Guderian did not expect such incidents would occur anything
more than occasionally and locally.[104]

Many false conclusions were drawn from the campaign in the west in
1940. The emphasis was often placed on the wrong factors. Quite simple
explanations took precedence over more complicated ones, despite the
fact that the latter were more important. The German propaganda added
to these misunderstandings.

However, it was not only non-German observers who drew false
conclusions from the campaign. Hitler also seems to have made the
same mistake. Significantly, he seems to have given himself a far larger
share in the responsibility for the victory than was due to him. At a press
conference on May 20, Hermann Goering had already declared that
Hitler himself had personally conceived the plan for the campaign in
the west. He went on to claim that the "military genius of Adolf Hitler
had caused a revolution in the art of war, where fundamental principles
thus far regarded as inviolable had been overthrown." In the German
propaganda, Hitler was portrayed as the creator of "Blitzkrieg" and "the
greatest commander of all time."[105]

Hubris is a dangerous trait when important decisions have to be made.

CHAPTER 5

INTERLUDE WITH CRUCIAL DECISIONS

After France had been defeated, the balance of power shifted dramatically. Until May 1940, Germany had been squeezed between France in the west and the Soviet Union in the east. The Molotov-Ribbentrop Pact had removed the threat from the east, but Hitler could not count on that in the future. However, the defeat of France left only one major land power remaining on the continent to oppose the Germans. Hitler found himself in a position where he had far more freedom to choose his future actions. Not only had the conquests opened up sources of raw materials for German industry, he could also count on the other nations to accept trade treaties with Germany, which appeared to dominate Europe in 1940.

The impact of the German victory over France was not confined to Europe—the repercussions were palpable in other parts of the world too. The French defeat allowed Japan to mount increasing pressure on the French colonies in Indo-China to enforce concessions. Similarly, the defeat of the Netherlands meant that that her ability to defend her possessions in Indonesia was reduced. This area, with its important supply of crude oil, had figured prominently in Japanese war planning. Japanese ambitions in southern Asia were also of concern to the United States. Of course, the Soviet Union was also very much affected. What Stalin thought is hard to know, but undoubtedly the German victory over France must have been a very unpleasant surprise to him.

The British were well aware of the serious consequences of the defeat. Not only had the Britain's Expeditionary Force been badly defeated, her strongest ally was gone and a new enemy had appeared in the

Mediterranean. The balance of power in the Mediterranean had thus shifted dramatically for the worse. No longer did the French Navy hold Italian sea power in check in the western Mediterranean. To cope with this situation, the British had to reinforce their Naval forces based in Gibraltar and Alexandria. As the British were alone in their struggle with the Axis powers and had a vast empire to protect, it was difficult to dispatch resources to the Mediterranean. Fortunately for the British, the German Navy was very weak after suffering losses during the campaign in Norway. Nevertheless, the prospects for the future were very bleak indeed. A sober analysis revealed clearly that Britain did not have the resources necessary to defeat Germany singlehandedly. A strong ally was indispensable, and there only remained two that were strong enough: The United States and the Soviet Union. Without such allies, only the Channel prevented the Germans from conquering the British Isles. However, it appears that the Soviet Union did not figure prominently in the British considerations. The nation on the other side of the Atlantic possessed a far greater industrial capacity than any other country, which, of course, was a huge advantage in a war of the scale that lay in the future. However, in 1940, the American armed forces were weak except for her Navy, and unfortunately Germany could not be defeated by naval forces alone. A strong army supported by air power was also required. Such resources could not be created immediately.

As Great Britain was no longer a major threat, Hitler found himself in an entirely new situation. Before the campaign in the west, the German dictator had been forced to navigate through very difficult waters, with his freedom of action severely curtailed. Improvisation had temporarily saved him from tricky situations, with the Molotov-Ribbentrop perhaps the most important example of this. Realistic long-term planning could hardly be conducted. Hitler seems to have had a kind of compass that roughly guided him, but he had frequently been forced to grasp opportunities as they appeared.

After the defeat of France, Hitler suddenly found that he could plan far into the future and choose from several substantially different strategies. The recalcitrant British were annoying, but they were not a threat to the German hegemony on the continent. One of the first decisions made by Hitler was to initiate planning for a large-scale attack on the Soviet Union. He initially wanted to attack the same year as the Fall of France, 1940, but he soon realized that such a campaign would not be concluded before the fall and winter brought adverse weather conditions. The planning soon shifted to a campaign in 1941.

As the planning and preparations had been initiated many months before the attack was to be launched, a final decision to proceed with the attack didn't have to be made in 1940. Hitler could have considered other options, but it is doubtful that he seriously considered any other alternatives. "Jewish Bolshevism" had long since been his main enemy, and the living space he craved would mainly be found in Eastern Europe. An attack on the Soviet Union fitted exactly with his worldview.

The dogged British were a thorn in Hitler's side, but he could not expect any significant dividends if they were defeated. On the other hand, if he were to attack the Soviet Union early in the summer of 1941, much of the German armed forces would not be committed for several months. Accordingly, that meant there was a period Hitler could devote to the stubborn opponent in the west.

The Battle of Britain must be seen against this background. The German attack had the character of a fumbling effort, quite unlike the three main campaigns conducted thus far. The Luftwaffe lacked a clear conception of how to defeat Britain, while the German Navy had little faith in a seaborne invasion. Admiral Raeder, the commander of the German Navy, preferred to direct military resources at the British overseas imports. He believed attacks on British shipping and ports would eventually bring the islanders to their knees. However, such a strategy would not produce significant short-term results. As the attack on the Soviet Union was scheduled for mid-1941, it was hardly likely that Britain could have been defeated by Raeder's strategy before the German armed forces crossed the border in the east. Raeder thus also advocated extensive operations against British possessions. He wanted a substantial German effort in the Mediterranean, where Mussolini's declaration of war had opened a new front against the British.

For the Germans, the war against Britain presented new problems that required strategies other than those that had been given priority during the rapid expansion before the war. Intellectual work on combined operations had been done; for example, war games had been conducted at the Armed Forces Academy in Berlin during the second half of the 1930s, when extensive inter-service operations had been dealt with. However, overall, such work had not been prominent in the German planning for war, and the Germans were not particularly well prepared for the situation they suddenly and unexpectedly found themselves in.[1]

Unlike in the previous campaigns, there was hardly even a hypothetical possibility of a quick victory over Britain. The key component in the German art of war was the Army. That was a choice that made very good sense when fighting almost any other country in Europe but Britain, which was shielded from the German Army by the Channel. In this case, the Luftwaffe and the Kriegsmarine had to fulfil their missions before the German Army could make itself felt. This, of course, resembled Operation *Weserübung*, but the Germans had been able to rely on the element of surprise for that operation, which was hardly possible during the summer of 1940.

There was only one circumstance that could lead to a quick German victory over Britain in 1940, and that was a sudden collapse of the British resolve to battle on. It was not feasible to defeat them militarily—at least not within the reasonably short period of time available. The situation in the summer of 1940 differed fundamentally from the previous campaigns, during which the Germans may have nurtured hopes of a speedy enemy collapse, but the results were effectively decided on the battlefield. By defeating the enemy's military units, the Germans had left their opponents bereft of the means to offer resistance. The fallen countries had lost after their army units had been defeated.

Britain was quite unlike anything the Germans had encountered before. Her Army had suffered disastrous defeats in Norway and Western Europe. The soldiers evacuated had lost all their equipment, but unlike the other countries, Britain was not mainly dependent on the Army for the defense of her home territory. She relied far more on the Air Force and the Navy. This resulted in a kind of deadlock in which neither power could deal the other a mortal blow. The Germans were utterly superior on the ground, but the British were similarly superior on the seas. Neither side had a clear-cut advantage in the air, although many observers believed the Germans held the advantage; the Luftwaffe had gained a fearsome reputation after its campaigns in Poland, Denmark, Norway, the Netherlands, Belgium and France.

The Luftwaffe was somewhat stronger than the Royal Air Force, aided by its tactics, training and experience. However there were advantages for the RAF too. Both sides had developed radar, but with radar development at the level it was in the summer of 1940, the technology was clearly more valuable to the defender, particularly along a coast. Another important advantage was perhaps not so obvious. During the interwar years, air power had been depicted as a means to avoid the costly war of attrition of World War I. This theory would prove to be incorrect, as aerial warfare during World War II would turn out to be very much a matter of attrition. Losses would be very heavy, and enormous numbers of aircraft would be produced to cope with mounting losses. The Luftwaffe was larger than the RAF at the beginning of the summer of 1940, but British aircraft production was greater. Time thus favored the RAF, particularly if both sides endured heavy losses.

The Germans initiated air attacks against Britain during the summer of 1940, but they could not deal a mortal blow. Instead, the Luftwaffe tried a succession of alternative targeting methods, but none of them met with the kind of overwhelming success that was required. The Battle of Britain turned into a campaign of attrition during which the Germans could not gain the upper hand. In September, Hitler shelved the plans for an invasion. The Battle of Britain deviated substantially from the general pattern of 1939–41. Most obviously, Hitler did not score yet another victory, but more fundamental was the fact that the German efforts during the summer campaign in 1940 were quite unlike the Blitzkrieg campaigns. The Londoners would call the German bombings of the British capital "The Blitz," but they were not in the best of positions to analyze the German methods of warfare.

By the time the fall weather ruled out any chance of a German invasion of Britain, the planning for the attack on the Soviet Union— Operation *Barbarossa*—was already very advanced. Unlike the Battle of

Britain, Operation *Barbarossa* would be a typical exponent of the kind of Blitzkrieg warfare the Germans had conducted. Still, it was clear that an attack on the Soviet Union presupposed suitable weather, meaning that it could not be launched until well into 1941. There was still a period that could be used for other efforts. It only remained to decide which.

Admiral Raeder maintained his opinion that Germany should pursue a maritime strategy to bring Britain down. His own ships—submarines as well as surface vessels—would be directed against British convoy routes on the Atlantic. He also wanted the Luftwaffe to attack British ports, where their cargo was unloaded. Finally, he also wanted a more vigorous German effort in the Mediterranean.

Two countries figured prominently in Raeder's plans—Spain and Italy. However, Spain was exhausted after the devastating Civil War of 1936–39, which ended with Franco as victor. Despite Hitler's urgent requests, the Spanish dictator did not intend to become a belligerent. He also turned down German requests to use Spanish naval bases. The Italian dictator, Benito Mussolini, was, unlike Franco, very enthusiastic. When he declared war on France and Britain on June 10, he had hoped to grab a share of the spoils, but Germany defeated France before Mussolini had achieved any success against the country. The Italian dictator would have to find laurels elsewhere.

Italy had already acquired colonies in Somalia and Eritrea at the end of the nineteenth century. Mussolini had attacked Ethiopia in 1935; it was one of very few areas in Africa not already under European control. In August 1940, Italian forces in Ethiopia initiated a limited offensive against the British colony in Somalia and captured it.

Mussolini was not satisfied. He urged Marshal Graziani, who commanded the Italian forces in Libya, to attack Egypt. The Marshal expressed concerns as he regarded his forces to be poorly equipped, and he believed that supply difficulties would arise as they penetrated into Egypt. Mussolini was not to be moved. Graziani's 10th Army advanced into Egypt in September 1940, but he halted the offensive after covering less than 100 km.

Albania had been annexed by Italy during the spring of 1939, giving Italy a land border with Greece. In the fall of 1940, Mussolini decided to attack the latter country as a step towards his ambition of establishing dominance in the Mediterranean. However, the attack would soon turn into the first of a series of humiliations suffered by the Italian armed forces. It had been launched at a time of the year when unfavorable weather could be expected. Also, the Italian troops were poorly prepared for the mountainous terrain. The Greeks were soon able to stop the Italian offensive and push the attackers back into Albania.

Some time later, a British counteroffensive was launched in Egypt. Despite being numerically inferior, the British force inflicted a series of appalling defeats on the poorly prepared Italian forces. The British conquered Cyrenaica and advanced to El Agheila, where they halted the offensive and took up defensive positions. Thereafter, the British launched an offensive on Mussolini's empire in East Africa. The Italians were defeated again and *Il Duce* lost most of his colonial empire.

News of the Italian setbacks arrived as the German armed forces worked on their plans for Operation *Barbarossa*. Hitler was dismayed, but the German Army was not unduly worried as it regarded the Mediterranean theater to be of secondary importance. Reassured by its string of victories, the German Army honed its art of war. The experiences gained from recent campaigns were analyzed, resulting in a refinement of the existing concept. An example of this is provided by the guidelines issued by the Army high command in December 1940 regarding the employment and command of a Panzer division. These guidelines rested on the foundations laid by the field manuals from 1921 and 1933. The guidelines emphasised that the mobility and high tempo the Panzer divisions could generate depended on commanders at all levels acting daringly and quickly made decisions that were expressed in concise orders. Of course, this was nothing new in the German Army. The employment of temporary battle groups was also discussed, but again the new guidelines confirmed previous points of view. There were, however, some new aspects in the guidelines. Among the most important was the clearly held view that the Panzer divisions were an operational weapon to be employed for decisive action. Furthermore, the Panzer divisions should not be employed piecemeal, but concentrated. The latter particularly applied to the tank component. The positive results of employing Panzer corps were confirmed. Breakthrough and encircle-ment were identified as the most important tasks for Panzer divisions, which should be used to destroy the enemy, not merely push him back.

The notion that the Panzer divisions were a decisive weapon was thus confirmed. During the fall of 1940, the number of Panzer divisions was also increased from ten (the number when the campaign in the west began) to twenty. This change indicated the increased importance attached to the Panzer divisions. As no ground operations were conducted during the fall and winter of 1940–41, the Germans could train the new formations properly. The new divisions were mostly formed by picking components and experienced officers from existing units. In some cases, new Panzer divisions were formed from infantry divisions. The new Panzer divisions were not green formations, but they needed time to conduct exercises to evolve into smoothly performing teams. This lull provided the time needed.

While the German Army could focus on preparing for the campaign in the east, both the Luftwaffe and the Kriegsmarine were involved in significant operations. The Luftwaffe's operations against Britain were the most important, and they resulted in heavy losses. Particularly serious were the losses of well-trained crews. Significant quantities of aviation fuel were also consumed.

The Italian reverses led the Germans to send air units to Sicily, thus further diverting scarce air resources, although the Luftwaffe units soon became a serious menace to the Royal Navy. Mussolini's setbacks induced Hitler to send further units to the Mediterranean, including ground combat units.

Lieutenant-General Erwin Rommel was given command of the German ground combat units sent to Libya. At first, he only had the recently formed 5th Light Division, but the 15th Panzer Division would follow some time later. Rommel's exploits in North Africa have occu-pied many pages in the books on World War II—perhaps too many. He and his soldiers performed very well in battle, but it would be wrong to portray their performance as something much different than that displayed by other German formations. However, the war in North Africa would eventually be decided by the ability to bring reinforcements and supplies to the theater. Rommel did not always pay due consideration to the logistical issues, which were quite complicated. First of all, ammunition, fuel, food and other necessities were to be brought across the Mediterranean and unloaded in North African harbors. Then all of it had to be brought across mile upon mile of desert by trucks before it could reach Rommel's units at the front. These transport routes were bottlenecks, and they became increasingly worse the further Rommel's units advanced.[2]

Within the German Army high command, the war in North Africa was regarded as rather unimportant. Few resources would be devoted to it as no significant objectives could be captured. If Germany captured Alexandria and the Suez Canal, the British Mediterranean fleet would have to cease conducting operations in the eastern Mediterranean. This would hardly bring Britain down. If Rommel was to continue east after overcoming the Suez Canal, he might attack towards the oil deposits at the Persian Gulf. They were indeed an important objective. Of course such a goal was tempting, but there was a very serious drawback—the very large distances involved, in an area where communications were poor, would make such an undertaking a logistical nightmare.

Against this background, the unwillingness to commit resources to the North African theater is quite understandable. It was acceptable to send German units there to prevent a complete collapse of the Italian forces in the area, but not to pursue more far-ranging objectives. Considering the logistical problems involved, the reluctance of the German Army high command appears quite sensible.

However, Lieutenant-General Rommel was a very ambitious person who would not be content with a passive role. On his own initiative, he launched an offensive into Cyrenaica. He used methods that were well established in the German Army. Thanks to the mobility and flexibility of his units—a result of the German emphasis on thorough training and great latitude for decision-making amongst junior commanders—Rommel could rapidly capture Cyrenaica and surround Tobruk. When reaching the Egyptian border, he halted. The distance already covered would result in significant supply problems.[3]

From a tactical perspective, Rommel's actions do not deviate from established practice in the German Army. They were, however, peculiar in one important respect. Periods of intensive action were separated by long lulls resulting from supply problems. As full-scale operations were conducted, the units—both German and Commonwealth—consumed ammunition and fuel at a greater pace than they were able to be resupplied at. When stocks dwindled, the units had to spend time on building them up again.

Much attention has been devoted to the battles in North Africa—far more than is warranted by their significance. The area remained secondary to the Germans. Neither is the area of particularly great importance to the study of the war. The events that took place in Eastern Europe from the summer of 1941 onwards are far more extensive and also more relevant for studying the German art of war.

The Germans did not only commit forces to North Africa during the first half of 1941. Events that Hitler found ominous took place in the Balkans, and he would use military force to change the course of events to a direction he preferred. It was the failed Italian attempt to conquer Greece that had set this course of events in motion. When the British saw that the Greeks offered tenacious resistance, they began to consider supporting them. The Romanian oil fields at Ploesti—one of the most important sources of crude oil to Germany—could be attacked from airfields in Greece. Hitler could not tolerate such a danger. Preparations for an attack on Greece were initiated—including diplomatic efforts, as the Germans would need access to Bulgarian territory to attack Greece.

Hungary had already been tied to Germany, and after the defeat of France, the Germans reinforced their position regarding Yugoslavia and Romania. An agreement with Romania allowed the Germans to pass their troops in transit to Bulgaria, as well as defending the oil fields at Ploesti. Planning and preparations for an attack on Greece continued during the early months of 1941, but a coup in Yugoslavia on March 27 upset the German plans. The new regime was not friendly to the Germans, unlike its predecessor. Instead, the new government chose to establish connections with the Soviet Union.

The unexpected events in Yugoslavia caused an enraged Hitler to attack the country. The armed forces hastily altered the plans for attacking Greece to include an assault on Yugoslavia. When the Germans attacked on April 6, they again made swift progress. Belgrade was captured within a week, and soon afterwards the Yugoslavian Army ceased to offer any significant opposition to the invaders.

Greece was attacked simultaneously. British units bolstered the Greeks, but to little avail. In a series of rapid maneuvers, the German Panzer units defied the mountainous terrain and outflanked the British positions. Most of the Greek Army was deployed against the Italians in Albania, and this position rapidly became untenable. Unfortunately, Greek attempts to retreat were in vain as the Germans quickly drove into central parts of Greece. The Greek soldiers, who had defended gallantly against the Italians, had to surrender to the Germans on April 23. The British units were again forced to evacuate hastily, leaving vast quantities of equipment behind.

The German armed forces had again defeated their opponents in a swift campaign. Germany's art of war had been further honed, which was helpful in the mountainous terrain on the Balkans. In this campaign, the Germans also enjoyed the benefit of greater resources in the theater than their opponents possessed. It would be the last time the Germans enjoyed such an advantage.

The German Balkan victory was, however, not without disadvantages. Worst of all, the campaign adversely affected Operation *Barbarossa*, something that became clear as soon as Hitler ordered Yugoslavia to be included in the operation. Neither had the battles come to an end when Yugoslavia and Greece had been captured. British forces had previously been sent to Crete, and a large part of the forces evacuated from the Greek mainland were sent to the island. The forces lacked most of their heavy equipment, but they could nevertheless contribute to the defense of the mountainous island.

As British bombers based on Crete would constitute a threat to the oil fields in Romania, the Germans decided to attack the island by assaulting it from the air. It was a daring operation—even more daring than the Germans realized, as they did not expect strong opposition. When the first wave of parachutists descended towards the Cretan soil, it was met by a hail of small-arms fire and suffered significant casualties. The German attack began so badly that the entire operation could have ended in a disaster. Confused Allied commanders did, however, allow gaps in their defenses at the Maleme Airfield. The local German commander seized the opportunity and captured it. This was the turning point. Although the British could still fire on the airfield, German reinforcements could be flown to Crete. The Germans were particularly helped when elements of the 5th Mountain Division arrived and drove the British away from the Maleme area.[4]

Once the Germans had secured the airfield, further elements of the 5th Mountain Division could be air landed. However, the Luftwaffe was not only a transport service. Excellent weather permitted it to attack British communications on Crete. Also, German air power dominated the skies above the sea surrounding Crete. The Royal Navy could only operate in daylight by endangering its precious warships, of which many were sunk.[5]

It soon became apparent that the British could no longer defend Crete. On May 23, the defenders began to retreat to the southern coast to be evacuated. Inevitably, Royal Navy warships became exposed to air attacks and suffered serious losses. Still, many soldiers were successfully evacuated, but 11,835 Commonwealth soldiers ended up in German captivity. 1,742 had been killed during the battles on Crete and another 800 died during the evacuation. German losses were also heavy; they amounted to 6,116, of which 1,990 had been killed and 1,995 were reported as missing. Few of the missing would be found alive.[6]

The losses suffered by the British and Commonwealth forces were much higher than the German casualties, but the latter mainly consisted of elite paratroopers as most of the German casualties occurred during the first phase of the operation. As Germany had few parachute units, these losses were serious. They did not signal the end of German airborne operations, but they at least suggested a pause until the units had been reconstituted.

During the period between the Fall of France and the attack on the Soviet Union, Hitler enjoyed a greater freedom of action than any he had been allowed before. It was a luxury that would not return. Despite the various options he had and the time he could devote to pondering them, Hitler seems to have settled for attacking the Soviet Union quite soon.[7] The other alternatives were regarded as secondary and unlikely to produce results favorable enough to Hitler. Instead, they tended to squander his energy. The main objective—the utter defeat of the Soviet Union—remained, but the escapades in the Mediterranean, in the Balkans and on the Atlantic meant that Germany could not devote all her strength to the enormous undertaking known as Operation *Barbarossa*. Clearly this was a disadvantage, but Hitler seems to have not been unduly concerned. In a sense, this is understandable. The critical resource for Operation *Barbarossa* was Army units, and particularly Panzer units. The German Army could send almost all its Panzer units and motorized infantry divisions into the Soviet Union. In the short term, the other theaters did not cause much of a drain of this most critical resource. However, if the war dragged on, they might provide far more of a distraction. Nevertheless, Hitler expected a rapid victory over Stalin.

CHAPTER 6

THE ULTIMATE ORDEAL

No fewer than 2.5 million German Army soldiers stood poised to attack the Soviet Union in June 1941. They belonged to an army that could look back at an impressive array of victories. Norway, Denmark, the Netherlands, Belgium, Luxembourg, France, Poland, Yugoslavia and Greece had fallen to the advancing German units. The British had been chased off the continent (except at Gibraltar, which the Germans could hardly reach as long as Spain remained neutral) and humiliated in North Africa. Quite understandably, the German soldiers were confident after garnering so many impressive victories in less than twenty-one months. However, this time they faced a task of monumental dimensions, but the individual soldiers did not know the extent of the operation called *"Barbarossa"* that was about to be launched. It seems that most of the German officers did not realize the magnitude of what lay ahead either.

None of the adversaries fought by the Germans thus far possessed military resources as vast as those that Stalin could rely on, but the Germans were largely ignorant about the true Soviet military capacity. The German intelligence services, like those of other nations, had not understood the magnitude of the Soviet armaments. It is possible that Hitler would have made other decisions had he been better informed about Stalin's military power. The number of tanks is telling; the Red Army possessed around 23,000 tanks in June 1941, of which 12,885 had been deployed in the military districts along the western border. Germany only had 5,694 tanks and assault guns, of which 3,648 were included in the units that were about to launch Operation *Barbarossa*.

Against such odds, an absolutely exceptional warfare concept would be needed.[1]

Hitler expected a quick victory. He took for granted that the Red Army was poorly trained, poorly equipped and poorly led. Stalin's regime was presumed to have a fragile grip of the vast country. Hitler was not the only person to nurture such opinions either; similar perceptions were prevalent among German officers as well as observers in other countries. Hitler's assessments contributed to him not making any efforts to gain popularity in the areas he was about to conquer. On the contrary, during the spring of 1941, preparations were made for an unusually brutal occupation as soon as new territory was conquered. It was an expression of Hitler's conviction that victory would be easily achieved as well as his quest for living space in the east.

The German Army intended to win the campaign by defeating the Soviet armed forces. Thereby control of the vast area would be secured. The focus on the defeat of the enemy armed forces is well in line with the previous campaigns. It appears to have been a realistic choice in this case too. Soviet raw materials were found far from the border, as were the Soviet industries. Neither German air power nor German ground units could be expected to adversely affect Soviet production during the initial phase of the war. It was not until the German armies had advanced deep into the enemy's territory that his war production could be adversely affected. Furthermore, as the Germans had poor knowledge about the Soviet war economy, effective targeting would be difficult.

Another alternative had been to undermine Stalin's regime, but it was hardly feasible to do that without also doing what the Germans planned to do—destroying the Soviet Army. Stalin could be overthrown following the defeat of his military. On the other hand, the Germans did not make any notable efforts to capitalize on the dissent Stalin's brutal regime had sown. The Germans remained focused on a military victory, at least during the initial period of the campaign.

The Luftwaffe also planned to destroy Soviet military units. By attacking the Soviet Air Force at its bases, extensive losses would be inflicted at the outbreak of war. The Germans would thus attain air superiority. Surprise was an important prerequisite.

Compared to the campaign in the west in 1940, the Luftwaffe suffered from important disadvantages as Operation *Barbarossa* was about to be launched. Costly battles still raged in the skies above Britain, although they were less intense than in the late summer of 1940. The Luftwaffe had also sent significant numbers of units to the Mediterranean. Finally, the Navy demanded more air assets to be used in the efforts against British transatlantic shipping. Consequently, the Luftwaffe could not devote all its resources to the attack on the Soviet Union.

The overall strength of the Luftwaffe had only risen marginally since May 1940, but the percentage of operational aircraft had fallen. On May 10, 1940, the Luftwaffe could field 2,589 combat-ready aircraft for the attack in the west, but only 1,916 combat-ready aircraft were available for Operation *Barbarossa* when the buildup had been completed.[2]

Not only were fewer aircraft available for the attack on the Soviet Union, but the theater was also considerably larger, which made the employment of air power more difficult. The great distances complicated concentration of effort. Reconnaissance units had vastly larger areas to cover, and extensive woodlands provided good opportunities for enemy units to hide. Large expanses made it very difficult to isolate the battlefield by air interdiction, although the less dense road and rail systems facilitated the task. Great distances would also strain the Luftwaffe's supporting services. As the German Army would advance very rapidly, air bases would soon be located far behind the front line. Extensive efforts would be required to constantly bring air bases within reasonable distance of the battlefield. Fighters, with their short range, were especially dependent on bases near the front line.

There were many arguments suggesting that the Luftwaffe would be less capable of contributing to success in the east compared to the campaign of May–June 1940. The Army would be the main instrument, and the Luftwaffe would support it in various ways. Considering the circumstances, there were hardly any alternatives. The Germans lacked the means to subjugate Russia by attacking her industry or other strategic targets.

The German ground units would advance very rapidly to defeat the Soviet Army. Thus the enemy combat units would be cut off from their supplies, becoming disorganized and prevented from escaping by retreating. Such a scheme placed particular emphasis on the Panzer divisions as their mobility and combat power made them singularly suited for the task. They were to receive a more dominant role than in previous campaigns.

It has been argued that the Germans made a mistake before Operation *Barbarossa* by reducing the number of tanks in their Panzer divisions. In some cases, it has been described as a reduction by almost half. Perhaps the argument has some merit, but the reduction was not that great. When the Germans attacked on May 10, 1940, they had ten Panzer divisions, of which six had four tank battalions each and four had three. On June 22, 1941, the twenty German Panzer divisions had three (eight divisions) or two (twelve divisions) battalions. On average, the reduction was by one third, not half.[3]

Roads in the Soviet Union were often poor and subjected the vehicles to wear and tear. Rain could render them impassable to wheeled vehicles. Photo courtesy of Krigsarkivet, Stockholm.

However, the number of battalions do not present a complete picture. The number of tanks is probably more relevant. On May 10, 1940, the ten Panzer divisions possessed 2,439 tanks, or an average of 244 per division. For Operation *Barbarossa*, 3,648 tanks had been assembled and the number of Panzer divisions committed was seventeen, resulting in an average of 215 tanks per division. This only suggests a reduction by 12 percent. Also, the very weak Panzer I made up 21 percent of the tank fleet in May 1940. This model had been almost wholly discarded by the summer of 1941. Therefore, the number of truly combat-capable tanks had actually increased for Operation *Barbarossa* both in absolute numbers and as an average per division.[4]

Against this background, it seems hard to conclude that the Panzer divisions were weakened before Operation *Barbarossa*, especially as the other components of the Panzer divisions were improved. It could, however, be argued that stronger Panzer divisions might have been created had their number not been doubled. On the other hand, it is doubtful that the Germans would have had much use of stronger Panzer divisions on June 22, 1941. The ones they had performed very well during the initial weeks. However, it might be argued that stronger Panzer divisions would have had greater staying power. During prolonged operations, the number of operational tanks would inevitably shrink, not least because of mechanical breakdowns. After months of operations, this could result in the average Panzer division having quite few combat-ready tanks. Nevertheless, as the Germans expected a brief campaign, this probably did not appear to be an important argument.

While a combat unit's equipment is of great importance, it is far from the only factor that decides its combat power. The rapid expansion of the Army 1935–39 had affected training adversely. The lull between the campaign in Poland and Case Yellow had been used to improve training, and after France had been defeated, the German Army units could again train extensively. The experiences gained in the campaigns could be used to improve the quality of the training. The Panzer divisions had probably never been as effective as they were on June 22, 1941, and the other German Army units were also very well trained. Few armies have had combat units as well prepared as the German Army in June 1941.

Deployment

Hermann Türk found the journey to Radzyń Podlaski very unpleasant. Rainsqualls followed each other on this day, June 11, 1941, and his motorcycle offered no protection against the elements. Smoke from burning buildings along the road added to the misery. The smoke troubled his lungs as well as his eyes. Türk's sole consolation was the high speed he was traveling at, which at least meant that his journey did not last unnecessarily long. Wet but otherwise unharmed, Türk reached Radzyń Podlaski, where I Battalion of the 394th Motorized Infantry Regiment was stationed. The unit was part of the 3rd Panzer Division.[5]

Radzyń Podlaski was located east of the river Wisła, approximately 50 km from the Bug tributary, which formed the border between the part of Poland occupied by Germany and the part controlled by Stalin. Most of the daily activities remained similar to what had occurred for more than a year. Trains still crossed the demarcation line between the German and Soviet occupation zones, many of them still carrying raw materials from the Soviet Union to Germany. The German soldiers stationed west of the Bug lived a life that resembled a peacetime assignment. On June 13, Türk went to the battalion staff together with another physician, Dr Marr, where they were invited to a meal. After dining, Türk continued to the companies in the battalion. During his visits, he was offered sparkling wine, cognac, brandy and other tasteful beverages. After a pleasant day, Türk began his journey back to his lodgings at 9 p.m. When he woke up on the following day, a less pleasant day greeted him. During the afternoon, Türk visited the ghetto at Radzyń. In his diary, he recalled that it was a terrible sight, with ramshackle houses and the faces of emaciated people.

Türk saw increasing indications of the impending war against the Soviet Union. Airfields were prepared and the fighter group "Mölders" was stationed near Radzyń. The soldiers of the battalion ensured that the equipment was in good order. Weapons were thoroughly cleaned. Officers approached the border to reconnoiter. Türk went to Warsaw on June 16. It was evident that the city had been badly damaged during the fighting in September 1939. Not only did the population suffer from damaged buildings, but prices had skyrocketed, including the price of bread. Conditions in the ghetto were even worse. The stench was almost palpable, even at distance. Türk was told that 750,000 Jews had been packed together in a small area. The noise was loud. Many Jews tried to sell various articles. Others, including many women and children, lay starving in the streets, barely capable of moving. The contrast between the ghetto and the adjacent district was stark.

Rumors of war flourished. Türk noted that detailed plans were made up. Every man had to know his task, and II Battalion of the 349th Motorized Infantry Regiment was already marching east on June 17. Türk found some of the orders issued to the supply units particularly interesting; they were to prepare themselves for biological and chemical warfare, such as gas and rats infected with plague. The Germans faced a new enemy with unknown weaponry.

On June 19, Türk saw numerous vehicle columns drive past him. The spectacle continued all day long, but in the evening it was time for his own battalion to march. The 3rd Panzer Division was regrouping to the Koden area, south of Brest-Litovsk. For Türk, this meant a chilly night march on very dusty roads, but the mood in the battalion remained good. It was said that around 180 divisions would participate in the attack. Moscow would be captured in two or three weeks, but the press and radio had nothing to say about the attack, which Türk, of course, did not find astonishing. The element of surprise was very important, and the media could not blaze the intention to attack abroad.

Türk reached the designated deployment area in the morning of June 20. Like the other men who had traveled by motorcycle, he was grey from road dust. So much dust covered their faces that familiar faces were hard to recognize. After washing, the only thing left to do was wait. The tension mounted. On June 21, they were informed that the attack would be launched early the next day. Nothing in the radio broadcasts suggested that a major attack would soon be launched. The weather was excellent; the soldiers called it "Hitler weather." The forests around Koden abounded with tanks, artillery and horses. The corps Türk's battalion belonged to also included the only German cavalry division. Everybody tensely awaited June 22.

Attack

The night was still dark, but undoubtedly a beautiful day would follow as soon as the sun rose. There were almost no clouds. Only slight mist was expected in the morning. Nothing obstructed the Luftwaffe aircraft as they took off to attack Soviet airfields, fuel depots, staffs and barracks. At 3 a.m., they flew into Soviet territory and set out for their targets. Meeting scant resistance, the German aircraft—fighters, bombers and dive-bombers—swept towards thirty-one Soviet air bases. Only scattered antiaircraft fire met the attackers, who daringly released their bombs and fired their automatic weapons on ground targets. The attack was an instant success and was followed by further waves. After the first day of the campaign, the Luftwaffe claimed to have destroyed 1,811 aircraft while only losing thirty-five. Most of the Soviet losses were said to have occurred on the ground. Although claims about enemy losses should always be treated skeptically, it is clear that the Soviet Air Force was dealt a severe blow on the first day of the campaign.[6]

Despite their great success on the first day, the senior Luftwaffe officers realized that the Soviet Air Force had not received a mortal blow. Air reconnaissance revealed previously unknown bases. The main task for the German air units would still be to establish air superiority. Support to the ground units would have lower priority for the time being. It would very soon become evident that the German Army units did extremely well in any case.[7]

What is probably the largest ground operation ever was launched at dawn on June 22. Immediately, the Germans noted outstanding successes. After just four days, the LVI Panzer Corps had captured Daugavpils and thus secured a bridgehead across the Dvina, which was very important for the continuation of the offensive. The corps had advanced 310 km in a very short time. Further south, the German Army Group Center achieved even greater success. On June 25, the XXXIX Panzer Corps had already reached a point east of Minsk, having advanced 325 km in less than four days—an unparalleled performance. The Germans also advanced very rapidly on the Army group's southern wing. On June 28, the XXIV Panzer Corps reached Bobruisk after advancing no less than 442 km.[8]

Such a rapid advance was—and is—exceptional, and it seemed to confirm the optimism permeating the German planning before the operation. The Soviet units also suffered grievous losses. In the area between Białystok and Minsk, large Soviet forces were surrounded. The Germans captured 324,000 prisoners, 3,300 tanks and 1,800 artillery pieces. Russian sources confirm the picture. For example, it was reported that 4,799 tanks were lost in Byelorussia.[9]

Less dramatic advances were made in the Ukraine, but after three weeks, German spearheads had captured Zhitomir and Berdichev, located approximately 300 km from the border. Soviet losses were very heavy in the Ukraine too; the Soviet defenders lost 4,381 tanks before July 6. Casualties, which amounted to more than 240,000 during this period in the Ukraine, were severe.[10]

It was however, along the Warsaw–Moscow axis that the German Army expected to decide the campaign. The Red Army was supposed to be defeated west of or along the Dnepr. The German commanders believed most Soviet reinforcements would be sent to the central sector. As the German Army intended to bring the Soviet Union down by defeating her armed forces, most German armor was committed where the enemy was expected to send the majority of his forces. Consequently, Guderian's and Hoth's Panzer groups raced eastwards. It was vital to capture bridgeheads across the Dnepr as soon as possible.

Stary Bychóv

Early in July, the 4th Panzer Division crossed the Berezina, a tributary to Dnepr. It was an important success, but a bridgehead across the Dnepr was even more important. Both Army Group Center and South would have to cross the large river. As a result of the lower advance rate and the reaches of the Dnepr, Army Group South would not, however, arrive on its banks as soon as Army Group Center. Hermann Hoth's Panzer Group 3, which operated on the northern wing of Army Group Center, did not have to cross the Dnepr as the river followed an east–westerly direction in the Smolensk area. However, Heinz Guderian's Panzer Group 2, on the southern wing of Army Group Center, could not avoid the Dnepr.

His lead formation was the XXIV Panzer Corps, consisting of the 3rd and 4th on the southern and northern wing respectively.[11]

In the morning of July 3, the 35th Panzer Regiment in the 4th Panzer Division received orders to cross the Berezina at Bobruisk, where a war bridge already spanned the river. The regiment was told to proceed east and ford the Drut, a minor tributary to the Dnepr. At 6 a.m., the tanks had been refueled and orders to march were issued. They reached the Drut in the evening, later than scheduled. Important elements of the division lagged behind, but at midnight the regiment was nevertheless ordered to attack Stary Bychóv and capture a bridgehead across the Dnepr by a *coup de main*. Colonel Eberbach was entrusted with the mission.[12]

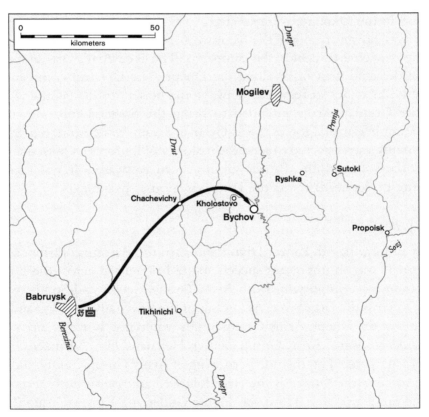

35th Pz.Rgt. attack on Stary Bychov July 4, 1941

A difficulty Eberbach had to consider was the Drut river crossing. The Red Army had blown up the bridge at Chinicy, but the Germans had found a ford. However, it was so deep that most vehicles could not use it. Even tanks had to negotiate it cautiously. Consequently, the task force could not be assembled quickly. At 7.30 a.m., the staff and three companies from I Battalion of the 35th Panzer Regiment had crossed the Drut. The 1st Company had already set off towards Stary Bychóv, and the other companies followed as soon as possible.[13]

As a result of the attack ordered, the 4th Panzer Division became stretched out. The distance from Bobruisk to Stary Bychóv was approximately 80 km as the crow flies. Radio communications were vital to mobile operations over such great distances. The German Army had been quick to realize the importance of radio communications and had fitted two-way radio sets in their tanks, except for the Panzer I, which had been conceived for training purposes. However, the insufficient availability of other types had nevertheless forced the Germans into employing the Panzer I in battle during the campaigns of 1939–40. By the time of Operation *Barbarossa*, few Panzer Is remained in service with the combat units. Thus almost all German tanks used in the operation had two-way radio communication, unlike most Soviet tanks.

Radio communications were important, but they also had limitations. One of them was range. In this case, when the 4th Panzer Division was spread over a large area, the limited range of the radio sets made wireless communication difficult. Independent action was indispensable as radio communications could not be relied upon. In any case, the Germans did not intend to use radio communications to centralize command and decision-making. Rather, the radio technology was used to enhance independence while still maintaining focus on the overall mission.

There were also advantages with the limited range of the radio transmitters—for example, when the Germans assembled large forces within a small area to break through enemy defenses through a concentrated blow. The radio network would be cluttered if too many units shared a limited number of frequencies. Radio sets with short range could make it easier to use a limited number of frequencies efficiently, without units interfering with each other. In such cases it could be an advantage that the range of individual tanks was limited to a few kilometers.[14]

When the 1st Company of the 35th Panzer Regiment launched its attack in the morning of July 4, radio communications soon became problematic. However, at first, the company was only hampered by chopped-down trees and blown bridges. It was not forced to fight until it reached Kholstovo, 6 km from Stary Bychóv. Soviet infantry supported by antitank guns tried to halt the German tanks. However, the German company was able to quickly overcome the defenders and attack the town that was their goal. At 8.30 a.m., the 35th Panzer Regiment received a radio message from the 1st Company, which reported that it had reached the rail station in Stary Bychóv. Fifteen minutes later, another message was received, stating that the company was engaged in fighting within the town. That was the last message received from the lead company for quite some time.[15]

Two other tank companies followed after the 1st Company, but at quite a distance behind. They were delayed by stubborn Soviet forces that included antitank guns. Fierce actions had to be fought by the German forces trying to catch up with the lead company. Meanwhile, the 1st Company fought to clear Stary Bychóv of Soviet defenders. This turned out to be a more difficult task than expected by the Germans. House-to-house fighting ensued, and the defenders enjoyed powerful artillery support. One by one, the buildings caught fire as they were hit by shells.[16]

The German 1st Company gradually fought its way east through Stary Bychóv. Five tanks managed to drive across the Dnepr bridge and reach the eastern parts of the town. The important objective thus seemed to be in German hands. However, soon afterwards, a direct artillery hit blew away a 15-meter-long section of the bridge. Four of the five German tanks that had reached the eastern bank were ambushed by well-concealed Soviet antitank guns after the defenders had allowed the Germans to come close.[17]

The damaged bridge could not be used by soldiers on foot either. Although the Germans cleared the part of Stary Bychóv that lay on the western bank of the Dnepr, they gained little advantage by doing so as another segment of the bridge was blown away by the Soviet defenders. The fire from the Soviet artillery was relentless, and one German tank took a direct hit.[18]

In the evening, Soviet infantry crossed the Dnepr south of Stary Bychóv by using inflatable rubber boats. Supported by the artillery, it attacked the German tanks in the western part of the town. The latter were hard-pressed to fend off the attack. Later in the evening, II Battalion of the 35th Panzer Regiment arrived, which allowed the Germans to firmly control the area. Still, the main goal, a bridgehead across the Dnepr, had eluded the Germans. The 4th Panzer Division had also incurred significant losses on July 4, amounting to seventy-four killed in action, 186 wounded and six missing.[19]

The attempt to capture the bridge at Stary Bychóv by a *coup de main* did not produce the intended result, but it illustrates the German penchant for independent action. The bridge at Stary Bychóv was essential to Guderian's entire Panzer group, but the action was wholly up to the commander of the 1st Company, 35th Panzer Regiment. He received the brief but clear mission early on July 4 and immediately set out to accomplish it. Almost as soon as his tanks had departed, he was left to his own means. Lack of reliable communications prevented him from receiving instructions as the attack progressed—and even if communications had been excellent, he would hardly have received many instructions. The German philosophy emphasized that the commander on the spot should make the decisions, and in this case the company commander was the senior officer in the area that mattered. Evidently, his decisions did not lead him astray. What prevented him from attaining his goal was a lucky shell from the Soviet artillery. Neither did the German company commander possess any means to knock out or suppress the Soviet artillery. His tanks could destroy the enemy fire directors, but the Soviet gunners could find the position of the bridge by a glance at the map.

There are many similarities between the attack on Stary Bychóv and Sorko's battalion at Stien, which was described in Chapter 3. Sorko was given an independent mission and he himself gave one of his company commanders an equally independent mission. It is hardly surprising that mountain troops and tankers both fought with great independence—it had been a basic tenet within the German Army before tanks became part of its inventory.

As the *coup de main* at Stary Bychóv failed, Guderian's Panzer group had to make a more elaborate assault on the Dnepr line. A few days were required to prepare and to bring up the units that were to conduct the attack. On July 10, the preparations were completed.[20]

Meanwhile, *Panzergruppe 3*, commanded by Colonel-General Hermann Hoth, had made spectacular progress on the northern wing of the Army group. Unlike with Guderian, rivers flowing perpendicular to his direction of attack did not unduly hamper him. Instead, he could attack in the area between the Dnepr and Dvina, where a passage almost 80 km wide could be used for the attack east. Guderian's Panzer group has received more attention in the literature, but the success attained by Hoth's Panzer group is at least as impressive.

With four Panzer divisions—the 7th, 12th, 19th and 20th—Hoth's Panzer group packed great striking power. Although Guderian had one more Panzer division, Hoth had more tanks. However, after the almost unbelievably rapid advance to Minsk, the lead units were difficult to supply. The Germans were fortunate to capture Soviet fuel depots and continued the advance. One of Hoth's goals was the city of Vitebsk, located on the Dvina.[21]

Hoth could not direct all his resources towards Vitebsk. The more westerly town of Polotsk was also an important goal. To capture it, Hoth directed the 19th Panzer Division towards Disna, located 30 km downstream along the Dvina. Disna was captured on July 3, and the following day, a bridgehead was established on the northern bank of Dvina, allowing the Germans to thrust eastwards on the northern bank of the river.[22]

Peremerka

After brief orientation on the morning of July 7, the 2nd Company of the 27th Panzer Regiment set out to advance along the northern bank of the Dvina. The first platoon, commanded by Second Lieutenant Mathieu, was in the lead. The tanks soon reached Myck, where they established connection with the motorcycle battalion of the 19th Panzer Division. The motorcyclists had become engaged by strong enemy forces and requested support. They had reached Peremerka, but the enemy had forced them back.[23]

When the commander of the Panzer company had been informed about the situation, he immediately decided to attack together with the motorcyclists to recapture Peremerka. The tanks continued in the same direction, with Mathieu's platoon ahead. About a kilometer southeast of Myck the company encountered weak opposition. It proceeded forward towards a bend of the river. There, the 4th platoon took up good firing positions, enabling it to support the remainder of the company, which continued to advance. Nearby, the terrain sloped downwards, but further away it rose and wooded hills prevented the Germans from observing further away. Although there were few trees in the area between the German tanks and the wooded hills, there were lots of bushes that made the terrain difficult to survey.

Second Lieutenant Mathieu continued to lead the attack, which proceeded swiftly. The German tanks only encountered infantry that did not have any heavier weapons than machine guns and mortars. The rapid advance allowed Mathieu to capture an intact bridge. His company could then assume a more suitable combat formation. So far, Mathieu had been fortunate, but then he ran out of luck after proceeding on the eastern side of the small river. A Soviet antitank gun opened fire and knocked out his tank. Two men in his crew were badly wounded.

The other tanks in the platoon followed Mathieu. One of them was commanded by Sergeant Stuppy, who silenced the Soviet antitank gun. Soon afterwards, another Soviet antitank gun hit a German tank, killing the commander, Umbach, and severely wounding two other men. Stuppy silenced this gun too, but the fighting was not over. Further Soviet antitank weapons opened fire and one German tank from the following platoon was set ablaze. The commander, Bürstinghaus, was wounded. While the remaining crew extinguished the fire, a major from the motorcycle battalion approached the tanks. He thanked the tankers and said that his men

The StuG III was intended for fire support, a role that suited its short-barreled 7.5-cm gun. Later versions would be fitted with a longer 7.5-cm gun, which was more effective against enemy tanks. Photo courtesy of Krigsarkivet, Stockholm.

would have been lost had the tanks not rescued them. The major ensured that the wounded were taken on board his truck and brought to the rear.

Meanwhile, the commander of the tank company had reached the bridge, but when the driver turned left immediately after driving off the bridge, the tank skidded sideways into a moat. The crew had to abandon the tank and the company commander went to the adjutant's tank. Meanwhile, the commander of the 2nd platoon, Sergeant Bürschgens, had taken over the lead with his tanks. He advanced towards the wooded hills while Sergeant Stuppy brought the wounded from the battlefield.

Bürschgens' platoon soon became embroiled in a firefight with Soviet antitank weapons and machine guns, while the 3rd Platoon, led by Sergeant Dölcher, took up positions to cover the left flank. Dölcher was not a minute too early as his tanks had just assumed their positions when a Soviet counterattack was launched. From their excellent firing positions, Dölcher's tanks opened withering fire and repulsed the Soviet attack.

The German company commander had so far not influenced the action significantly, but at this moment he ordered the tanks to fire on the nearby brush. He assumed that Soviet soldiers were hiding in it and he turned out to be correct. Many Soviet soldiers surrendered when exposed to the German fire and approached with their hands held high. The German motorcyclists brought the prisoners to the rear. The crew of the company commander's tank captured twenty prisoners.

Some time later, the Germans discovered vague shadows on the edges of the woods on the higher ground. By carefully studying them in their binoculars, the Germans realized that the shadows were Soviet tanks. Bürschgens' platoon had advanced further than the other and engaged the recently discovered enemies. According to the Germans, four Soviet tanks were knocked out.

Fierce fighting also raged near the bridge. The German tanks encountered Soviet infantry armed with machine guns and mortars. The latter made daring attempts to attach explosives to the tanks, but they were fended off by the Germans. However, the Soviet artillery increased the pressure on the Germans at the bridge and Soviet air power also joined in.

The 2nd Company did manage to hold its positions until the other elements of the battalion reached the area. This reinforcement could have allowed the Germans to attack, but they received an order not to enter the wooded hills. The prospects of a successful attack thus appeared slim, as Soviet artillery fire directors positioned on the hill could observe the Germans and call down fire. For the Germans, this meant that the position on the further side of the bridge was not suitable for defense. As they were not allowed to enter the woods, the German tankers decided to retreat across the bridge and assume positions that allowed them to fire on any enemy approaching it.

The fighting at Peremerka petered out. The Germans made attempts to recover the company commander's tank, and on July 10 they finally succeeded.

While the action at Peremerka was being fought, Hoth's Panzer Group continued east. The 19th Panzer Division operated on the left wing, while the 7th and 20th Panzer Divisions captured Vitebsk and continued advancing along the so-called "land bridge" between the Dvina and the Dnepr. Such a constriction might have been easier to defend, but Hoth's Panzers made good progress. If Guderian, on the right wing, overcame the Dnepr, the stage was set for yet another large-scale encirclement. The Soviet units could be caught in a trap in the Smolensk-Orsha area.

The Battle at Ryshkovka

On July 10 and 11, the 4th Panzer Division crossed the Dnepr. The Germans found the Soviet defenses disorganized and decided to advance rapidly on Propoisk, where important river crossings could be secured. The 35th Panzer Regiment would attack on the left wing and conduct an offensive along a crescent-shaped line towards Propoisk. The regiment commander placed I Battalion in the lead, closely followed by II Battalion. Lieutenant Krause's 3rd Company was at the very tip of the attack. His company had been reinforced by a Panzer IV platoon as well as a towing vehicle from the engineers. Krause and the other company commanders had been instructed by the battalion commander during the morning of July 12.[24]

Krause felt proud to advance with the rest of the battalion behind him as his driver speeded along the dusty roads. Krause's men were well prepared for battle. Not only had they ensured that the tanks had been provided with plenty of ammunition, they had also put hand grenades in their pockets and ensured that they had plenty of cartridges for their pistols. They initially had no use for the ammunition as they only encountered undefended roadblocks. These were quickly overcome, but the tankers were nevertheless very vigilant as they drove forward. Soviet defenders might open fire at any moment from well-concealed positions.[25]

After a while, the Germans were halted by a stream with marshy banks that prevented them from fording it. A light platoon had been sent forward to reconnoiter and it reported that Soviet antitank guns had opened fire and knocked out one of the tanks near the stream. Krause reported to the battalion commander, who immediately instructed Krause to disengage and attack further east instead, while Lieutenant Rachfall would attack further north with his company. The intended maneuver would outflank the difficult passage on both sides. Soon, Krause could hear distant firing from around where Rachfall's company was expected to be. Shortly afterwards, Krause received a report that told him that two enemy antitank guns and infantry had been fought on the edge of Ryshkovka.

After receiving the report, Krause directed his company towards Ryshkovka, but when he reached the village, the fighting appeared to be over. Two abandoned enemy antitank guns were silent witnesses to the enemy's flight. However, the German tankers could not relax. The gunners gazed through the hatches like watchful lynxes. Krause also strained his eyes to see anything suspicious in the surroundings.

Suddenly Krause's eyes picked something out. On a side street to the left, he observed Soviet soldiers unloading from trucks. They had tried

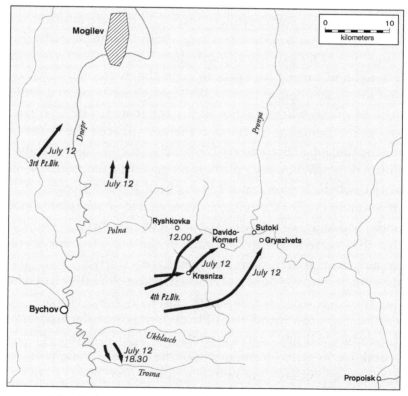

3rd and 4th Pz.Div. in the Bychov-Ryshkovka area July 12, 1941

to remain concealed behind trees and bushes, but this was in vain. Krause quickly moved his head and limbs into the turret and closed all the hatches as he ordered, "High-explosive shell, ten o'clock, 100 meters, at the bushes, trucks, FIRE!"

The Soviet soldiers had hardly seen the muzzle flashes from the German guns before the exploding shells hit them. Krause's loader rejoiced like a child when he saw the shells hitting the vehicles, which were set ablaze. Krause did not waste any time rejoicing. He realized he had to act quickly. Over the radio, he ordered his III Platoon, which was the rearmost in his company, to outflank the village to the left. The platoon commander led his unit in the new direction. It soon moved abreast of the other platoons.

At this moment, Krause's plans were thwarted as his company was subjected to fire from Soviet artillery pieces. They were positioned at the edge of a forest, around 500 meters away, with buildings nearby. Luckily for Krause, one of his platoon commanders, Sergeant Wallowsky, immediately acted and turned his tanks to fight the Soviet guns. Krause did not give any orders before he saw Wallowsky's tanks open a withering fire at the area from where the Soviet fire originated. The German shells set some of the buildings on fire and thereby silenced the Soviet guns.

Once the threat had been averted, Krause gave his platoon commanders new instructions. Wallowsky's platoon remained in the northern part of Ryshkovka, where it took a small bridgehead across a stream, while the other platoons in the 3rd Company maneuvered to attack Ryshkovka from the south. Suddenly, two Soviet antitank guns opened fire on Krause's tank, but they missed. Perhaps the gunners did not have enough time to aim properly at such very short distance. Krause's driver steered the steel colossus straight onto the guns and crushed them before they had reloaded.

After running over the antitank guns, Krause ordered Second Lieutenant Lange, commander of I Platoon, to pursue the Soviet defenders whose guns had just been overrun. The light platoon, commanded by Second Lieutenant Honstetter, was instructed to support Lange's advance. Krause's orders were probably quite good, but as so often happens in war, unexpected events take place. The second after Honstetter had received his mission, a hailstorm of Soviet artillery shells rained down on his platoon. Despite the fire, Krause ordered Honstetter's tanks to remain in their positions and wait until Lange had begun attacking.

Honstetter's men did not have to wait long. In the corner of his eye, Krause saw Lange come rushing forward—as usual, with his head far above the protective armor of his tank. A moment later, Krause heard Lange's voice on the radio. It told him that I Platoon had reached as far as Krause had intended, thus prompting him to order III Platoon and the light platoon to attack. Krause had just issued the orders when he heard a dull thud in the tank. The engine stopped running as an armor-piercing shell had penetrated the side armor and entered the engine compartment. The tank was immobile, but Krause and his crew had not been hurt.

Honstetter sent a tank for Krause to allow the company commander to continue leading the unit. After switching tanks, Krause ordered Lange to continue the attack. The crew of Krause's damaged tank remained in position, firing in support of the attack and relaying messages to and from the battalion commander. In the German tank companies, the commanders' tanks usually had extra radio sets—one shorter-range set for communication within the company and one longer-range set to communicate with the battalion and regiment commanders. The two sets also operated on different frequencies. When he switched to another tank, Krause could not count on being able to communicate with the battalion commander, and thus he wanted the crew to remain in his tank and operate the radios.

Unfortunately, the damaged tank was in an exposed position. Krause's driver jumped out from the tank and ensured that a towing wire was attached to another tank, which pulled the stricken vehicle into cover. Meanwhile, Krause attacked the Soviet position from which the fire had originated. He put the defenders to flight and jumped out of his new tank when it had come near the Soviet guns. After opening the breeches, he inserted hand grenades into the barrels and then sought shelter. As soon as the grenades had exploded, he returned to the tank.

While Krause was busy, Wallowsky's platoon continued attacking at the northern end of Ryshkovka. His tanks had been fired upon from a piece of woodland next to the edge of the village. The fire was well aimed and included shells from artillery pieces. Wallowsky did not waste time. He immediately ordered his platoon to attack the Soviet forces in the woods. The fire from the German guns and machine guns soon persuaded the Soviet defenders to abandon their positions. Sergeant Hildigard brought his tank so close that he could throw hand grenades at the Soviet artillery pieces, causing the last defenders to flee.

Wallowsky reported on the radio what had transpired in the north, but as Krause had abandoned his tank, problems occurred. Krause could receive Wallowsky's messages, but Wallowsky could not hear Krause. Wallowsky decided that his platoon should dismount and clear the piece of woodland on foot, while he himself would drive south to see if he could communicate with Krause. The scheme succeeded, but the fighting in the south intensified.

Krause had ordered Honstetter to clear the woods and then support Lange. However, some of the German tanks became stuck in the woods. When the crews attempted to tow them, they were fired upon by Soviet small arms. One of the tank commanders was hit and killed. Honstetter was in trouble, but the Soviet defenders were engaged. Lange realized that this gave him a chance, and he seized it. He led his platoon in a maneuver around the Soviet position to attack it from behind. His tank soon came very close to the as-yet-unaware Soviet gunners. Lange would order his tanks to open fire very soon.

Lange had carefully studied the terrain, but he was nevertheless surprised by fire from Soviet antitank guns at the fringe of a wooded area on the left flank. One or more shells hit Lange's tank, rendering it immobile. Sergeant Dreizner's tank also was hit. He was known as the company's daredevil, but this time luck betrayed him. His tank was hit in the turret and he was severely wounded in the head by metal splinters. The two tanks of the platoon that had not yet been hit drove to a small depression, where they could avoid the antitank guns and still fire on the vehicles belonging to the artillery unit they had intended to attack. Lange tried to lead the fight on foot, while Dreizner's driver drove his tank to a dressing station with the badly wounded commander inside.

Krause was oriented on the radio. He ordered Honstetter to attack, thus bringing some relief to Lange's exposed platoon. Honstetter's platoon defeated the Soviet artillery unit, whereupon the tanks of I Platoon joined in. Boosted by the success, Honstetter continued, but he drew fire from the same antitank unit that had decimated Lange's platoon. Sergeant Söffge's tank was the first to be hit. He and his crew could bail out unharmed, but when Söffge and the radio operator sought cover, they were badly wounded by an exploding Soviet shell. The other crew members managed to bring the two wounded men into cover while Honstetter used the radio to urgently call a doctor to the site. His efforts would prove futile; Söffge and the radio operator had been mortally wounded.

At this stage, Krause discussed the situation with the battalion commander and suggested that another attack should be launched. The battalion commander concurred. Krause ensured that Wallowsky's platoon rejoined the company before resuming the attack. After instructing his platoons, Krause's remaining tanks attacked again. Krause himself moved in the center and soon reached higher ground, from where he could see his company advancing. Honstetter's platoon formed up next to Lange's, on Krause's left, and headed towards a piece of woodland. So far, everything seemed to be going to plan, but soon Krause was informed on the radio that the two platoons on the left flank had encountered a marsh that prevented them from advancing any further.

Despite the problematic obstacle, Krause was determined to proceed with the attack. He ordered his tanks to fire intensively at the edge of the forest beyond the marsh and then move around it on both flanks. Krause's plan was not adhered to. After the powerful firing, Lieutenant Lange believed the enemy was very weakened. As the distance was short, he climbed out of his tank and assaulted the position on foot. The other tankers followed his example. The gunners and loaders remained in the tanks to provide supporting fire while the commanders, radio operators and drivers attacked the Soviet position. There was little Krause could do while his men captured the Soviet position in such an unorthodox fashion, but the goal was accomplished and that was what mattered.

Krause was not allowed much time to enjoy the success. Soon afterwards, his tank was hit twice by Soviet antitank guns. One shell damaged one of the tracks. The other hit the side armor at an oblique angle and ricocheted. Krause ordered his crew to bail out. Leaping like cats, the men reached shelter in the woods. At this moment, Krause realized that all his maps, code tables and other vital papers remained in the tank, which was still intact except for the damaged track. He decided to retrieve the documents. The gunner and loader would cover him with their pistols. When the Soviet fire paused, Krause dashed to the tank. To his great surprise, he saw the driver do the same, and he even managed to start the engine and drive the tank into a depression, where it was not exposed to the Soviet gunners.

When he was in cover, Krause calmed down and realized that the tank was not badly damaged. He decided to move to the right to get a better overview of the situation. Krause briefly glimpsed about fifteen Soviet soldiers who disappeared among the trees. Soon afterwards, after slipping closer to the edge of the forest, he discovered a Soviet soldier in a foxhole aiming his weapon at him. Krause instantly threw two hand grenades. As far as he could see, a few soldiers sank to the ground. He wanted to take advantage of the shock caused by the hand grenades and told his gunner to dash forward and disarm the enemies while he provided cover. The loader also hurried forward on his own initiative and helped to disarm the stunned Soviet soldiers, who were captured and brought to the rear.

After this brief episode, Krause caught sight of Söffge's knocked-out tank and then another. The doctor treated the wounded and ensured that they could be brought away, while Honstetter supervised from his tank. With a red-and-white flag rattling in the wind, the doctor's vehicle drove off. Krause decided to resume the attack. He believed the Soviet defense was stronger to the left and weaker to the right. For this reason, he chose to let II and III Platoons fire at the enemy forces to the left while Honstetter's light platoon and I Platoon attacked on the right wing.

Krause issued the necessary instructions before the attack, giving particular attention to the marsh that had halted III Platoon. However, the attack could not immediately be launched as many of the tanks were low on ammunition. Redistributing ammunition between the tanks alleviated the situation.

When the preparations had been completed, Krause ordered the attack to begin. II and III Platoons opened fire against the area where the Soviet defense was believed to be strongest. The tanks on the right drove at full speed towards a curtain of trees along a road. There, they would be concealed from the Soviet gunners. At this moment, Krause received a disquieting message on the radio. Honstetter's gun had malfunctioned. Despite the severe handicap, Krause ordered him to remain in his firing position. Krause urged the other tanks on and drove forward at full speed to break into the Soviet position. Krause soon realized that Honstetter was following behind, at an angle. His gun remained useless, but the machine gun belched out bullets at presumed enemy positions.

The German tanks penetrated the Soviet position while firing violently. The defenders fled and left around ten guns and numerous vehicles behind. Krause's men became afflicted by a kind of euphoria, but he urged them to continue forward and harvest the fruits of victory. Krause indicated further targets to destroy while men from knocked-out tanks, including Second Lieutenant Lange, attached themselves. They came in handy when rounding up the prisoners.

The Soviet defense was still not completely broken. At a range of 800 meters, Soviet antitank guns opened fire on the Germans. However, Krause had anticipated this and had detached tanks for this kind of threat. They immediately returned fire. At this moment, Krause was ordered by the battalion commander to hold fire, but he ignored the order. He wanted to complete the destruction of the enemy before breaking off the action.

The fighting continued into the evening, but Krause's company had got the better of the enemy, and when he considered his soldiers to have achieved enough, he broke off the battle. The damaged tanks were recovered from the battlefield and sent to workshops. Krause's men sought positions where they could bivouac for the night. He and his soldiers were convinced that their effort on July 12 had opened the way to Moscow. They had captured around 200 prisoners and estimated that about twenty artillery pieces and ten antitank guns had been destroyed.

Krause's hope that the road to Moscow lay open was more than a little premature. The 4th Panzer Division had been fighting hard battles on July 12; they had won some success, but the Soviet defense would recover. The fighting began again on the following day.[26]

It is interesting to observe how independently Krause's company fought. On one occasion, he discussed the situation with the battalion commander, but the latter did not interfere; instead, he just gave his consent. There was one case when the battalion commander actually gave an order to Krause, who ignored it. However, not only did Krause act independently, so did his subordinates on many occasions, and this was not regarded as remarkable. It was a consequence of the command philosophy the German doctrine rested upon. Until the summer campaign of 1941, the German Army had had ample time to train and foster the spirit desired. This had not been the case before Poland was attacked in 1939, and the willingness to take initiative had not been at a level deemed satisfactory. The twenty-one months that separated the campaign in Poland from Operation *Barbarossa* had, however, provided the opportunity to train, gain experience and weed out less competent commanders.

On July 12, Krause's company fought on its own, without cooperating with other arms. The Luftwaffe is not mentioned at all in the extensive report Krause wrote, and that is quite common. Most German Army units' after-action reports do not mention any cooperation with the Air Force, suggesting that such cooperation was not particularly common.[27]

Battles like the one fought by Krause's company on July 12 were not particularly costly to the German Panzer formation, but as they were fought frequently, the cumulative effect was far from negligible. On July 17, the 35th Panzer Regiment reported that it only had forty combat-ready tanks. Most of the reduction resulted from the wear and tear accumulated during the more than 500 km covered by the tanks since June 22.[28]

Luga, Smolensk and Kiev

After establishing a bridgehead across the Dvina on June 26, the LVI Panzer Corps' advance on Leningrad halted temporarily. The other components of Army Group North had not matched the breakneck speed at which von Manstein's corps had advanced. Soviet reinforcements had also gathered in the area north of Daugavpils, forcing the LVI Panzer Corps to fight fierce battles. However, in early July, the Germans were ready to strike again. Once again, they advanced very rapidly, but this time the XXXXI Panzer Corps made faster progress than its neighbor. In mid-July, the XXXXI Panzer Corps crossed the river Luga. Only 100 km remained to Leningrad, the second largest city in the Soviet Union.[29]

Further south, Army Group Center continued its offensive, and on July 16 Panzer Group 2 captured Smolensk. In the area north of Smolensk, Panzer Group 3 had reached even further east. The 7th Panzer Division captured Yartsevo on July 15, while the lead elements of the 20th Panzer Division reached the area northeast of Yartsevo. These performances meant that Panzer Groups 2 and 3 had covered almost two thirds of the distance from the Soviet western border to Moscow.[30]

The success achieved thus far by the Germans was undoubtedly spectacular, but there were problems on the horizon. The advance in the Ukraine had picked up speed after the initial battles had ended, but the Soviet resistance was not broken. Field Marshal von Rundstedt, who commanded Army Group South, could rejoice over the fact that his Panzer divisions had reached a point 100 km west of Kiev on July 12. However, after this success, the advance on Kiev would stall. Instead, von Rundstedt directed his units southwards.[31]

Unlike Army Group Center, von Rundstedt's armies had not encircled any significant Soviet units. Without cutting off substantial enemy forces, Army Group South could not inflict as high losses on the enemy as would otherwise have been the case. This allowed the Soviet high command to send most of its reinforcements to the sector where the German Army Group Center attacked. A well-known quote from the German chief of general staff, Colonel-General Franz Halder, reads: "We had expected to encounter 200 divisions, but have already identified 360." Most of these extra divisions had appeared before Army Group Center.[32]

The imprecise intelligence was not the only cause for concern. The Panzer divisions in Army Group Center had performed impressively, but most of the German formations were infantry divisions, relying on the feet of men and hooves of horses for their mobility. Even Army Group Center, despite having around half the German mechanized divisions, was mostly made up of infantry divisions. In mid-July, they lagged behind the armored spearheads. Consequently, the relatively few Panzer

Eastern Front June–October 1941

divisions and motorized divisions had to assume a share of the fighting exceeding their rather small numbers.[33]

The German generals had, of course, realized that the infantry divisions would hardly be capable of keeping pace with the Panzer divisions. The situation that had arisen was not surprising, but it required measures.

As Panzer Groups 2 and 3 reached the area east of Smolensk, a pocket was created west of the city, where large Soviet formations were compressed. For reasons that are unclear, the Germans left a narrow opening along the Dnepr that allowed some Soviet forces to sneak out. Nevertheless, the Red Army suffered a very costly defeat. The Germans counted 301,110 prisoners and a large booty that included 3,205 tanks and 3,000 artillery pieces, but the fighting in the pocket did not end until August 5.[34]

Most of the infantry divisions caught up with the mechanized units as the Smolensk pocket was being defeated. The Germans also found the time to repair railroads to such an extent that the trains could bring the supplies closer to the front. The limited capacity of the trucks and roads of those days prohibited long distances between the lead combat units and the railheads. Before the campaign, the German planners had estimated that the distance ought not to exceed 300 km. In the first weeks of July, that distance had been exceeded considerably. The supply difficulties were eventually mastered, but they could become intolerable in the future. To allow the trains to unload further east was thus a prerequisite for the continuation of the offensive.[35]

At this stage, a series of discussions on the future direction of the offensive ensued. From the very outset, the Germans had discussed several goals. To some extent, these coincided with the Army groups' axes of advance, and the geography of the Soviet Union tended to take the German Army groups in diverging directions. Army Group North attacked towards Leningrad, approaching it on a northeasterly axis, while Army Group South attacked eastwards. The terrain in the Toropets area was difficult, and in July the Germans had advanced so far that the two Army groups were separated by the woodlands around Toropets. Army Group South attacked from Poland and into the Ukraine, taking it in a southeasterly direction. Army Groups Center and South were separated by the Pripet area, a marshland that was not suitable for any significant operation during the summer. Neither was it easily negotiated during the winter, as the roads and railroads were few and of low capacity. However, approximately 100 km east of the Dnepr, the swampy area ceased and the terrain became more favorable. By mid-July, Army Group Center had already advanced beyond the Pripet marshes, but Army Group South had not yet crossed the Dnepr. Consequently, Army Group Center developed a long and problematic flank, which tied up units.

The German military commanders and Hitler disagreed about how the campaign would be continued, resulting in indecision in August. The operations of Army Group Center became particularly delayed due to the disagreements. Instead of attacking east, von Bock's forces tended to attack on the northern and southern flanks. The Red Army was thus afforded a respite and brought reinforcements to the sector west of Moscow. Hard battles would be fought.

The Battle On the Sozh

Unlike the previous Blitzkrieg campaigns, the attack on the Soviet Union would result in prolonged fighting. The campaign in Poland had been decided in the first two weeks. The battles in Norway had dragged out longer, but the Germans clearly had the advantage after a few weeks, except at Narvik. The campaign in the west in 1940 had been decided during the first ten days, when German Panzer divisions reached the Channel. Although costly battles remained to be fought after the initial phases of these campaigns, the swiftness of the operations prevented the casualties mounting to alarming levels.

Operation *Barbarossa* immediately resulted in tremendous German success. The advance rates were spectacular and the Red Army suffered losses at a level previously unheard of. However, the vast Soviet reserves saved the country from collapsing under the German onslaught. Gradually, German casualties accumulated to significant levels, though far lower than the immense Soviet losses. Up to July 31, the Germans recorded 213,301 casualties, of whom 58,228 had been killed in action or were missing. Such casualties exceeded previous campaigns and forced the Germans to send replacements to the combat units, or else their combat power would deteriorate.[36]

Lieutenant Georg Hoffman was a twenty-five-year-old officer who had served at front sectors where little fighting had occurred, such as on the front along the Rhine in May and June 1940. When France had been defeated, Hoffman was stationed at Belfort, not far from the Swiss border. He was still there on July 28, 1941. Together with Lieutenant-Colonel Garbsch, he visited a casino to play cards. Both men knew that Hoffman might never return to France, as he would board a train the following day that would take him to the Eastern Front. He was to serve in an infantry unit.[37]

His train made a brief stop at Warsaw, where around 100 officers who were to serve on the Eastern Front had been assembled. There was a lack of officers trained for or with experience of antitank units. Hoffman mentioned that he had attended a course with an antitank company, and it was immediately decided that he would assume command of an antitank company himself. In the evening of August 1, he climbed aboard a train that was destined for Minsk.

When he arrived at Minsk, Hoffmann could not help noticing how mangled the city was, but he had little time to inspect the Byelorussian capital. The journey continued to Bobruisk, from where he proceeded by car. On August 6, Hoffmann finally reached the front, at the 34th Infantry Division. He reported to the division commander, Lieutenant-General Hans Behlendorff, who instructed Hoffman to go to the 80th Infantry Regiment. He found the regiment commander, Colonel Walter Hörnlein, at Khostorov. Hoffman was told that he would be entrusted with the best company of the regiment, the 14th. Like most German infantry regiments, the 80th had three infantry battalions, with companies numbered 1–4, 5–8, and 9–12 respectively. There was usually also a company equipped with infantry howitzers, which carried the number 13, and an antitank company, with number 14. The 80th Infantry followed this pattern.

Hoffman assumed command of the company on the following day. Lieutenant Reitz, a reserve officer who used to command IV Platoon, had temporarily commanded the regiment, but now he returned to his established position. Hoffmann spent August 8 meeting as many of the soldiers serving in the company as possible. He visited them at their battle positions. Most of them had already served in the company during the campaign in the west, more than a year ago. They were clearly more combat-experienced than Hoffman, but he hoped he would gain their confidence soon. In a few days, he would be tested in battle, as the 34th Infantry Division would force the Sozh River.

The attack on the Sozh was prepared during August 9. The division commander and most of the other senior commanders participated. Hoffman learned that he would serve under a new regiment commander, as Walter Hörnlein would assume command of the elite regiment

Grossdeutschland. The other commanders completed the planning. The following day was spent on establishing the enemy positions and studying the terrain in the area. Hoffmann did not know when the attack was to begin, but as he scrutinized the terrain near the Sozh river, he realized that his baptism of fire lay only hours in the future, or a few days away at most. He thought of his father, who had been killed in the last year of World War I. Hoffmann, born in 1916, had not seen much of his father before the old man passed away.

On August 11, it was decided that the attack would be launched on the following day. In the evening, Hoffmann and his men, like the other units that would participate in the attack, crept to the positions near the river, from where they would launch the attack. Hoffmann's company would follow as soon as the first rubber boats had taken infantry across the river. First they would take the light 3.7-cm antitank guns to the other bank, and then they would get the heavier 5-cm guns across.

The night was dark and hardly any noise was heard. Hoffmann had plenty of time to ponder difficult questions. Who would die tomorrow? Which soldiers would not return? Nobody had an answer. The Soviet artillery briefly interrupted Hoffmann, but the thoughts again haunted him when the noise from the bursting shells had faded away. Hoffmann did not know if the other men in company, who had already seen much fighting, were beset by similar thoughts.

The attack was launched early on August 12. Hoffmann was among the first to reach the opposite bank of the river. Bullets from rifles and machine guns whizzed close to his head as the rubber boat carried him across the river. Hoffmann was lucky, unlike one of the antitank guns being ferried. It was destroyed by a direct hit, but the German attack did not relent. When one of his platoons had reached the eastern bank, Hoffmann established a provisional command post. Soon, a platoon equipped with 5-cm guns was brought across the river.

The first day of the attack proceeded according to plan. A bridgehead across the Sozh was captured and consolidated. The attack was quickly resumed at 3.10 a.m. on the following day. Hoffmann advanced with one of the light platoons and the heavy platoon into no man's land. A German patrol was encountered, but it was identified before any fratricide incident developed. Soviet forces were found somewhat later, but they retreated immediately. The recently appointed regiment commander, Colonel Warmuth, ordered Hoffmann to prepare an ambush with his heavy platoon and a platoon from the 13th Company. Hoffmann issued the necessary instructions to the platoons, which quickly moved into suitable firing positions. On Hoffmann's command, they opened fire on retreating Soviet units. Thus, Hoffmann had experienced his baptism of fire.

On the following day, the 80th Regiment continued attacking. The regiment commander forwarded acknowledgments from the neighboring 17th Infantry Division, which had been helped by the ambush Hoffmann had arranged. Some time later, Hoffmann's company became embroiled in hard fighting near Vasilyevka, where he endured the unpleasant experience of being shelled by enemy mortars.

The second half of August was mainly spent regrouping by Hoffmann's company, which gradually moved east. In early September, the 34th Infantry Division had reached the Desna River, northwest of Bryansk. On September 1, intelligence indicated that Soviet armor was heading straight towards the division.

The Battle at Ugost

The information on the approaching Soviet tanks strained the commanders of the German 80th Infantry Regiment. Heavy Soviet artillery fire that hit the German positions on September 2 appeared to confirm the fears of an imminent enemy attack. In a meeting with the regiment commander, various options were discussed. Lieutenant-Colonel Warmuth wanted the 14th Company to split in such a way that each of the three battalions in the regiment was reinforced by one antitank platoon. The fourth platoon would be directly subordinated to the regiment. Hoffmann objected; he wanted to retain control of the entire company and argued that he knew best where and how the guns should be deployed, how they could be used to greatest effect and also how they could effectively cooperate with the other units. Warmuth was somewhat skeptical, but he acquiesced. He added that Hoffmann would assume responsibility.

Hoffmann was determined to pursue his line of thought and visited his platoon commanders to ensure that everything was adequately prepared. The battle positions were given better camouflage and protection against fire. Hoffmann made certain that the crews could easily serve their weapons. As Hoffmann wanted to hold fire until the enemy tanks were at a range of 200 meters, the crews had to be able to reload their guns quickly. Also, the Germans would try to hit the flanks of the enemy tanks. The platoon and gun commanders were allowed to open fire at their own discretion. To ensure that the enemy tanks caught fire, Hoffmann instructed them to use high-explosive shells in addition to the armor-piercing shells. He also held a discussion with the antitank company of the neighboring regiment to ensure that they could cooperate smoothly. That was all he could do; all that remained was to wait through the night.

At 9 a.m. on September 3, the suspense came to an end. Soviet artillery and heavy mortars bombarded the German positions. As Hoffmann expected the fiercest Soviet attack to be directed at the boundary between the 80th and 253rd Infantry Regiments, he went to Second Lieutenant Frentz, whose platoon defended the positions near the 253rd Regiment. He also found a fire director from the artillery at Frentz's positions. Hoffmann was reassured by what he saw and hurried to the other flank to find out what was going on there.

Soviet artillery fire was also directed at the area behind the main German defense line, rendering Hoffmann's journey to the other flank dangerous. On his way, he encountered a soldier who told him that a wounded second lieutenant from the 14th Company had died at the dressing station. Hoffmann realized that it was most likely Frentz. He hurried to the dressing station as quickly as possible; it was located around 300 meters away. It turned out that Hoffmann was right. Second Lieutenant Frentz had been struck in the shoulder by a bullet soon after Hoffmann had departed. Now he was dead. Deeply shaken, Hoffmann told his driver to get the car. The corpse of Frentz was lifted into the rear seat as Hoffmann was assailed by thoughts about what would happen during the next days and weeks. How many more would die?

The car brought Hoffmann and his unusual cargo to Frentz's platoon, where Frentz's remains were placed at one of the battle positions.

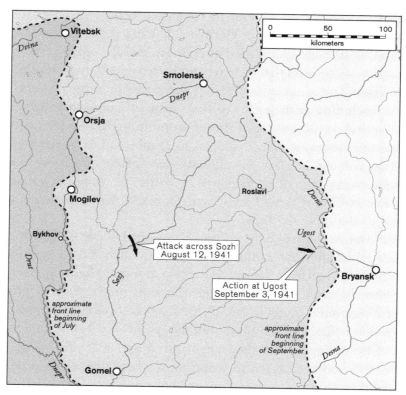

Actions at Sozh and Ugost August 12 and September 3, 1941

Hoffmann was informed of the situation at the platoon and learned that it had accomplished its mission gallantly, despite the fact that the commander had been mortally wounded. The Soviet attack had been repelled within an hour and the other platoons reported similar success. German claims included thirty-eight destroyed Soviet tanks.

The Maintenance Service

Combat vehicles had not been extensively employed in the Norwegian campaign, but the German tanks had figured prominently in Poland and Western Europe. In the latter campaigns, many vehicles had been hit, suffered mechanical breakdowns, or became stuck in difficult terrain. The

Germans had chosen to recover the damaged tanks and bring them to centrally located workshops in Germany. During the brief campaigns of 1939 and 1940, this meant that they were usually repaired when the fighting was over. Tanks that were repaired often ended up in another unit.

Operation *Barbarossa* differed from the previous campaigns in many respects, including with regard to the repair of damaged vehicles. The large distances in the east made it time-consuming to transport damaged vehicles. Furthermore, heavy vehicles like tanks had to be mostly transported by rail, but the Soviet railroads were sparse and those available to the Germans were often damaged by battle; the different gauge used in the Soviet Union caused additional problems. Later, partisans would also add to the difficulties.

As the war in the east dragged out, it was inadvisable to wait to repair damaged tanks after the campaign had been concluded. A considerable number of tanks had been damaged after two months of fighting. According to a report discussing the situation for the units on the Eastern Front on August 23, the units ought to have 3,152 tanks according to the prescribed organization tables. However, up until that point, 706 had been destroyed or so badly damaged that they were not considered worthy of repair. Another 718 had been taken to workshops, where they awaited repairs.[38]

Evidently, many tanks were damaged but not yet repaired, and reports from individual units confirm this picture. A 4th Panzer Division report from July 21 shows that the division only had forty-four combat-ready tanks, while forty-two had been lost. The division was also in possession of eighty-nine tanks that needed repairs. Of these, forty could not be repaired as necessary spare parts were not available.[39]

Tank engines were an important component. They were subjected to much wear and tear during battles and long advances. Dirt from the dusty roads was sucked into the air intakes and caused excessive damage. In many cases, it was better to replace the entire engine, but as such measures might interfere with the production of new tanks, Hitler was unwilling to send new engines to the units on the Eastern Front. However, on August 4 he acquiesced and permitted 400 new tank engines to be sent there.[40]

The great distances traveled, lack of spare parts and difficult terrain made the work of the repair services demanding. NCO Rudolf Ruyter served on the staff of the 35th Panzer Regiment and spent a great deal of time with the repair services. He could see with his own eyes how richly varied this activity could be. In addition to recovering and repairing tanks, the men had to bring supplies forward and quite often also found themselves engaged in combat.[41]

During the initial period of the campaign, Ruyter did not face great dangers. His main concern appears to have been one of the tires on his car, a Kübelwagen, which was losing pressure. Few vehicles were damaged at this stage, and they had received all the necessary maintenance before the offensive was launched. However, with time, more breakdowns would occur. As long as few vehicles needed repairs, time could be devoted to bringing food, ammunition and fuel to the combat units. The rapid advance resulted in high fuel consumption. Also, the distance between the combat units and railheads and depots rapidly increased as the spearheads drove into the Soviet Union.

Rivers might prove to be difficult obstacles. When Ruyter was about to cross the River Drut, it turned out that retreating Soviet troops had blown up the bridge. However, German engineers had prepared a ferry. Only the most important vehicles were to be brought across the river by the ferry, but, as Ruyter put it, "everyone considered himself important and the higher the rank, the greater the eagerness." At last, Ruyter and his Kübelwagen, after being fully laden with rations, were ferried across the river. He set out for Stary Bychóv to provide the combat elements of the Panzer regiment with much-needed rations. The car proceeded along very dry roads. Enormous clouds of dust were created behind the car. Later, Ruyter would learn that he passed a Soviet unit that had been close to the road, but perhaps the dust clouds obscured his car. He did not notice any firing. Once he had made it to Stary Bychóv, Ruyter had to find the combat units. It was not easy as they were almost constantly on the move, and of course they also tried to conceal themselves as well as possible.

Ruyter realized that supplying the combat units was a very difficult task. He considered how the supply officers had to use their flair to judge many things. One example was the supply of ammunition for the tanks. They mainly used two types of shells—high-explosive and armor-piercing, depending on the type of target to be engaged. As ammunition could not be brought forward instantly, the relative consumption of the two types of ammunition had to be estimated in advance. Furthermore, the two main types of tanks, the Panzer III and Panzer IV, did not carry the same armament and used different kinds of ammunition. It was necessary to ensure that no type of ammunition was exhausted at the front.

Soldiers serving with the supply and maintenance services also found themselves occasionally engaged in combat. On one occasion, Ruyter was sent on a mission to the 10th Motorized Infantry Division, which was also part of the XXIV Panzer Corps. Three tanks would support the division, but they of course required supply and maintenance. The NCO, Reinhardt, to whom Ruyter was subordinated, received hand grenades he distributed to his men, including Ruyter. Then they were dispatched together with the tanks for the combat mission. The hand grenades would remain unused, but Ruyter had to wait several hours for an enemy attack that never materialized.

There was hardly any time for leisure in the repair and maintenance services. When the combat units were allotted a day of rest, the tank crews could relax, but for the mechanics, such days were as arduous as any other. Damaged tanks had to be returned to service and combat-ready tanks had to be carefully checked to ensure that they remained usable. Before attacks, the maintenance companies often had to work all night long to allow as many tanks as possible to participate. Ruyter noted that the companies made it a competition to have the most tanks serviceable. A large amount of imagination, initiative and knowledge was required for the work. Captured vehicles were often used to replace lost vehicles, but the companies competed fiercely for the captured cars and lorries.

During attacks, the repair services followed close on the heels of the combat units. At Baturin, on September 9, Ruyter followed immediately behind the tanks during a night attack. It was not particularly dark, allowing the tanks to make swift progress against the weak opposition. However, at Makeyevka, the visibility was reduced by fog. As far as

Ruyter could see, no other German forces followed. It appeared that the lead attacking elements had no connection to other friendly units. At a crossroads, Sergeant Jüppner saw something move in what appeared to be a foxhole. He immediately threw a smoke grenade at the suspected enemy. The grenade belched out smoke for what Ruyter thought was a very long period of time, before a Soviet soldier came forward with his hands held above his head.[42]

The German formation searched the terrain for further enemies. A few wounded Soviet soldiers were found, but no other signs of the enemy were encountered. The Germans reassembled at the road, but they were almost immediately fired upon by small arms from the left and the right. The faint light did not allow the Germans to respond accurately, but there was a farm approximately 200 meters away that appeared to offer some cover. The Germans raced to it without suffering any casualties.

No more action took place overnight. In the morning, Ruyter returned along the road where the unit had advanced less than twelve hours before. After an uneventful journey, he found other parts of the repair service fully occupied with recovering whatever might be useful from a Soviet column that had been shot up during the dark hours. It had encountered a battalion from the 35th Panzer Regiment.

Terrain often made the repair services' work difficult. Most of their vehicles had limited cross-country capacity. Although the vehicles designed for recovering tanks had good cross-country capabilities, they were strained to the utmost when towing a tank weighing more than 20 tons. Ruyter was often sent to reconnoiter the terrain in advance, which was one of the best ways to avoid difficulties. However, sometimes even the most careful reconnaissance was insufficient. At Bachmach, Ruyter experienced how one day of rain could turn beautiful meadows and fields into impassable seas of mud. His car got stuck, but it seemed that he would be able to get away.

After some hard work, Ruyter's car was brought free from the mud. He went over to a few houses next to a group of trees, hoping to find a road with better surface. There was indeed a road, and he waved to his driver, who managed to reach the better road without getting stuck again. This episode took place in September, before the fall arrived, when more continuous rain could be expected. The weather could thus be expected to become worse in the future, but Ruyter did not ponder on it for long before seeing a gasoline truck sink to the drive shafts in the soft ground. A captured Soviet tracked vehicle managed to pull the truck along, but its engine overheated after a while.

It was clear that only tanks could negotiate the mud because the gasoline truck was far from the only vehicle to get stuck. Ruyter's car again sank in the mud, as well as many other vehicles. Later in the day, a tank arrived to tow some of the trucks away from the worst mud, but a few days would elapse before all had been recovered. The German vehicles stuck in the mud were excellent targets for the Soviet Air Force. As might have been expected, three Soviet aircraft appeared and attacked the stationary German vehicles. Ruyter and the other German soldiers sought cover some distance away. The Soviet aviators targeted the vehicles, but their precision was poor. When the aircraft had left the scene, the Germans inspected their vehicles. A bomb had struck the ground only a few meters from Ruyter's car, but except for punctures and small holes in the bodywork caused by splinters, the vehicles were intact.

The importance of bringing supplies forward and recovering damaged vehicles and those stuck in the terrain was, of course, paramount, particularly for a Panzer division. This was obviously nothing new to the Germans and they had made arrangements to cope with the problems, but the arrangements were insufficient to maintain a high number of operational tanks in the Panzer divisions. As a result, the Germans would have to decentralize the repair services. This would allow more rapid repairs, but the low production of spare parts could not be remedied locally at the front. Of course, the field workshops could cannibalize damaged vehicles to obtain parts to repair others, but such measures could not be regarded as a viable long-term solution to the shortage of spare parts.[43]

The German system for repairing tanks had been designed for short campaigns fought near the home country. Such conditions permitted tanks to be recovered after the fighting had ceased and carefully repaired at proper facilities in Germany. The prolonged fighting in Russia made such a system impractical. At the end of August, more than 700 tanks were waiting for repairs at workshops—around one third of the pre-scribed number of tanks for the units in the east.[44]

It was not only tanks that suffered from wear and tear. Other vehicles, such as trucks, were also damaged. Approximately 15 percent of them were awaiting repairs at the beginning of September. The decline was less steep than for tanks, but nevertheless this meant a reduction of the German capacity to bring supplies to the front units.[45]

The wear on the tanks was especially critical as their importance seems to have been greater in Operation *Barbarossa* than in the previous campaigns. The German operations in the Soviet Union fit better with the popular image of "Blitzkrieg." This can be partly attributed to the improved firepower and protection of the German tanks in Operation *Barbarossa*.

After a few months, the punching power of what was probably the most important German arm had been thus diminished, with tanks being destroyed or damaged and not yet repaired or replaced. However, war is a struggle between two sides, and the problems on one side may very well be overshadowed by problems suffered by the other side. It is therefore better to compare your problems with those of the enemy rather than with some abstract ideal. The Soviet losses were greater than those of the Germans by several orders of magnitude. For example, almost 12,000 Soviet tanks had been lost up to July 9, and the losses continued to mount, allowing the Germans to attack deeper into the Soviet Union.[46]

The Kiev Pocket

The extended discussions about the future employment of Army Group Center after it reached the Smolensk area finally resulted in the two Panzer groups being sent in diverging directions, despite the objections raised by the Panzer group commanders. Panzer Group 3, commanded by Colonel-General Hermann Hoth, was sent north to assist Army Group North. This allowed the gap between the two Army groups to be closed and Toropets to be captured. Army Group North could seal off Leningrad and begin a long siege of the city, which was to result in a very high death toll.[47]

The fighting in the Toropets area was not particularly Blitzkrieg-esque. The Germans came out victorious, but the rate of advance was not particularly high and no significant haul of prisoners was taken. It was Hitler who had pushed for the Toropets operation, going against the opposition of the Army high command. The latter saw little value in the Toropets area, except possibly as a springboard for an attack on Moscow.

If the fighting at Toropets can be regarded mainly as a waste of time, the attack conducted by Panzer Group 2 on Hitler's initiative was not without dividends. The terrain in the Toropets area was unsuitable and offered few chances of encirclement. In contrast, the Kiev area offered better terrain and the Soviet forces there were in a precarious position.

By participating in the Kiev operation, Guderian's Panzer group would turn south, something he strongly opposed. He tried to prevent his divisions from being used in this operation as he wanted to continue towards Moscow. Guderian's two most powerful units were XXIV and XXXXVII Panzer Corps, which had been engaged in hard fighting for weeks. At 7 p.m. on August 22, the Panzer Group was asked if it could shift the direction of its attacks 120 degrees south. Guderian opposed this and flew to Field Marshal von Bock, the Army group commander, on August 23. That afternoon, both officers flew to Rastenburg to try and persuade Hitler to alter his decision. They did not succeed, and on the morning of August 24 Guderian ordered his Panzer divisions to turn south. They broke through the Soviet defense on the same day, and by the evening of August 25 they had already penetrated 120 km into the Soviet defenses.[48]

This is an excellent example of the great operational flexibility the German Army was capable of. In very little time, an entire Panzer group had altered the direction of its main attack and immediately advanced very rapidly. It seems clear that this flexibility was the result of the German command philosophy, which emphasized initiative. This allowed the senior commanders to focus their attention on the goals to be pursued while the practical problems were attended to by their subordinates.[49]

The very high advance rate of the first two days could not be sustained. The reason for this was possibly that the German divisions were very worn down. The 3rd Panzer Division, which spearheaded the attack,

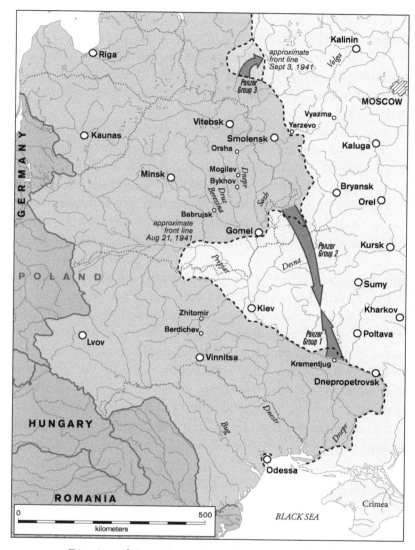

Diversions of Army Group Center August–September 1941

only had sixty combat-ready tanks on August 22, compared to 198 when Operation *Barbarossa* began. Guderian had argued that his units needed a pause to rest and repair equipment, but the new mission assigned to him thwarted his plans.[50]

The tank component of the 3rd Panzer Division was not the only one worn out; the infantry battalions were operating at only 50 percent of full strength. Guderian estimated that a lull could bring the battalions to 75 percent of the prescribed strength. The 10th Motorized Infantry Division, which was the other spearhead, was similarly worn out.[51]

After the divisions had broken through, the sectors they had to cover became extended as they drove into the depth of the enemy grouping. In their weakened condition, they had to devote a larger share of their limited resources to protect their flanks. As the roads also turned out to be very poor and the enemy resistance did not collapse, Guderian's advance slowed down from August 27. The 3rd Panzer Division captured Novgorod Severskiy on August 26, and on September 7 the Panzer group reached Konotop, only 85 km further south.[52]

While Guderian attacked from the north, Panzer Group 1, commanded by Colonel-General Ewald von Kleist, was to cross the Dnepr southeast of Kiev and advance north. This attack also developed rather slowly. Had the Soviet commanders been instructed to retreat from the Kiev area, they would probably have been able to escape encirclement. Except for the initial days, the German advance rate was too low to seal off the encirclement before the Soviet units withdrew. Of course, such a course of events would have handed the Germans Kiev as well as a very large bridgehead across the Dnepr, but they would not have obtained a large haul of prisoners. Hitler would not have had a major victory to boast about.

Hitler would turn out to be lucky. No Soviet retreat order was given in time. Instead, XXIV Panzer Corps crossed the Seym River near Konotop on September 9. The 3rd Panzer Division subsequently broke through and captured Romny early on September 10. This would prove to be a decisive victory.[53]

However, problems again occurred. Rain turned the roads into canals of mud, making it very difficult to supply the lead units. At Romny, the 3rd Panzer Division had the great fortune to find a Soviet depot that contained around 400 cubic meters of fuel. This allowed the division to continue and reach Lokhvitsa on September 12.[54]

While the 3rd Panzer Division attacked from the north, von Kleist's Panzer group established a bridgehead across the Dnepr at Kremenchug and attacked north. The 16th Panzer Division made particularly good progress, and in the evening of September 12 the gap to be closed had been reduced to 75 km. The Soviet units were up to 220 km west of the gap separating the two German Panzer groups.[55]

By now, it was too late to retreat out of the forming pocket. Scant resistance faced the German spearheads. On September 15, the ring had been closed around the Soviet forces in the Kiev area. Formations from five armies had been surrounded and were defeated over the following ten days. The haul of prisoners was huge—the Germans captured 665,000 men during the operation, a number that has seldom been exceeded.[56]

Considering the immense haul of prisoners and booty, the operation was a tremendous success. However, in fact, it hung on a single, very weak thread. Had Stalin ordered his armies to withdraw, the German success would most likely have been reduced significantly. In most of the other encirclement operations, the Germans had advanced so quickly that most Soviet forces would not have been able to retreat quickly enough even if they had received timely orders. The Kiev operation was different, but thanks to Stalin's unintentional cooperativeness, the Germans could destroy a very large share of the units defending the Ukraine.

The German victory in the Kiev operation can thus be regarded as rather lucky, but there were also disadvantages resulting from it. Admittedly, the road towards Kharkov now lay open for Army Group South, but the time lost could not be made up. As the fall rains were expected to occur earlier in the Moscow area than in the Ukraine, the loss of time was more alarming to Army Group Center. Also, Guderian's units had become even more worn out. For example, on September 27, the combined tank strength of the 3rd and 4th Panzer Divisions only amounted to ninety-three combat-ready tanks.[57]

Orel

After the Kiev cauldron had been cleared, Army Group Center could again set its eyes on Moscow. A large-scale attack on the Soviet capital—Operation *Typhoon*—was to be launched. In addition to Panzer Groups 2 and 3 on the southern and northern wing respectively, Army Group Center had been reinforced by Panzer Group 4 from Army Group North. The latter had been positioned in the center of the Army group. The fresh 2nd and 5th Panzer Divisions had also arrived on the Eastern Front, including Colonel-General Erich Hoepner's Panzer Group 4.

The forces available to Field Marshal von Bock were impressively large, but on the other side of the front line, equally large Soviet forces were ready to defend. The latter had also enjoyed ample time to prepare their defenses as the front line had been almost static for several weeks. Reinforcements had arrived, but there were also many worn-out units in the Red Army.

Guderian's Panzer group had the greatest distance to cover, a result of his detour into the Ukraine. Unlike the other units of Army Group Center, which were to attack on October 2, he would strike on September 30. The first goal was Orel, which was an important road and railroad junction. As so often before, Guderian assigned the most important mission to the XXIV Panzer Corps, which was led by General Leo Geyr von Schweppenburg. The corps attacked from the Glukhov area and immediately made spectacular progress, particularly the 4th Panzer Division.[58]

The 4th Panzer Division launched its attack at 6.35 a.m. on September 30. The division commander, Major-General von Langermann und Erlencamp, instructed a battle group commanded by Colonel Eberbach to lead the attack. The battle group soon encountered Soviet tanks, but Eberbach rapidly concluded that his tanks and the subordinated antiaircraft guns would be able to master the threat and continue to advance. However, a short while later, the Germans were halted by heavy KV tanks, which fought from positions partially obscured by mist. Infantry was sent out to neutralize the heavy tanks in close combat, but the attempt was discovered by the Soviets. The KV tanks moved to other battle positions that were protected by minefields. The Germans solved this problem by sending tanks on an outflanking move while directing heavy artillery fire at the area where the Soviet tanks were located. The latter found it was better to withdraw.[59]

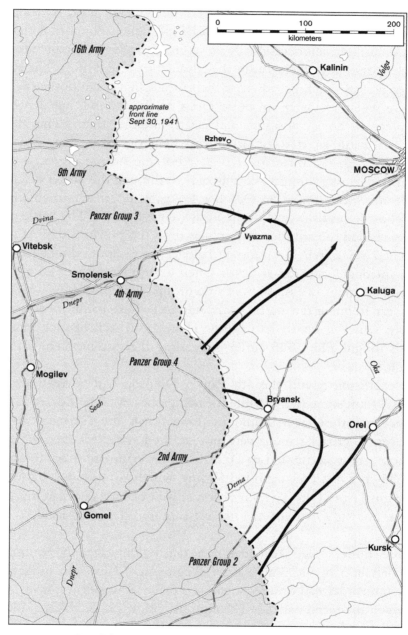

Initial thrusts by Panzer units during operation Typhoon

Eberbach and his battle group continued northeast. During the afternoon, twin-engine Messerschmitt Bf 110 fighters supported his units. The German airmen occasionally drew fire from Soviet antiaircraft units, but they could nevertheless assist the advancing ground units. The aircraft did not possess much firepower, which meant they were not particularly effective when attacking Soviet positions on the ground, but they could spot prepared Soviet positions and clearly indicate them. This allowed Eberbach's battle group to either outflank them or destroy them rapidly. In the evening, Eberbach reached Kruglaya Polyana, having advanced almost 30 km. His battle group had cleanly broken through the Soviet defenses.[60]

The attack continued on October 1. Again, Eberbach's men enjoyed air support—this time dive-bombers as well as fighters. The battle group even exceeded the advance rate achieved on the previous day. At noon, it reached Sevsk, where important bridges were captured intact. A fratricide incident occurred at Sevsk when a German aircraft accidentally bombed elements of Eberbach's battle group. Such problems, which had been very frequent during the campaign in Poland, had not been solved entirely, which is hardly surprising. There is no lack of such incidents in wars fought after 1945 either, suggesting that the problem is indeed difficult to solve.[61]

By capturing Sevsk, the 4th Panzer Division had covered approximately 70 km since the morning of September 30. The Soviet defenses had been shattered and could no longer halt the German advance. However, Eberbach's men were not satisfied with this success. In the afternoon, they continued to Dmitrovsk, covering another 60 km. On the following day, they captured Kromy, which lay almost 170 km from the original front line. The Soviet forces west of Orel faced an imminent disaster, but the Germans had not yet captured the town itself.[62]

Private Schöffel served as a loader in the tank belonging to the commander of II Battalion of the 35th Panzer Regiment, Major von Jungenfeldt. The commander had ordered a halt at a piece of woodland, from where he scoped the terrain ahead. Through his vision slit, Schöffel could also see the open field and further woods around 500 meters away. Behind the latter, Schöffel glimpsed the buildings of Orel.[63]

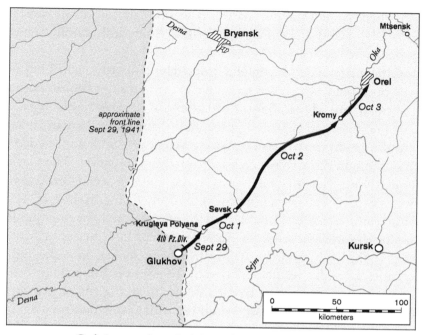

Guderians attack on Orel September 30–October 3, 1941

Fighting in built-up areas was risky. On September 9, 1939, the 35th Panzer Regiment and other elements of the 4th Panzer Division had attacked Warsaw and sustained heavy losses. Colonel Eberbach, who commanded the battle group, had been the commander of the 35th Panzer Regiment when it attacked Warsaw. On that occasion, his tanks had slinked away after failing in their objective. This time, circumstances were more favorable. Orel was much smaller, with a population about one tenth the size of Warsaw's. Additionally, the very rapid German advance towards Orel had not allowed the defenders much time to prepare.[64]

Schöffel was not thinking about the history of the regiment; he had been distracted by a ray of light that had been suspiciously reflected into his field of vision. Perhaps it was the just sun reflecting off a glass surface. As a precaution, the gunner, Lieutenant Euler, decided to fire upon the mysterious target. Schöffel placed a high-explosive round into the breech, while Euler aimed the gun. A very sharp crack indicated that the shell had left the gun barrel. A second later, it hit the target and exploded. To avoid any unnecessary risks, Euler and Schöffel repeated the procedure.[65]

A moment later, von Jungenfeldt ordered his tanks to attack. They drove into the open field, which was rather flat except for a few mounds of earth. The German unit advanced in a formation that roughly resembled a wide wedge. The field had appeared peaceful, but after the German tanks had advanced into the open terrain, Soviet defenders suddenly opened fire. Schöffel thought shots were cracking from every direction. The Germans responded with their machine guns as the tanks proceeded towards the outskirts of Orel. The gases from the intensively firing machine guns were irritating, and Schöffel switched on the ventilation system. Suddenly, fire swept through the tank. A Soviet rifleman had thrown a Molotov cocktail at the tank, and the flames had been sucked into the fighting compartment by the ventilation system. Major von Jungenfeldt ordered the crew to bail out. Despite being a stocky man, the Major managed to leave the tank impressively fast, as did the other crewmembers.[66]

Schöffel sought cover behind the tank with the rest of the crew. In the heat of the battle, he found it amusing that he, as a tanker, was outside his armored vehicle. His thoughts were soon interrupted as Soviet infantry opened fire from their foxholes. The German crew tried to cope as well as it could and was assisted by some infantry that had accompanied the tanks. Such help was desperately needed as the tankers had no heavier weapons than their Luger pistols and not much ammunition. Despite the help, the five crewmembers were being pressed hard. The gunner, radio operator and driver were wounded. Schöffel fired his last bullet. At that moment, he heard a loud crash behind him. He turned his head and saw Sergeant Gabriel's tank. Alongside the other tanks in his platoon, he had set out for the damaged tank and managed to silence the opposition.[67]

Schöffel looked around and found Major von Jungenfeldt sitting next to the damaged tank's left track. He still wore his headset and throat microphone, but the torn-apart wire dangled from his belt. In spite of this, he pushed the transmit button and repeated: "Leckschat, forward! Leckschat, forward!" Schöffel took a few swift strides towards the Major, grabbed the loose end of the torn wire and held it before his eyes. With his peculiar dialect, Schöffel said, "Don't you see that the cable has been torn apart?" The Major stared incredulously at Schöffel for a brief moment before throwing away the microphone.[68]

This kind of erratic behavior could befall virtually anyone in the heat of battle. The stress caused by the obvious mortal danger could make people gravely misunderstand what was taking place. They were also prone to misjudge time; what may have appeared as a very long sequence of events might, in fact, have taken place over the course of a few seconds. Probably not more than a few minutes had elapsed from the moment von Jungenfeldt's tank was hit to the arrival of Gabriel's platoon. Soon, Leckschat arrived in his tank. He had obviously been unable to hear von Jungenfeldt's request, but he had nevertheless understood that the battalion commander's tank had been knocked out. By now, von Jungenfeldt had regained his composure and entered Leckschat's tank to drive into Orel.[69]

Medics soon arrived and attended to the wounded. They also asked about the damage to the tank. A quick inspection showed that only parts of the baggage lashed on the outside of the tank had caught fire, meaning the flames could rather easily be extinguished. Later in the evening, the tank was driven to the rail station at Orel. The following day, the crew received supplies and the men again met Major von Jungenfeldt. Schöffel found that he was back to his old self, perhaps thanks to the excellent tuna fish served at the field kitchen.[70]

Overall, Eberbach's battle group had been more successful than von Jungenfeldt's. Although Soviet air power had attacked his advancing units—no fewer than thirty-five Soviet air attacks had been counted before the end of the day—they moved swiftly towards Orel. No German fighter cover appeared until the evening. Tanks and motorcyclists advanced in the lead and they managed to capture Orel. The city was so surprised that the Germans found the trams were still operating according to schedule when they arrived.[71]

Eberbach's battle group had not sustained heavy losses during this very rapid advance. Altogether, thirty-four had been killed in action and 121 wounded. Tank losses were also modest—five Panzer IIIs and one Panzer IV had been lost. In four days, Eberbach's men had captured 1,136 prisoners and fifteen tanks.[72]

Over the course of four days, the 4th Panzer Division had advanced approximately 210 km as the crow flies, a remarkable performance against a prepared enemy. The Soviet defenses were spilt wide open and Guderian's Panzer group made good progress. The southern wing of the Soviet defenses before Moscow had been set rocking. Furthermore, it was not only Guderian's success that had caused concern among the Soviet high command; further north, Army Group Center had begun Operation *Typhoon* on October 2.[73]

Vyazma

Colonel-General Hoepner's Panzer Group 4 was moved from the Leningrad area to the central sector of Army Group Center before Operation *Typhoon* was launched. Hoepner mainly brought the staff and some supporting elements. The Panzer divisions that had belonged to the Panzer group when it advanced towards Leningrad were sent to other sectors. At the beginning of Operation *Typhoon*, he would control five Panzer divisions. Two of them were the recently arrived 2nd and 5th Panzer Divisions and three were divisions that had fought from the very beginning of Operation *Barbarossa*, but with other Panzer groups—the 10th, from Panzer Group 2, the 11th, from Panzer Group 1, and the 20th, from Panzer Group 3.

The Desna River lay ahead of Hoepner's units. As his Panzer group had no useful bridgeheads across the river, the infantry divisions would make the initial attack. Prisoner interrogation had provided information on the Soviet defenses that was useful for the planning of the attack. There was little time for planning and preparations, but the experienced units could cope with such difficulties.[74]

It was cold and rainy when the soldiers of the 7th Panzer Regiment, which belonged to the 10th Panzer Division, drove their vehicles to the staging areas they had been allotted. Few of them knew the reasons behind the redeployment, but the soldiers were accustomed to such uncertainty. Secrecy demanded that information on the overall purpose was restricted,

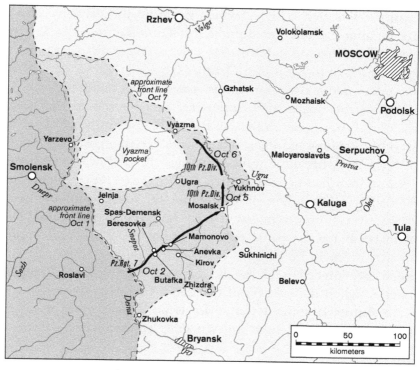

Closing of Vyazma pocket by 10th Pz.Div.

and at this stage, secrecy was more important than the ability to improvise and take initiative. Once the battle had begun, matters would be different; then the importance of local initiative was much greater, and successful initiative demanded at least some knowledge of the overall mission.[75]

Information about the overall aim would soon trickle down the command structure. At 2 p.m. on October 1, Colonel von Hauenschild, the commander of the 7th Panzer Regiment, held a briefing with the officers in the regiment. They were informed of the plans for the attack that would begin early the next day. A few hours later, they also received written orders. As it was still daylight, the instructions did not result in any activity, but after dusk, the regiment began to move to the positions from which the attack would be launched. Engineers had reinforced the roads to make them capable of carrying the high volume of traffic. The engineers had even constructed some new roads. Despite these efforts, some of the wheeled vehicles, which made up the majority even in a Panzer regiment, encountered problems. Tanks had to pull away trucks that became stuck and this resulted in delays. The regiment was not fully ready to attack until 5 a.m. on October 2.[76]

An order of the day from Hitler was read aloud. It described the operation as the final major battle that would result in the death of Bolshevism. It was noted in the 7th Panzer Regiment war diary that the spirits of the soldiers and their morale were very high. Perhaps the optimism was somewhat more muted amongst the staff of the 10th Panzer Division, which had been informed that no more replacements would arrive and winter equipment would not be issued until the coming battle was over. If everything went according to plan, that would not be problematic, but if the battle failed to produce the results desired, the consequences might be grave.[77]

Unlike the preceding days, the weather was clear and gentle on October 2, when the soldiers of the 258th Infantry Division attacked. The 7th Panzer Regiment waited in its positions slightly west of the Desna. For example, II Battalion remained approximately 10 km west of the river.[78]

The initial assault succeeded. Bridgeheads across the Desna were captured and war bridges were quickly prepared. The 7th Panzer Regiment was ordered to advance as soon as 8 a.m. At first, the tanks moved slowly. The first reached the Desna at 9.30 a.m. and drove to the eastern bank on the river via one of the war bridges. They wasted no time and hurried towards the tributary Snopot. A railroad bridge had been captured there intact; it was used by the wheeled vehicles, the tanks could ford the river. After crossing the Snopot, the regiment commander instructed I Battalion to capture Butafka and II Battalion was informed that Beresovka would be its goal.[79]

While I Battalion waited for orders to attack, it was subjected to Soviet artillery fire. A little later, the Soviet artillery was attacked by German dive-bombers. Major von Grundherr, who commanded the battalion, had been instructed to hold his position until he received new orders, but when he saw the Stuka aircraft hurl themselves at the Soviet batteries, he immediately ordered his battalion to attack. Grundherr instructed his 2nd Company to cover the right flank and the 4th Company to secure the left flank. The 3rd Company would attack in the center, immediately followed by the 1st Company and the battalion staff.[80]

Grundherr's initiative is a rather typical example of how the Germans chose to act according to the situation and disregarded given orders if the situation warranted it. Nothing in the war diaries or reports of those involved units suggests that they had been informed about the air attack on the Soviet artillery. Despite this, the opportunity was effectively taken advantage of when Grundherr ordered his battalion to attack. I Battalion of the 7th Panzer regiment was very successful and fought its way to Beresovka in the evening, where it joined Major Gerhardt's II Battalion.[81]

The 7th Panzer Regiment had thus achieved a decisive success, but it did not rest on its laurels. The tanks continued after the sun had set and aimed for Kirov. It soon became apparent that the maps issued were not fully reliable. The Germans had to find another means of navigating in the darkness. Local farmers accompanied the lead tanks as guides, allowing the attack to continue during the night of October 2–3.[82]

After midnight, I Battalion encountered a tank ditch that was defended by Soviet antitank guns. The fighting that took place was only awarded a laconic comment in the battalion's after-action report: "Weak enemy. Antitank guns destroyed." After the brief battle, I Battalion continued forward and captured Anevka at 1 a.m., pausing there afterwards.[83]

Meanwhile, II Battalion had also attacked during the night, and before dawn it reached Mamonovo, where Soviet defenders opposed the advancing Germans. I Battalion reached Mamonovo almost simultaneously. The Germans quickly broke the resistance and occupied the village. They destroyed three Soviet aircraft at the airfield nearby. A bridgehead across the nearby river was also established, as the tanks could ford the watercourse.[84]

Overnight, the 7th Panzer Regiment had advanced in such a way that it split the Soviet defenses to an extent that could be regarded as a breakthrough. Conventional military wisdom did not encourage night attacks by tanks, but the Germans often disregarded this principle. They had done so many times during Operation *Barbarossa* and they had also done it frequently during the campaign in the west in 1940. It can be interpreted as an indication of the great importance the Germans attached to time. They accepted the disadvantages associated with night fighting in order to derive advantages in the overall context of the battle. In this case, the enemy defenses were severely upset, and the night of October 2–3 was also comparatively light. By pushing on through the night, the 7th Panzer Regiment managed to penetrate more than 40 km into the Soviet defenses during the first twenty-four hours of the offensive.

The rapid German advance on the first day of Operation *Typhoon* had resulted in a breakthrough of the Soviet defenses, but on the following day the Germans could not fully capitalize on the success. Lack of fuel hampered the continuation of the offensive. The tanks had outpaced the supply vehicles, and little fuel remained in their petrol tanks. The division commander, Major-General Wolfgang Fischer, set out in the direction where the tank regiment could be found, but on the way he was halted by Soviet antitank guns. However, the opposition was soon brushed aside. The Soviet defenses were disorganized following the Panzer regiment's thrust. The motorized infantry of the 10th Panzer Division could take the lead and continue towards Mosalsk. Thereby the main direction of the attack was shifted slightly to a more northeasterly direction.[85]

Assisted by a few tanks that had received fuel, the motorized infantry could continue the rapid advance. The 69th Motorized Infantry Regiment was particularly successful on October 3 and 4. It reached a point just south of Mosalsk in the evening of October 4. The 10th Panzer Division had thus advanced more than 120 km in two and a half days. The first objective had been attained; now it was time to encircle the Soviet forces to the north, in the Vyazma area.[86]

The 10th Panzer Division was the most successful of the German divisions that made up the right pincer of the developing encirclement at Vyazma. From positions northeast of Smolensk, Panzer Group 3, commanded by Colonel-General Hermann Hoth, had also attacked successfully. The 6th and 7th Panzer Divisions broke through the Soviet defense and advanced in a southeasterly direction, towards Vyazma. To seal the bag around the Red Army formations along the Smolensk–Vyazma axis, units from Panzer Group 4 had to turn north, while the advance northeast on Moscow was also continued. It was vital to reap the most that could be gained from the chaos of the Soviet defense. Fischer's 10th Panzer Division was directed towards Vyazma to close the ring around the Soviet forces that had defended along the main road from Smolensk to Moscow. The SS-Division "Reich" would advance towards Moscow.[87]

II Battalion of the 7th Panzer Regiment received the mission to lead the advance on Vyazma. Major Gerhardt instructed his company commanders, but they knew as well as he did that the tanks were low on fuel. Only parts of the battalion could attack. As the Soviet defense was weak—a consequence of the rapid German advance thus far—the Germans could nevertheless advance successfully towards Vyazma.[88]

The 7th Panzer Regiment was hampered as much by lack of fuel as the Soviet defenders. Occasionally, the advancing German tanks encountered Soviet vehicle columns, which they instantly attacked. When the tanks approached a railroad, the commanders, with their heads up through the turret hatches, discovered a train. They promptly opened fire. The wrecked train blocked the railroad as the German tanks hurried towards Vyazma, which they reached before dawn on October 7. Simultaneously, the 7th Panzer Division had reached Vyazma from the north.[89]

When the German pincers met at Vyazma, several Soviet armies became encircled west of there. Also, Guderian's attack in the south resulted in a pocket near Bryansk. Consequently, the operation would also become known as the "Vyazma-Bryansk" battle. It resulted in an enormous haul of prisoners; on October 19, Army Group Center reported that it had captured 673,000 prisoners since the beginning of the operation.[90] To this figure can be added an unknown number of dead and wounded. As both sides had deployed close to 1.3 million men when the offensive began, more than half the Soviet force had been destroyed in under three weeks.[91] Furthermore, the Germans had covered about two thirds of the distance to Moscow in this short amount of time.[92] Operation *Typhoon* can be seen as a textbook example of how devastating a Blitzkrieg operation could be to those who faced it. The German casualties numbered fewer than 60,000 killed, wounded and missing. In other words, the German losses were not even one tenth of the Soviet casualties.[93] For a World War II operation, the German casualties were exceptionally small compared to the results achieved.

Fall Rains

The Soviet disaster in the Vyazma–Bryansk battle opened the gates to Moscow for the Germans. However, there was a factor that strongly hampered further German advances. As we have seen, the 7th Panzer Regiment had on several occasions lacked the fuel to continue the offensive, and there were other units that suffered similarly. However, during the first week of October, the weather had been favorable, allowing the roads to cope with the large volume of traffic that a major offensive inevitably resulted in. When the 10th Panzer Division joined the 7th Panzer Division at Vyazma, the weather changed considerably. Rain and sleet combined to make the soldiers' existence in their foxholes miserable. As very few roads in the Soviet Union had a hard surface, they quickly became impassable after precipitation. On October 13, Army Group Center reported that the roads were unlikely to improve until frost made them hard again.[94]

The difficult conditions made the Germans unable to reap the ultimate fruits of the great victory won in the first week of Operation *Typhoon*. Nevertheless, Army Group Center persisted and tried to advance on Moscow, but the extremely high advance rate could not be maintained in the mud and slush. However, the very weak Soviet defenses permitted the Germans to gain ground despite the atrocious weather. The 19th Panzer Division, which was one of the units in Hoepner's Panzer group, was one of the German units that attacked towards Moscow. During the late afternoon and evening of October 17, parts of it, particularly I Battalion of the 27th Panzer Regiment, attacked towards Maloyaroslavets, but they stopped at nightfall. A more determined attack would be launched the next day.[95]

The soldiers of the 27th Panzer Regiment, which was the armored component of the 19th Panzer Division, tried to snatch as much sleep as possible during the night before October 18. However, this was not easy. Ingenuity was often needed to get a good night's sleep. The tank crews had an advantage; they could dig a hole in the ground and park the tank above it. The steel hull provided shelter against nature as well as shells, but the heat from the engine could also lend comfort to the soldiers sleeping beneath the hull. Other men tried to find buildings, but often the German soldiers had to rely on the fabric of tents for protection against the weather during the night.

The early reveille often prevented the soldiers from getting as much sleep as they would have liked, and there was no exception on the morning of November 18 for the company commanders of I Battalion in the 27th Panzer Regiment. They were woken up at 5 a.m. by messengers who urged them to report to the battalion commander fifteen minutes later. As they slept in almost full battle equipment, they managed to make it to the commander's briefing in time.[96]

The battalion commander described the forthcoming mission and gave his orders. The 19th Panzer Division should capture Maloyaroslavets and thereby create conditions for a successful continuation of the offensive. The 27th Panzer Regiment would lead the attack in cooperation with the 74th Motorized Infantry Regiment. A task force was composed for the attack, and Lieutenant von Werthern was appointed to command it. He received four Panzer IVs from the 3rd Company, the tanks from the 1st Company, one company from the 19th Antitank Battalion and an engineer platoon. I Battalion and its tanks would follow immediately behind, reinforced by engineers. One of the tank companies had been dispatched to cooperate with the 74th Motorized Infantry Regiment. The attack force was not given much time to prepare; it would have to be ready to attack at 7 a.m.[97]

Combining various elements into battle groups, as the 27th Panzer Regiment did on the morning of November 18, could almost be regarded as everyday fare for the German Army units. The practice had been a fundamental tenet within the Army since the 1920s, and training programs had been designed accordingly. The campaign in Poland had revealed shortcomings caused by the rapid expansion, but they were subsequently attended to, and by the fall of 1941, the German units had formed various kinds of battle groups innumerable times.

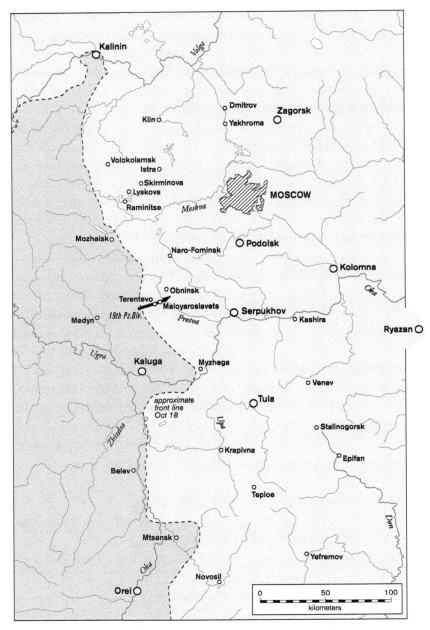

Army Group Center October 20, 1941 and 19th Pz.Div. attack

The soldiers ate their breakfast while they prepared for the mission. Everything was completed by 7 a.m., and a minute later the word "Forward!" was heard in the headsets. Sergeant Nause was eager and took the lead in his tank. The Germans initially met no opposition as they advanced along the main road to Maloyaroslavets. They captured a bridge approximately 12 km east of the town. Lieutenant von Werthern detailed Second Lieutenant Jordan and his platoon to secure the bridge while the other elements of the battle group continued on. Soon afterwards, the Germans were surprised when huge flames shot up on both sides of the road ahead. Several dug-in flamethrowers had been triggered, blinding the driver in the lead tank. Nevertheless, the drivers in the first platoon gave full throttle and drove straight through the fire. The soldiers could feel the heat through the steel walls surrounding them, but they suffered no other discomfort. The following tanks fired on the area from which the flames spouted and managed to extinguish the fires, allowing the other vehicles to proceed.[98]

The Germans soon realized that the flamethrowers had been employed to delay them and thus allow Soviet units to retreat. As the German tanks continued along the main road, the crews saw abandoned vehicles and horse-drawn carts. A little later they also encountered some Soviet stragglers, but no regular units attempted to fight the advancing Germans. The latter could rapidly continue towards Maloyaroslavets and capture a bridge over a stream at the village Terentevo. After fifteen minutes, the German advance elements were within a few kilometers of Maloyaroslavets.[99]

The Panzer regiment commander was informed over the radio about the swift advance conducted by the lead elements. He ordered them to defend the positions taken until further elements of the battalion arrived. Lieutenant von Werthern chose to follow the order and discovered that one of the Panzer IVs had been damaged by the flamethrowers. The heat had been intense enough to cause one of its radiators to partially melt. It would be unable to participate in the subsequent attack.[100]

After shooting up some Soviet vehicle columns and being subjected to artillery fire, the German tank commanders spotted an aircraft. It was a

German reconnaissance plane, and it reported that Soviet vehicles were moving on the roads northeast of Maloyaroslavets, towards the bridges across the Protva River that the Germans aimed for. As the Soviet artillery fire intensified, Lieutenant von Werthern wanted to continue the attack—and grasp the opportunity to strike at the retreating Soviet forces—rather than remain in the current position. He reported this on the radio and the regiment commander soon consented.[101]

At this moment, the battalion commander reached the lead tanks, as did the 3rd Company. No time was wasted. The attack on Maloyaroslavets was launched immediately. The Germans encountered a roadblock within one minute, but it caused only a trivial delay. The tanks rapidly entered firing positions and covered the engineers, who cleared the obstacle. The road into the town thus lay open and it turned out that Maloyaroslavets was abandoned. Not a single shot cracked as the German tanks drove into the streets in two columns. Not until they reached the northeastern outskirts did the German observe something that alarmed them, but they soon realized that the threat was almost harmless. Trucks and cars approached, but when the drivers saw the German tanks, they halted and the men in the vehicles fled.[102]

The Germans hardly glanced at the abandoned vehicles as they drove past them. They increased their speed, hoping to capitalize on the apparent confusion the enemy suffered from. Lieutenant von Werthern pulled out an aerial photo of the target and studied it while his driver sped along the road between Maloyaroslavets and Obninsk.[103]

The tanks proceeded at high speed. They had to reach the bridge across the meandering Protva River before it was destroyed. Suddenly, von Werthern glimpsed a column of Soviet vehicles. The Germans drove straight into it while shooting wildly. Despite being surprised, the Soviet soldiers tried to prepare an antitank gun ready for firing, but their efforts did not meet with success. None of the shots hit any German tanks before the gun was destroyed.[104]

The Soviet force began to panic. Soldiers were fleeing in every direction. Some of the drivers tried to take their trucks off the road and onto the muddy terrain. Others tried to escape northeast, towards Moscow, but the Germans showed no mercy. They shot at every conceivable target. Some tanks simply drove over the vehicles. The edges of the road were soon littered with damaged, destroyed or abandoned guns, carts, trucks and other equipment. Lieutenant von Werthern did not bother to count the booty. Over the radio, he urged, "No delay! We must capture the bridge."[105]

The tank crews realized why von Werthern spoke with such gravity. They soon saw their objective, a double wooden bridge, which Soviet engineers were trying to prepare for demolition. Suddenly, Sergeant Nause saw something remarkable. A herd of cows was about to cross the bridge, oblivious to the war around them. Nause did not hesitate. He ordered the driver to drive towards the bridge at full speed. The steel colossus rapidly approached the bridge, the squeaking noise of its tracks and the roaring engine attracting the cows' attention. For many of them, it was too late. The tank drove straight into the herd and crushed some of the cows, while others managed to escape to the sides. Nause drove over both bridges. No Soviet antitank guns opened fire, which allowed him to scare away the Soviet engineers who were preparing the bridges for demolition. German engineers that followed close on the heels of the lead tanks immediately began to remove the charges and detonators. The Protva bridges were soon securely in German hands.[106]

The tank's tracks allowed them to negotiate the mud better than the wheeled vehicles. Still, the attack on the Protva bridges mainly followed a major road, which was expected to cope with traffic better than minor roads or the surrounding terrain. This resulted in the tip of the attack consisting of a very small force, which would have been a serious disadvantage had the Germans encountered stiff opposition. However, the Soviet defenses in the Maloyaroslavets area turned out to be very weak as a result of the Vyazma-Bryansk disaster. Thus, the Germans could advance swiftly and attain their goal before powerful Soviet countermeasures were taken.

The successful thrust also illustrates the many disadvantages the fall rain created for a major attacking force. The German task force was subjected to Soviet artillery fire during their attack, and the task force was unable to call on any artillery support to counter the Soviet fire due to the mud. The weak roads had deteriorated seriously, and very little ammunition could be brought to the 19th Panzer Division's artillery regiment. Had the Germans encountered strong Soviet defenses, the lack of artillery support could have had grave consequences.[107]

In the end, the Germans would not be able to capitalize on the Protva bridgehead as intended. The terrain beyond the river turned out to be marshy and wooded. The Soviet defenses were also better prepared in this area than west of the Protva. They could not be overcome unless they were attacked on a broader front and with ample artillery support. The prevailing weather ruled this out for the Germans, and the 19th Panzer Division could not make much progress over the following two weeks.[108]

The 19th Panzer Division's actions at Maloyaroslavets show that it was not only the mud that halted Army Group Center at this stage. Had there not been any Soviet defenses, the Germans could have entered Moscow despite the mud. However, the mud caused such difficulties for the attacking side that even sporadic defense could cause significant delays.

The actions around Maloyaroslavets were not unique. All of Colonel-General Hoepner's 4th Panzer Group became stuck in a similar fashion. The 3rd Panzer Group, where General Reinhardt had replaced Colonel-General Hoth as commander, was also stranded after capturing Kalinin on October 14. Moscow received a badly needed respite.

Circumvention and Retreat

As the mud deepened, the battles became less intensive and far less mobile. Consequently, the armored units had proportionally less influence on the operations than the infantry. The infantry had to shoulder a heavy burden even within the Panzer divisions, despite the fact that the rifle companies were depleted after months of fighting. The remaining soldiers were also exhausted from the hardships they had endured.

The men of III Platoon, 3rd Company, of the 394th Infantry Regiment were woken early in the morning of November 5. It was one of the two motorized infantry regiments in the 3rd Panzer Division. Recent fighting had brought them to the area near Tula, south of Moscow. The messenger who had woken them up brought orders from the company commander, who instructed them to prepare for a special mission. Without knowing any further details on the mission, the half-asleep soldiers tottered out from the stable and formed up behind it. They almost immediately received marching orders. Engineers would take over the defense of the present positions.[109]

After marching for a short while, the platoon reached the company commander's post. Three tanks were waiting for the platoon, and the riflemen climbed on board them. They were told that air reconnaissance had discovered a weakly defended road that might allow the Germans to circumvent the Soviet defenses ahead. After the short briefing was concluded, the drivers fired up the engines and set out. The infantry riding on the tanks enjoyed the journey. They expected the tanks to make their fighting easier. Also, they soon discovered that they could warm their frozen feet and hands on the exhausts on the rear of the tanks.[110]

When the small force reached a village, the order was given for them to dismount and ready themselves for battle. The men jumped off the tanks, which slowly continued and passed German soldiers crouching in their foxholes. They made up the forward defensive line, and after passing this, the tank drivers began to move more cautiously. They tried to drive as often as possible in low-lying areas, despite the increased risk of becoming stuck in the mud. The soldiers of the rifle platoon were very attentive, but the noise from the tanks' engines and tracks forced them to rely primarily on their eyes. They kept a finger on their safety catches so they were able to open fire as soon as any enemy was seen.

At this moment, Russians appeared—but they were just civilians from the nearby village. They approached the Germans in a friendly way and offered them milk to drink. The Germans had little time to enjoy the hospitality as the tanks were continuing forward, and the infantry could not risk becoming separated from them. A little while later, the small German force halted as it confronted some brushwood. Suddenly, a wildly gesticulating lady appeared and ran towards the tank in the lead. As there was an interpreter in the German force, they were able to ascertain that she was telling them about an enemy position within the brushwood. Shortly afterwards, the German infantry heard a command they were unaccustomed to—"Prepare for break-in!"

Their rifles were cocked almost instinctively. Many men reached down to their trousers to ensure that their grenades were in their pockets, and then they climbed up on the tanks, where the commanders closed the turret hatches. The engines revved. Accompanied by the ringing sound of the tanks, they set off at high speed towards the Soviet position. They drove around the brushwood and caught sight of torn-up earth, which suggested that the defenders had dug in. The Germans immediately opened fire with their machine guns. A Soviet soldier was seen running towards his machine gun, but he was unable to reach it before the German bullets hit him.

The German infantry jumped off the tanks and dashed to the nearest trenches, threw hand grenades into them and hurried on to clear the position. Soon, the first Soviet soldiers appeared with their hands raised. The Germans brought them to a depression and managed to incite more Red Army soldiers to surrender after shouting in Russian that they would throw hand grenades. So far, the German attack had developed perfectly, but a moment later, other Soviet units opened fire on the Germans. The tanks returned fire, but when a Soviet antitank gun joined the fighting, the armored vehicles withdrew to find protection among some buildings.

The German infantry tried to grasp the situation. The trench system appeared to be extensive and continued towards Tula. The Germans could also see that Soviet reinforcements were approaching. The captured position was not suited to defending against an enemy attacking from the current direction, and therefore it was not easy to hold. Retreat was not an appealing option either, as that would force them to move 500 meters across an open field that offered no protection. The German soldiers hunkered in the trenches while they tried to figure out which option was the least unpleasant. Finally, they decided to retreat.

The German riflemen barely dared to raise their heads above the trench. Bullets whistled above them and the Soviet antitank gun also fired. Among the soldiers in the platoon, there were veterans as well as young replacements who had recently arrived. The inexperienced were relieved to withdraw, but the veterans reminded them that the wounded had to be helped back to safety first.

Exercising great caution, the German soldiers managed to reach the depression where the prisoners were keeping low to the ground. Only one German soldier was wounded, and his wounds were not serious. He could make it on his own. As the enemy gunners would not immediately find their mark, those who ran first were less likely to be hit. For this reason, the wounded soldiers went first in situations like this.

As the German machine guns fired rapidly, the wounded soldier rushed towards the village located 500 meters away. Other soldiers followed him almost immediately, and at last the commander and the machine gunners left their positions and hurried towards the village. They felt like rabbits trying to run away from a hunter as they alternated between running and crawling. They reached the village all out of breath, but unscathed.

The German platoon had hardly returned to the village before a Soviet attack was launched. Noise from shooting filled the air. The sharp cracks from exploding hand grenades occasionally drowned the rattling sound of small-arms fire. At that moment, III Platoon was bringing its prisoners to the company staff after their ignominiously aborted "special mission." The engineers defending the village requested help from III Platoon. After conferring with the company commander, the riflemen were sent to the long and narrow village.

The men of III Platoon were met by whizzing bullets as they approached the village, but they were nevertheless able to establish contact with the engineers, who assigned them to suitable battle positions. At that moment, a few German tank destroyers arrived. Their support allowed the Germans to launch a counterattack along the main street. The shells from the guns hit buildings along the straight street as the infantry advanced through the gardens to the left and the engineers advanced on the right side of the main street. Some of the houses caught fire and Soviet soldiers were seen fleeing from them. A Soviet machine gun temporarily halted the German advance, but it was silenced by the tank destroyers, which drove to the end of the village.

The tank destroyers briefly fired upon the fleeing Soviet soldiers before the noise of battle faded away. The German soldiers assembled on a village street and thought about what to do next. The long and narrow village was not suited to defense. The question was whether it should be defended or abandoned. While the German soldiers conferred, villagers crept out from hideouts dug into the earth, despite the fact that shots could still be heard. The Germans decided to abandon the village and take up defensive positions behind it. The villagers thus found themselves in no man's land.

Twilight soon began to fall over the cold village. A snow squall soon wiped out the traces of the battle fought in the day. The German attack had not resulted in any positive result except for the prisoners. This was actually unsurprising; the war had turned into innumerable small battles as the larger offensive operations stalled. Their outcome was often difficult to gauge, but they inexorably wore the units down.

The Dressing Station

As Operation *Barbarossa* was more extensive and prolonged than any previous campaign, the accumulated German casualties were considerably greater. Far more replacements had to be introduced into the combat units, but the medical services also had far more work to do. On November 10, the Chief of General Staff, Franz Halder, noted in his diary that the casualties up to November 6 amounted to 686,108 officers and men. Of these, the 512,076 wounded made up the majority. Their wounds could vary greatly, from being so severe that they eventually proved fatal to those that only required brief medical treatment. Those suffering illness have to be added to this number, as the medical services had to treat them as well.[111]

The doctors and nurses had a heavy workload and their resources were scarce. When the fall rains turned the roads into seas of mud, the supply problems multiplied. This obviously affected the medical services as well, as they received less medicine and found it difficult to evacuate the wounded and sick. As the conditions near the front were harsh, the Germans strived to bring the wounded to medical facilities far from the front as soon as possible. Such transports were made in several stages, the first of which was usually sending the wounded to dressing stations in field ambulances. Emergency care was conducted there. The intention, however, was for the wounded to be moved to field hospitals or, preferably, for them to be evacuated to the home country.

Wounded soldiers serving in the Panzer divisions could be fortunate enough to be transported in half-track ambulances. This was particularly advantageous when the fall rains made the ground difficult to negotiate for conventional vehicles. Perhaps the infantry divisions suffered worst, as their field ambulances were often horse-drawn. The animals fought a losing struggle with the sticky ground, which virtually sucked the wagons down. As time was crucial for a wounded soldier's chances, this was very serious.

The harsh weather also affected the Panzer formations. Dr Altemüller served as regiment physician in the 7th Panzer Regiment, and he was forced to change his procedures to cope with the climate. The regiment fought in the Skirminova area, but its main medical facility was located at Raminitse. The muddy roads made the movement of wounded far too time consuming. Altemüller decided to establish an additional facility at a local hospital at Lyskova.[112]

Altemüller would have preferred the facility to be located at Skirminova, but the poor state of the buildings and occasional Soviet artillery fire excluded this option. Lyskova was the second-best option, and work began there on November 3. Conditions were definitely better here than at Skirminova, but difficulties were nevertheless encountered. Up to November 9, the dressing station received 121 wounded, of which only twenty-six belonged to the Panzer regiment. The remainder arrived from other elements of the 10th Panzer Division. Around thirty were brought to the rear area as soon as they could be transported on tanks and other tracked vehicles.[113]

The low transport capacity made it difficult to provide the wounded with sufficient food. A field kitchen did not reach the station at Lyskova until November 6. On the same day, the commander of one of the motorized infantry battalions in the division, Lieutenant-Colonel Maus, sent approximately 40 kg of bread baked by his soldiers, as well as approximately 5 kg of honey they had found. Bandages were also in short supply, but by exercising great care and thrift, it was possible to change bandages on the wounded when needed.[114]

Despite all their efforts, Dr Altemüller and his staff could not prevent five of the wounded from dying at the dressing station. However, all the other wounded men survived, and in the evening of November 9, a platoon from a field ambulance company arrived at the dressing station. Around sixty wounded were taken on board the ambulances on the following day and brought to Rusa and then Moshaisk, where they were transferred to a train. During the fall, the mud meant the railroads were far more reliable than the roads.[115]

Tula

After capturing Orel, elements of the 4th Panzer Division resumed the advance northeast after a few days and reached the Mtsensk area, where Soviet armor was encountered. At the same time, the weather deteriorated drastically. Guderian's Panzer army also had to clear the large pocket created near Bryansk, where a large haul of prisoners was taken. As a result, Guderian's units could not begin to close the distance to Moscow until several weeks later. Nevertheless, early in November, elements of his Panzer army had reached the outskirts of the industrial city of Tula. Guderian's lead elements temporarily became stuck in this position and the battles fought near Tula in mid-November quickly assumed a more static character, unlike the rapid operations that had dominated the initial days of October.[116]

The 394th Motorized Infantry Regiment, where Hermann Türk served as field surgeon in I Battalion, was among the German units that fought near Tula. The regiment belonged to the 3rd Panzer Division, which, after more than four months of continuous fighting since the beginning of Operation *Barbarossa*, had suffered over 5,000 casualties (mostly wounded). Approximately 3,000 of these losses had been made up either by returning convalescents or replacements. Many faces had thus arrived and disappeared during the months Türk had served in the regiment. The infantry usually suffered the vast majority of the casualties, resulting in much work for the doctors in these units. Like the other Panzer divisions, the 3rd had two motorized infantry regiments—the 3rd and 394th—and their soldiers faced the greatest risk of dying or becoming wounded.[117]

As a doctor, Türk often accompanied the combat units and frequently found himself exposed to enemy fire. The ever-deteriorating weather resulted in more cases for him to attend to. Some German soldiers suffered from frostbite during the fighting outside Tula. On November 14, Türk noted in his diary that a soldier had been brought to him with one of his feet frostbitten. It turned out that half the foot was already dead. The poor soldier had not noticed how the numb part of his body had gradually died. There was little Türk could do but note how awful the war was.[118]

The supply problems were slightly reduced every three days, when Junkers Ju 52 aircraft landed to deliver supplies, but the needs of the dressing stations far outweighed what the Ju 52s were able to deliver. The shortages notwithstanding, it was decided to attack southeast of Tula. Türk had a difficult job caring for his medicines; the glass vessels in which they were contained were prone to breaking open when the temperatures fell. Several bottles of vaccines and other medicines were lost due to the freezing conditions.

On the afternoon of November 16, Türk was summoned to a briefing where the plans for the forthcoming attack were discussed. The doctors also had to be briefed to enable them to make best use of the scarce medical resources. After the briefing, Türk made his preparations for the attack. He went to bed early in the evening and slept well until 4 a.m., when an infernal noise woke him. A salvo from the Soviet artillery crashed down in the area and the ground shook from the force of the explosions. Shrapnel shattered the window and landed in the room where he slept. Still drowsy, he saw three nearby buildings ablaze. Another three salvos hit the area and Türk tried to make himself as small as possible. He crouched low to avoid being hit. As suddenly as the shells had landed, the fire ceased. An eerie silence followed before the Germans regained composure and began to investigate the damage.

Except for the Soviet artillery's abrupt morning greeting, the German preparations proceeded according to plan. The attack force set out in the evening. As it was frozen, the Upa River was easily negotiated. Türk was

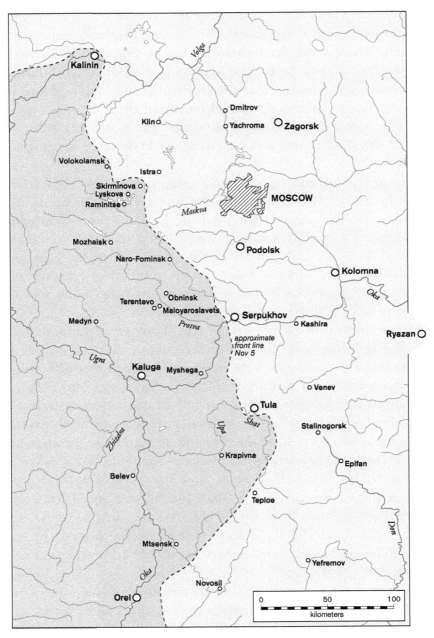

Army Group Center front line November 5, 1941

pleased with the easy river crossing, but he soon found that the frozen ground was slippery—a difficulty aggravated by the fact that the vehicles had to proceed with their headlights switched off. By midnight, he reached the village of Krutoye, where he found a hut to spend the night in. It had no heating, and the soldiers were packed into the buildings like sardines to avoid the severe night cold.

The protection offered by the walls and the roof only lasted a few hours. The journey was swiftly resumed at 3 a.m. on November 18, this time on foot. Türk and the other men negotiated a ravine in the cold night before they reached their intended positions. All that was left was to wait there silently, but they did not have to wait for long. The German artillery opened fire punctually at 6.05 a.m. Türk thought it sounded like there was thunder everywhere, and he presumed that the Soviet soldiers must have been rudely awakened by the noise. He must still have remembered his own recent experience.

The Germans reached Sergiyevskoye without much difficulty, but the fighting became intense there. Shells and bullets belched out from barrels as the German infantry thrust forward in leaps. In the midst of the fighting, Türk reflected on the soldiers' clothing. The German soldiers wore their warmest clothes but nevertheless froze like dogs as soon as they stopped moving. Some time later, the first wounded were brought to Türk. They convulsed and screamed from the cold. Just seeing and hearing them tormented Türk. They had to be brought to places where they could be better protected against the cold. Türk sent a motorcycle orderly to get a car while bullets and shrapnel whizzed around them. Despite the danger, the car managed to reach Türk and bring the wounded to a safer place.

The fighting had only just begun; there would certainly be more wounded to attend to. The fighting became more intense as the 3rd and 4th Companies attacked Soviet bunkers. The German infantry managed to overcome the opposition and capture a hill beyond the Upa River. Türk observed that the 2nd Company encountered stronger defenses. Soviet snipers fired from the left. One man from the engineer platoon next to Türk was hit, falling down and dying within seconds. Türk himself sought cover behind trees, but he soon found a barrack near the river, where he could take care of the wounded and get them warm.

Many of the wounded soldiers brought to Türk's barrack had severe injuries. One of them had been hit in the stomach, and he died around half an hour after arriving at the improvised clinic. Next to arrive was a tanker. He had been hit in the eye after a Soviet sniper shot a bullet through a vision slit in the tank. Türk was exasperated by the Soviet snipers, who were said to have arrived from Siberia. They obstinately remained in their hideouts, continuing to menace the Germans until a hand grenade hit their hideout.

The flow of wounded soldiers brought to Türk increased. Many of them suffered from fractures of their thighbones and arms. Türk's decision to establish his clinic at the barrack was fortunate as it had been much more difficult to put the soldiers' arms and legs into splints in the cold weather outside. As Türk's small surgery was the first link in a chain of medical facilities, he wanted the wounded to be transported to better-equipped facilities as soon as possible. Unfortunately, the vehicle that took the wounded away arrived irregularly. The wounded moaned loudly as they waited in the barrack. Türk attempted to arrange for an extra transport and finally managed to requisition a truck, which took ten of the wounded to a better facility.

More of the wounded were brought to Türk as the battle continued. He eventually had to transport the wounded from the barrack himself. The journey was especially hazardous as Türk was forced to make a detour. It took him to a section of the Upa River where it flowed through a gorge and the bridge spanning it had been destroyed. It was unthinkable to turn back with the wounded. Instead, Türk drove along the river, the sun setting in the sky; after driving for 8 km, his efforts were finally rewarded with success. A railroad bridge spanned the river. The rails and sleepers were not intended for cars and trucks, but Türk had no choice. The wounded wailed as the vehicle jolted, but they understood that the uncomfortable journey would take them to a suitable medical unit.

Soon after crossing the river, Türk reached a burning village that he could not identify. His compass allowed him to establish a direction that seemed appropriate. He again drove near burning villages and began to suspect that he had ended up on the front line. However, he was lucky.

After an uneasy and worrisome journey, he found the battalion staff in a depression near a small river, where he could contact almost all the companies by phone and ensure that all wounded had been taken care of. A little later, he established communications with the last company, which reported that eight soldiers had just been wounded by mortar fire. Türk ensured that the wounded could be treated in a fully heated building.

Hard fighting had occurred in the 394th Regiment's sector on November 18, but no rest was allowed over the subsequent days. The goal of the attack had been attained, but the flanks remained vulnerable and fighting continued there. Türk compiled the November 18 casualty report for the battalion; it turned out that seventy men had been lost—twelve killed in action and fifty-eight wounded. Türk found some time to read the German newspapers arriving at the front at irregular delays. According to them, "the Russians were no longer capable of offering much resistance. Only scattered remnants of units surrendering and wandering about remained."

To the soldiers fighting at Tula—and the doctors like Türk who attended to the wounded—the rosy picture of the situation as given in the newspaper appeared ridiculous. The Soviet defenses clearly did not consist of stragglers without any command. The climate was also making itself felt. The cold made bread inedible unless it was thawed over a fire. The water in the water bottles froze. Fresh sausages sparkled with ice crystals and the winter was taking an ever-firmer grip.

The Soviet fall was succeeded by the Soviet winter. The mud was replaced by frost, which the Germans were poorly prepared for. However, from the perspective of the generals, the frost brought an advantage. When the mud froze, trucks and other vehicles could negotiate the roads more easily. This permitted the Germans to resume the attack on Moscow, but the chance to capture the Soviet capital had been forfeited. When the mud virtually glued the German supply transports to the ground, Stalin received the respite he badly needed. From October 19 to November 19, Army Group Center made very small gains indeed. What Türk witnessed at Tula would turn out to be part of the final German attack on Moscow. Guderian's forces broke through the southeast region of Tula around November 20 and then turned north. Simultaneously, Hoepner's Panzer group attacked northeast of Moscow and advanced to the canal north of the Soviet capital.[119]

By this time, the Germans could no longer sustain the high tempo of their previous offensives. The worn-out units lacked the power to quickly punch holes in the Soviet defenses and make immediate deep thrusts. The Germans persisted in their attacks towards Moscow for two weeks, but the offensive finally stuttered to a halt during the first days of December.

Operation *Barbarossa* had failed.

Winter

The German generals' hopes that the winter would bring better conditions for offensive operations were soon dashed. Again, serious supply difficulties occurred. This time, it was the railroads that faltered. German rail engines were not designed for the stern cold, which caused water pipes to freeze and burst, thus rendering the engines unusable. The Germans tried to use Soviet engines instead, but they had not captured enough of them. The wider gauges of the Soviet railroads also added to the difficulties. This was a particular problem as the only way the great distances across the Soviet Union could be covered was by rail. If they could not be relied upon, little ammunition, fuel, food, spare parts, lubricants or any of the other items needed by a modern army would reach the front.[120]

The advent of winter meant that equipment had to be adapted to cold and snow. For example, everything from vehicles to howitzers required lubricants. Those used by the Germans during the summer were poorly suited to low temperatures, so the already worn-out equipment was often rendered totally inoperable after the lubricants froze. The soldiers' uniforms were not suited to the winter either. They were rather thin and light, which was an advantage during the warm summer days but very dangerous in a cold climate. Furthermore, the comparatively dark German uniforms contrasted starkly against the white snow. However, the worst thing about them was their inability to keep the soldiers warm.

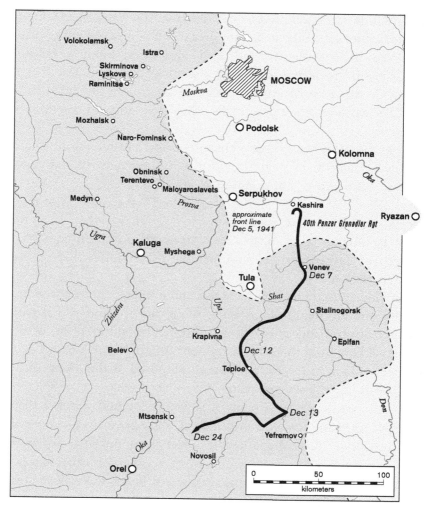

Army Group Center December 5, 1941 and 40th Pz.Gren.Rgt. retreat

The positions held by the Germans early in December had come about as a result of offensive operations that had stagnated, so they were not necessarily suited for defense. As always, the infantry was very exposed to the hardships of the climate. The 40th Motorized Infantry Regiment, which was part of the 17th Panzer Division, was among the units that experienced the rigors of winter retreats.[121]

When Guderian attempted to cut off Tula, the 17th Panzer Division advanced further east and reached the area south of Kashira, approximately 100 km south of Moscow. The 63rd Motorized Infantry Regiment defended positions on the front sector south of Kashira, along the Oka River, while the 40th Motorized Infantry Regiment defended the east flank. They would not get any further than that, and in December they would retreat.[122]

At first, the 40th Regiment retreated almost entirely along the road it had advanced on in November, but the soldiers nevertheless encountered new difficulties. They hardly received any rest for almost four weeks. During the daylight hours, the soldiers were fighting or digging positions. The latter task was, of course, very hard when the ground was frozen. During the nights, they regrouped, stood sentry, took care of equipment and performed innumerable other duties that prevented them from resting.[123]

Fatigue increases the risk of accidents and injuries. As they were numb from cold, the German soldiers quite often did not notice that parts of their bodies were dangerously frozen. From December 1–26, no fewer than 349 soldiers from the 40th Regiment suffered from various degrees of frostbite. Their feet were particularly exposed as the German boots were too thin for the severe winter.[124]

One example shows how badly smaller units could suffer. I Platoon of the 7th Company took up positions at Yablonovo on December 15. The commander, Second Lieutenant Spier, brought forty-seven men. His platoon held battle positions in open terrain for nineteen hours, without any kind of cover from the weather. When it was relieved on the evening of December 16, two men had been killed and eight wounded by enemy fire. Additionally, thirty men were suffering from frostbite. Only seven soldiers remained fit for combat. Spier was so badly frozen and exhausted that he could no longer command the pitiful remnants of his platoon.[125]

While his soldiers fought the Red Army as well as the elements on the Eastern Front, Hitler made one of his most inexplicable decisions. Early in the morning of December 7, carrier-based Japanese aircraft attacked Pearl

Harbor, where most of the US Pacific Fleet was stationed. The attack not only surprised the Americans; Hitler was taken by surprise as well. After reflecting for a few days, he decided to declare war on the United States. As the Japanese attack had been launched without any consultation with the Germans, the latter were not obliged to join their ally, but Hitler nevertheless made his mysterious decision to declare war on the United States.

Hitler's decision to declare war on the United States would eventually prove a very grave mistake, but as the US armed forces were not immediately ready to make a substantial contribution to the war against Germany, the immediate consequences were rather small. However, the Japanese action clearly confirmed that she would not attack the Soviet Union. Instead, she would conduct offensive operations in Southeast Asia and the Pacific area. This meant Stalin was free to bring in further reinforcements from Siberia.

The men of the 40th Motorized Infantry Regiment were too busy surviving to ponder on the implications of events in the remote Pacific Ocean. In their world, even Berlin was very distant. They were mainly concerned with enemy fire, the bitter cold and the shortage of food. The persistent supply difficulties made food scarcer at the front. Snow and cold made it more time consuming to bring hot meals from the field kitchens to the shivering soldiers. Often, sledges had to be used for the last 2–3 km. In the stern cold a warm meal was even more desirable than usual, but unfortunately it was not very easy to obtain. For example, the regiment's 6th Company fought at Yablonovo for three days without receiving a single warm meal.[126]

Personal hygiene was often difficult to maintain in the harsh climate. Many of the men of the 40th Regiment did not receive any laundered clothes—not even underwear—during December 1941. Furthermore, laundry equipment had been lost during the retreat and could not be replaced with the transportation system in shambles. Lice thrived and the soldiers became more exposed to various diseases.[127]

To a large extent, the German difficulties in the winter were caused by one of the pillars of their art of war collapsing—the capacity to move and transport supplies. High-tempo advances and operational mobility were the keys to success in the kind of warfare the Germans preferred. When the fall rains turned the roads into mud, they were deprived of the chance to achieve great success. The winter brought difficulties that endangered the health of the individual soldier. All that remained for the German Army was to try and survive for a few months until the spring arrived and potentially provided some hope of new victories.

Causes and Consequences

Operation *Barbarossa* was Hitler's most outlandish military project. Its scope and ambitions far exceeded any previous Blitzkrieg campaign. Furthermore, Hitler's armed forces had reached their pinnacle in terms of training, experience and confidence. The long string of victories had allowed the Germans to finely hone their methods of warfare. Experience had been used to create appropriate training programs and exercises conducted between the campaigns. Perhaps the German Army reached its qualitative peak in June 1941; it was clearly better prepared then than in early May 1940. Nevertheless, Operation *Barbarossa* was the campaign that would eventually bring Hitler down, after four years of brutal warfare.

Why did Operation *Barbarossa* fail when the Germans had better-prepared forces than in the previous campaigns? The most fundamental reason is the extent of Stalin's military resources. He possessed means far greater than any of Germany's previous opponents. The enormous Soviet losses exceeded the forces other countries could field. The battles at Kiev and Vyazma-Bryansk resulted in Soviet casualties of approximately 1.5 million men. Despite such disasters, the Red Army survived, and at the end of the year it actually had more men on or near the front than it had had on June 22. Meanwhile, the German forces had been reduced as their casualties—despite being far smaller than the Soviet losses—had not been fully replaced.

The vastly incorrect German intelligence on the Soviet Union was, of course, of paramount importance. However, the Germans seem not to have been far off the mark concerning the Soviet forces in the border military districts. The real error was that they grossly underestimated the reserves deeper in the Soviet Union as well as the Soviet capacity to create new military resources. Had the capacity of the Soviet military forces, including reserves and units that had not yet been created, followed German preconceptions, the Germans would most likely have won. They did inflict a shattering defeat on the forces they expected to meet, but new Soviet units arrived and left the Germans with no alternative but to battle on. Admittedly, the arriving Soviet units were often hastily trained, but they nevertheless fought.

The Germans were far from alone in underestimating the Soviet military capacity. When Germany and the Soviet Union had signed the Molotov-Ribbentrop Pact in August 1939, they had also agreed on a trade treaty. Accordingly, oil was exported from the Soviet Union to Germany. This led the British and French to consider attacking the Soviet oil fields at Baku. Such considerations suggest that decision-makers in Britain and France did not realize the magnitude of the Soviet military capacity.[128]

Evidently, the French and particularly the British had reasons to assess the Soviet military potential, but there is hardly any evidence suggesting they were much more successful than the Germans. Stalin's purges of 1937–38 led to the execution, dismissal or imprisonment of tens of thousands of officers. It was widely assumed in other countries that the Red Army had become far less effective following the purges. The poor Soviet performance during the Winter War against Finland in 1939–40 seemed to confirm this conclusion. The French commander-in-chief, Gamelin, regarded the Red Army as almost useless after the purges. Even G. S. Isserson, a professor at the Soviet war academy (and survivor of the purges) regarded the Army as "beheaded" after the purges.[129]

The widespread misjudgments of the Soviet military capabilities are far from unique. There are many examples of intelligence services either exaggerating or underrating the military capabilities of another country. Military intelligence is far from an exact science, and there are many examples of similar gross errors in modern times. However, this suggests that caution should be a guiding principle when planning, allowing for margins of error. The German preparations for Operation *Barbarossa* lacked such margins. Consequently, the German armed forces assumed an insurmountable task.

Compared to the campaign in the west in 1940, the German casualties during Operation *Barbarossa* were not much greater relative to the number of divisions employed and the duration of the campaign. Casualties per week were slightly higher during Operation *Barbarossa*, but larger forces were committed.[130] Consequently, individual divisions could suffer losses at a lower rate during Operation *Barbarossa*. For example, the 4th Panzer Division lost 1,571 killed, wounded and missing from June 22–August 3, 1941, a period almost exactly as long as the 1940 campaign in the west had been, during which the division suffered 2,049 casualties.[131]

However, there was a significant difference between the Germans' opponents in the two offensives. The Soviet forces suffered significantly higher casualties than the military units of the western powers had done in 1940. It could thus be said that the Red Army units had to pay a higher price without inflicting greater damage on the Germans. The Soviet units—particularly the reserves—were, however, far more numerous than the forces fielded by the western powers in 1940.

The German disagreement on where to place their main effort has often been discussed. This dissension hardly surfaced until Army Group Center crossed the Dnepr and captured Smolensk; however, it clearly affected German decision-making from the second half of July until well into August. Hitler wanted to concentrate on the flanks, while the Army high command preferred to continue towards Moscow. This dispute came about at the same time that the Germans began to battle the second Soviet echelon. It had already been broken through in the Smolensk area, but Army Groups North and South had not done that yet.

The disagreement between Hitler and most of his Army officers can be regarded as part of a more general question—how does one bring an opponent down? In this case, Hitler emphasized the economic factors, while the generals wanted to destroy the enemy armed forces. The characteristics of the German armed forces and the geography of the Soviet Union spoke against Hitler's plan. Furthermore, even successful attacks against the economic assets of the enemy were unlikely to result in a quick victory. It seemed illogical to alter the direction of a campaign that had been conceived as an attempt to win a rapid victory, unless the ambition of winning a quick victory was abandoned. Hitler's focus on the flanks was also the result of fear of flank threats. On this occasion, he displayed the same kind of anxiety he had evinced in May 1940.

The loss of time caused by the disagreement was serious, but this does not automatically mean that the Germans would have won if the generals had had their own way. Their chances of capturing Moscow would most likely have been better, but it is far from evident that Stalin's regime would had fallen if Moscow had been captured.

An alternative would have been to design Operation *Barbarossa* from the very outset as an attempt to win a war of attrition against the Soviet Union. The Soviets' manpower resources and weapons production undoubtedly outstripped those of Germany. On the other hand, the Germans inflicted far greater casualties than their counterparts. In 1941, the Soviet casualties were at least five times greater than the German losses.[132] Such an uneven casualty exchange ratio would be intolerable in the long run, but it would take more than half a year to deplete the Soviet reserves. Hence, to choose such an option would have forced the Germans to plan for a longer war. On the other hand, it is doubtful that they could have planned such a campaign without far better intelligence on the Soviet economy, industry and population. Furthermore, such as scheme could be jeopardized by an increased threat in the west if the United States entered the war.

Operation *Barbarossa* illustrates the German dilemma well. On the one hand, her Army was tactically and operationally more skilled than its adversaries. On the other hand, the strategic situation was not favorable to the Germans. This had been clear since 1939. The surprising victory over France afforded Hitler more freedom of action, but when the Soviet Union was attacked, the Germans again found themselves in a situation where long-term factors, such as economy and geography, would settle the issue.

As Operation *Barbarossa* petered out, World War II turned into a war of attrition. The capacity to bring new weapons and men to the front would eventually tell the difference between victor and vanquished. Such a struggle was unfavorable to Germany.

CHAPTER 7

SUCCESS OR FAILURE?

The German art of war has been presented as a revolution, but it actually built on traditions established quite long ago.[1] New types of weapons—developed in Germany or elsewhere—were fitted into the existing concept rather than spurring the Germans to create a completely new mode of warfare. In many ways, the German "Blitzkrieg" warfare was a consistent refinement rather than a revolutionary departure from the past. One example of this is the balanced composition of the Panzer divisions, allowing them to combine arms to great effect. This concept was well established before the invention of the tank. Furthermore, the combined-arms principle was one of the fundamental pillars upon which the first German Army field manual after World War I rested. At that time, the tank was still in its infancy and it was not clear that tanks would develop quicker than the antitank weapons.

Another example is the role of air power. Although the Luftwaffe was established as a separate arm in 1935, cooperation with the Army remained high on the German list of priorities. During the campaigns of 1939–40, close air support was often abysmal, but the Germans made progress. Judging from the after-action reports and war diaries, close air support worked better during Operation *Barbarossa*, but it seems to have improved even further into the summer of 1942. However, by then, the war was no longer going to be decided by swift Blitzkrieg campaigns.[2]

Combined arms was thus not a novel concept originating from new technological means invented during or immediately before World War I.

It was a principle permeating the German entire armed forces—not only the armored units and the Luftwaffe. The infantry divisions, which made up the majority of the Army, also adhered to the combined-arms principle. Compared to their opponents, German infantry divisions were more diverse and composed in such a way that junior commanders could combine different arms.

The German emphasis on combined arms was linked to two other tenets—mission-oriented command and high-quality training. As the weapons systems were often combined very low in the command structure, junior commanders had to be well-trained and eager to take initiative. The emphasis on initiative and adequate training was not only motivated by the desire to attain synergy between various arms; these traits were valuable for many other reasons, and this was repeatedly shown on the battlefield.[3]

Given this background, it appears more reasonable to regard the German warfare of 1939–41 as the culmination of a long development rather than a revolutionary departure. Quite often, and not unjustifiably, the contemporary world regarded the results of the German warfare as revolutionary. However, it does not follow that German warfare must have been revolutionary. With hindsight, we can see that the Germans were rather keen to use new means, such as airborne troops, tanks and an independent air force, but these novelties were incorporated into an existing framework.

The geographic position of Germany (as well as her predecessor, Prussia) since the eighteenth century contributed to the focus on mobile operations and quick victories. Given the large number of potential enemies, there was little choice. On the other hand, it can be concluded that military excellence did not necessarily ensure survival. During the Seven Years' War of 1756–63, Frederick the Great had won many battles, but in the long run, the large coalition he fought gradually won the upper hand. He was saved by the accession of a new monarch in Russia. In this war, a large coalition could clearly be superior despite Prussian tactical and operational skill.

During the nineteenth century, when Germany was united under Prussian dominance, Bismarck maneuvered skillfully, using diplomacy to his advantage. He thus avoided a strong coalition, allowing his armed forces to fight one adversary at a time. After Germany had been united following the victory over France in 1870–71, Bismarck continued his diplomatic efforts to prevent the formation of an overwhelming anti-German coalition. However, the results of his efforts did not last. The subsequent generation of German politicians did not manage to maintain the balance Bismarck had created. Neither can the German military escape criticism on this issue. Instead, the two world wars saw Germany pitted against coalitions that eventually proved overwhelming.

Experience thus indicated that wise diplomacy and foreign policy was essential; however, this obviously does not contradict the idea that military capabilities allowing mobile operations, based on high tactical skill, would be able to achieve a rapid victory should it be required. The Germans evidently had incentives to create the kind of warfare the country had practiced during World War II, and these incentives had existed for a very long period of time.

Geography may have influenced the compositions and character of the armed forces in many ways. For Germany, a large-scale conventional war dominated by ground combat was always in the forefront of her military thinking. The German colonial escapades in the decades preceding World War I were not particularly important. This contrasts with Great Britain and the United States, whose geographical positions and colonies motivated force structures that differed notably from Germany's. The most likely scenario for those powers was not a major land war on the European continent.

It can be argued that the British were more revolutionary during the interwar years. They experimented with tank formations that were more thoroughly dominated by tanks, compared to the more all-arms divisions created by the Germans. The Royal Air Force placed far more emphasis on strategic bombing than the Luftwaffe and intended mainly to target the enemy's cities and industries. This must be regarded as a more radical departure from previous warfare than the German development of the Luftwaffe. Aided by hindsight, we can see that the British decisions were, to a considerable extent, based on false assumptions. The more down-to-earth German concept appears more realistic. Furthermore, it can be argued that the Germans mainly strived to develop tactical and operational levels while the British attached more importance to the strategic level.

Even within the field of conventional warfare, the Germans remained rather traditional. Theoreticians like J. F. C. Fuller had advocated that tanks should penetrate deep and strike against enemy staffs, which, according to him, would paralyze the enemy. The Germans were of course pleased when they captured or destroyed enemy staffs, but they did not aim for such targets. Rather, they strived to cut off supply lines and put enemy combat units in very unfavorable positions. These were the governing thoughts behind the encirclement operations, including the dash to the Channel coast in May 1940. If the Germans paralyzed their opponents, they did so by acting so quickly on the battlefield that the enemy's actions tended to take place at the wrong place and the wrong time.[4]

It can be argued that the qualities of the German art of war were most prominent at the lower levels in the military organization, but they obviously also had positive effects at the higher levels. The operational level was mainly manifested in the corps and Army levels and benefited greatly from the qualities within the divisions. German generals such as Guderian and Rommel could conduct high-tempo operations with great flexibility because their tools—the combat units—were well trained and manned by individuals willing to take initiative. This allowed the generals to focus on the overall direction and aims rather than working on detailed plans. As always in war, various problems occurred that threatened to upset the ongoing operation, but the Germans usually overcame them thanks to local initiative. The operational commanders were often unaware of the problems that arose before they had already been solved. This was the most important German secret, and it was more difficult to replicate than the introduction of new weapons systems.

This also points at some of the German weaknesses. They focused heavily on the military aspect of conventional warfare. They were not eminent in the political, strategic and economic aspects of war.

Non-conventional warfare, such as guerrilla warfare, was poorly handled by the German armed forces. Still, the Germans hardly lost the war due to their lack of skill in dealing with irregular units. When Operation *Barbarossa* floundered, the partisan movement in the German rear areas had not yet reached a considerable scope.

Neither did traitors in other countries make much difference during the Blitzkrieg campaigns of 1939–41. The most well-known was probably Vidkun Quisling, but although he may have influenced Hitler's decision to attack Norway, he was not involved in the actual conduct of either the German planning or the actual attack.

The most fundamental factors behind the eventual German defeat were economic assets. Hitler led his country into a war against major powers that could produce weapons and field soldiers to an extent that German skill on the battlefield could not overcome in the long run. The production of tanks and aircraft is particularly illuminating, as shown by the following tables:

Table 2: Production of Combat Aircraft

	1939	1940	1941	1942	1943	1944
Germany	1,746	6,201	7,624	11,266	18,953	33,804
Italy	?	1,765	2,093	2,054	631	0
Japan	45,363 in total during the war					
USA	?	1,785	8,531	23,396	53,343	73,876
Great Britain	3,161	7,771	11,732	16,102	18,455	18,633
Soviet Union	?	8,145	12,377	21,480	29,841	33,209

Table 3: Production of Tanks

	1939	1940	1941	1942	1943	1944
Germany	743	1,743	3,701	5,245	9,179	17,483
Italy	40	250	595	1,252	336	0
Japan	?	315	595	557	558	353
USA	?	?	4,052	24,997	29,497	17,565
Great Britain	969	1,399	4,841	8,611	7,476	4,600
Soviet Union	3,110	2,666	6,274	24,693	24,006	28,933

As seen above, Britain, the Soviet Union and the United States produced four times as many tanks as did the Germans in 1941. During the following year, the Allies ramped up their production considerably and completed eleven times as many tanks as the Germans. The contributions from Japan and Italy did little to even the scales. As these two years saw the events that inevitably turned the fortunes of war against the Germans, they are particularly relevant.

It was pretty much the same story with aircraft production. Particularly illuminating is the fact that British aircraft production alone remained higher than Germany's through 1942. By then, the war had already turned decisively in favor of the Allies—not only in the factories, but also on the battlefields.

The production ratios also show that the Allies would eventually win by defeating the Germans at the fronts, where the German armed forces were gradually worn down. When Operation *Barbarossa* did not produce the Soviet collapse the Germans had expected, World War II turned into a long war of attrition. However, the basics upon which the German art of war rested proved very useful in attrition warfare too. Considering the vastly superior material resources of the Allies, the war dragged out longer than it ought to have done, and the price paid for victory was disproportionally high.

The fact that the German principles of warfare were suited to the kind of defensive war fought from 1942–45 suggests that they were not strictly connected to a particular kind of warfare. This fits well with the notion that the Germans did not develop any particular Blitzkrieg doctrine, but rather focused on developing such characteristics that were advantageous to fighting in general.

Perhaps the most important fundamental aspect of the German Army was that it emphasised war as an activity shaped by human action. Consequently, the role of the individual soldier was seen as decisive, but this did not, of course, mean that that soldiers were free to do whatever suited them. They were encouraged to use their capabilities to increase the combat power of the unit. For this purpose, they would take initiative, make decisions and act. Aims not in line with this overarching goal were unacceptable.[5]

The penchant for initiative was not only evident in field manuals or memoirs written after the war. The reports that have been the most important source for this book show innumerable examples of initiative. The willingness to take initiative was more distinctive than the practice of giving mission orders. To be sure, the importance of mission is emphasized in German manuals, but it is rather a method than the core of commanding and acting on the battlefield.[6]

As already emphasized, the German command style was not limited to the armored troops; the style permeated the entire Army, and its roots could be traced far back in time. However, it was not as prominent within the British, French, Soviet or American armies, which may explain why they did not copy the German methods. Interestingly, the Israelis seem to have adopted a style of warfare more similar to the Germans, and this included their style of command.[7]

The Panzer divisions proved important during the initial campaigns, but they were not out on their own. Infantry divisions were also given attack missions, and they usually accomplished them with merit. However, we can see that the Panzer divisions became ever more important as one campaign followed another. This trend continued after 1941, and it can probably be attributed to the greater firepower, protection and mobility of the tanks. During the last three years of the war, Panzer divisions conducted almost every significant German attack.

The emphasis on attaining great combat power was perhaps the most fundamental aspect of the German art of war, but time was also regarded as vital. One manifestation of the latter focus was the German penchant for using the night to launch surprise attacks or maneuvers. The battle at Sedan in May 1940 is a telling example.

Another important component was surprise, which could be achieved through many different means and affect the enemy in various ways. The German habit of acting rapidly was among the most important causes, but the use of new methods, deception and choice of unexpected areas to attack also figured prominently. The German efforts to surprise were mainly directed against the enemy's armed forces, which is hardly unexpected as the Germans were generally focused on conventional warfare.

It has been argued that the opponents learned from the Germans, both in terms of how the Blitzkrieg could be stopped and how they should conduct Blitzkrieg operations themselves. This is a notion that seems dubious. The Soviet armed forces were the main opponent to the Germans from the summer of 1941, and the Soviet art of war hardly resembled that of the Germans. Neither did the Soviet armed forces develop a specific method for halting the German Blitzkrieg.

From 1941 onwards, the western Allies mainly fought the Germans in theaters that were of lesser importance to the German Army. It was not until the Allied forces assaulted the beaches of Normandy on June 6, 1944 that the German Army faced a major threat from a direction other than east. However, the Red Army remained the major opponent. Nevertheless, by 1944 it had become clear that a German defeat was only a matter of time. The task facing the Allies was no longer stopping the German Blitzkrieg, but rather winning the war—and the sooner the better. However, their advance rate seems unimpressive given the circumstances.

Although the Germans' methods were not copied during the war, they exerted some influence afterwards. Many armies tried to adopt some of the German methods, but it was not easy; they required a specific philosophy, and it is difficult to introduce such changes quickly in large organizations. Therefore, it is perhaps no surprise that the Israeli Army, which was created after World War II, proved to be very adept at conducting Blitzkrieg operations.

NOTES

Chapter 1

1 For example, Fritz Sternberg used the term in the title of his book *Germany and a Lightning War*, released by Faber and Faber, London, in fall 1938.

2 See Adam Tooze, *The Wages of Destruction, The Making and Breaking of the Nazi Economy* (London: Penguin, 2007) for an excellent description of German rearmament and how it was obstructed by raw materials shortages and affected by the Great Depression.

3 For more on this, see A. J. Echevarria, *After Clausewitz, German Military Thinkers Before the Great War* (University Press of Kansas, 2001).

4 B. I. Gudmundsson, *Stormtroop Tactics—Innovation in the German Army, 1914–1918* (Westport, CT.: Praeger, 1992).

5 For more, see M. Samuels, *Command or Control? Command, Training and Tactics in the British and German Armies, 1888–1918* (London: Frank Cass, 1995); S. Leistenschneider, *Auftragstaktik im preußisch-deutschen Heer 1871 bis 1914* (Hamburg: Mittler & Sohn, 2002); D. W. Oetting, *Auftragstaktik: Geschichte und Gegenwart einer Führungskonzeption* (Frankfurt am Main: Report Verlag GmbH, 1993); and Gudmundsson, *Stormtroop Tactics*.

6 W. Murray and A. Millett, ed., *Military Innovation in the Interwar Period* (University of Cambridge Press, 1996), 36–37.

7 BA-MA RHD 487/1. In 1933, the *Führung und Gefecht der verbundenen Waffen* was replaced by a new field manual, the *Truppenführung* (see BA-MA RHD 300/1). A close reading of these two manuals reveals that the *Truppenführung* is largely a refinement of *das FuG* from 1921.

8 *Ibid.* and W. Murray and A. Millett, ed., *Military Innovation in the Interwar Period*, 37–38.

9 *Ibid.*, 47.

10 *Militärattachen i Berlin*, No. 427, Appendix 2, August 5, 1938, Fst/Und, B I, Vol. 4 (426–625), Krigsarkivet, Stockholm. It should be noted that von Fritsch mainly

argued that the commanding officer would be allowed to finish before the subordinate voiced his opinion. Von Fritsch did not promote any departure from this openness.

11 Olaf Groehler, *Selbstmörderische Allianz: deutsch-russische Militärbeziehungen 1920–1941* (Berlin: Vision Vlg., 1992).

12 *Militärwochenblatt*, No. 38, 1366, 1370, 1926; *Militärwochenblatt*, No. 28, 998f, 1926; *Militärwochenblatt* Nos. 19 and 22, 1927–28; *Militärwochenblatt* No. 18, 1926–27.

13 *Militärwochenblatt* No. 22, 1924–25, a separate supplement called *Der Kampfwagen* in January 1925 and No. 47, 1926–27.

14 *Militärwochenblatt* No. 37, 1927–28.

15 Peter Chamberlain, Hilary Doyle and Thomas Jentz, *Encyclopedia of German Tanks of World War Two* (London: Arms and Armour Press, 1978), 18.

16 For an extensive description of Beck's career, see Klaus-Jürgen Müller, *General Ludwig Beck* (Boppard am Rhein: Harald Boldt Verlag, 1980).

17 See Tooze, *The Wages of Destruction* for more on the German rearmament.

18 *Militärattachen i Berlin*, No. 454, Meddelande 94, August 26, 1938, Fst/Und, B I, Vol. 4, 426–625, Krigsarkivet, Stockholm.

19 *Ibid.*

20 Wilhelm Deist, Manfred Messerschmidt, Hans-Erich Volkmann and Wolfram Wette, *Das deutsche Reich und der Zweite Weltkrieg, Bd.* 1, 421; *OKH (Chef H Rüst u BdE) AHA/Ag/H IIa Nr 1911/41, 15.4.41*, BA-MA RH 15/205.

21 For more on this, see Roger R. Reese, *Stalin's Reluctant Soldiers* (University Press of Kansas, 1996).

22 Information on Soviet tank strength in 1941 has been gathered from A. Frankson, "Summer 1941," in *Journal of Slavic Military Studies* (September 2000), No. 3, Vol. 13, 132–137.

23 The dispute between Poland and Czechoslovakia illustrates the divisions between European countries at that time. With the benefit of hindsight, we know the result of Hitler's ambitions, but it was not so clear for the European statesmen of 1938. Hitler was far from the only threat; in Spain, a civil war raged; the Soviet Union appeared to be a menace; democracies were a minority. Hitler capitalized on the situation and managed to pursue a series of bloodless conquests.

24 Manfred Messerschmidt in A. R. Millett & W. Murray, ed., *Military Effectiveness, Vol II: The Interwar Period* (Allen & Unwin, Boston 1988), 230f.

25 *Ibid.*, 231–233.

26 J. S. Corum, "The Luftwaffe in the Spanish Civil War," in J. Gooch, ed., *Airpower—Theory and Practice* (Frank Cass, London 1995), 84f.

27 For more on this, see Williamson Murray, *The Luftwaffe 1939–45—Strategy for Defeat* (Washington, D.C.: Brassey's, 1996).

28 *Statistisk Årsbok 1938, Statistiska Centralbyrån*, Stockholm 1938.

29 See John Ellis, *Brute Force: Allied Strategy and Tactics in the Second World War* (London: Andre Deutsch, 1990), 558 for data on vehicle production.

30 Maier, Rohde, Stegemann and Umbreit, *Das deutsche Reich und der Zweite Weltkrieg,* Bd. 2 (Stuttgart: Deutsche Verlags-Anstalt, 1979), 268.

31 *Ibid.* and Chamberlain, Doyle and Jentz, *Encyclopedia of German Tanks of World War II* (London: Arms and Armour Press, 1978), 261f; S. J. Zaloga and J. Grandsen, *Soviet Tanks and Combat Vehicles of World War II* (London: Arms and Armour Press, 1984), 108, 225; Ellis, *Brute Force,* 555–558.

32 Gudmundsson, *Stormtroop Tactics,* 93–97.

33 RHD 4/300/1 (Heeresdienstvorschrift 300/1 "*Truppenführung I. Teil*" 1933), 2–4.

34 *Ibid.,* 10–11.

35 Robert A. Doughty, *The Breaking Point—Sedan and the Fall of France 1940* (Hamden: Archon, 1990), 27–30.

36 Karl-Heinz Frieser, *Blitzkrieg-Legende—Der Westfeldzug 1940* (Munich: Oldenbourg Verlag, 1996), 413f.

37 The German Army seems to have been more interested in the operational level compared to, for example, the British and US armies. On the other hand, the Red Army also placed great emphasis on the operational level. To what extent this shared interest can be attributed to the cooperation during the interwar years is unclear. Such a hypothesis may appear plausible, but the Germans had been thinking along these lines before the cooperation began, and the Red Army seems to have developed their view independently. Furthermore, their views differed on the value of initiative at lower levels.

Chapter 2

1 For more on the 1919–1920 war, see Norman Davies, *White Eagle, Red Star: the Polish-Soviet war, 1919–20* (London: Orbis, 1983).

2 For more on the Soviet military buildup, see Lennart Samuelson, *Soviet Defence Industry Planning—Tukhachevskii and Military-Industrial Mobilisation 1926–1937* (Stockholm School of Economics, Stockholm Institute of East European Economies, 1996).

3 Marco Smedberg and Niklas Zetterling, *Andra världskrigets utbrott—Hitlers anfall mot Polen 1939* (Stockholm: Norstedts, 2007), 66f.

4 *Ibid.,* 68, 101ff, 161f. Also see Herbert Schindler, *Mosty und Dirschau* (Freiburg: Rombach, 1979) for details.

5 Of 102 divisions, only fifteen were armored, light or motorized. The remaining ones were either infantry or mountain divisions. See Leo Niehorster, *German World War II Organizational Series, Vol. I* (Hannover: Leo Niehorster, 1990), 10f.

6 G. Tessin, *Verbände und Truppen der deutschen Wehrmacht und Waffen-SS* (Osnabrück: Mittler & Sohn, Frankfurt am Main und Biblio Verlag, 1966–1975); Klaus-Jürgen Thies, *Der Ostfeldzug, Heeresgruppe Mitte—Ein Lageatlas der Operationsabteilung des Generalstab des Heeres* (Bissendorf: Biblio Verlag, 2001); *AOK 10 Qu, "Truppenkrankennachweis 26.8.39–31.8.39,"* NARA T312, R79, F7600622; *AOK 10 Qu, "Truppenkrankennachweis 1.9.39–10.9.39,"* NARA T312, R79, F7600958.

7   XVI Corps, commanded by Erich Hoepner, was part of von Reichenau's army. In addition to two infantry divisions, it included two Panzer divisions—the 1st and 4th. Also, von Wietersheim's XIV Corps, with the 13th and 29th Motorized Divisions, belonged to the 10th Army. Furthermore, Hermann Hoth's XV Corps, with the 2nd and 3rd Light Divisions, was part of the 10th Army. Finally, another corps with two infantry divisions had been placed under von Reichenau's command, as well as one light division initially held in reserve. There were also two infantry divisions belonging to the OKH reserve immediately behind von Reichenau's army.

8   See Niehorster, *German World War II Organizational Series, Vol. I.*

9   Smedberg and Zetterling, *Andra världskrigets utbrott*, Chapter 6.

10 *Ibid.*, 110–112, 149–152.

11 *Ibid.*, 121–132, 162–167.

12 *Ibid.*, 152–154, 187.

13 *Ibid.*, particularly Chapter 6.

14 *Ibid.*, 110–112, 149–152, 162–167.

15 *Ibid.*, 179–182.

16 This narrative is based on the description Collin gave in his diary. See BA-MA RH 39/511. Collin commanded the 8th Company of Panzer Regiment 7, which was part of *Panzerverband Kempf* during the campaign in Poland.

17 *KTB XIX. A.K. (mot) Ia, 1.9.39*, NARA T314, R611, F606-9.

18 This narrative is based on Schroeder's description given in BA-MA M VII b 24.

19 *The Rise and Fall of the German Air Force 1933–1945* (Kew: Public Record Office, 2001), 46.

20 For more on this, see Smedberg and Zetterling, *Andra världskrigets utbrott*, 99–171.

21 *Ibid.*, 144ff.

22 *Ibid.*

23 *Ibid.*, 186–194.

24 *Ibid.*

25 *Ibid.*; *KTB 1. Krad.Sch.Btl.*, BA-MA RH 39/31.

26 *Ibid.*

27 *Ibid.*

28 BA-MA RH 39/31; *Die Aufklärungsabteilung 4 in Polen*, BA-MA MSg 2/3552.

29 *Ibid.*

30 *Ibid.*

31 *Ibid.*

32 *Ibid.*

33 *Ibid.*

34 For the T/O&E of the battalion, see Niehorster, *German World War II Organizational Series, Vol. I*, 19.

35 BA-MA RH 39/31.

36 *Ibid.*

37 *Ibid.*; Smedberg and Zetterling, *Andra världskrigets utbrott*, 172–210.

38 *Ibid.*, Chapters 9 and 15.

39 *Aus meinem im Polen geführten Notizheft (Lt. Scharnagl)*, BA-MA MSg 2/3232.

40 *Ibid.*

41 Smedberg and Zetterling, *Andra världskrigets utbrott*, 223ff; AOK 8 Ic, "Die 10. Division im polnischen Feldzuge', NARA T312, R37, F7545470ff.

42 BA-MA MSg 2/3232.

43 *Ibid.*

44 *Ibid.*

45 *Ibid.*

46 *Ibid.*

47 *Ibid.*; NARA T312, R37, F7545470ff.

48 *Ibid.*; *Aus meinen Notizen als Bataillons-Adjutant (Oberleutnant Bürger)*, BA-MA MSg 2/3232.

49 *Ibid.*

50 *Ibid.*

51 *Ibid.*

52 *Ibid.*; *Aus meinen Notizen als Bataillons-Adjutant (Oberleutnant Bürger)*, BA-MA MSg 2/3232.

53 See Smedberg and Zetterling, *Andra världskrigets utbrott*, Chapter 16.

54 *Ibid.*, Chapter 15.

55 Rüdiger Alberti, *Als Kriegspfarrer in Polen* (Leipzig: Verlag Ludwig Ungelenk, 1940).

56 *Ibid.*, 16f.

57 *Ibid.*

58 *Ibid.*, 18.

59 *Ibid.*

60 *Ibid.*

61 *Ibid.*

62 Robert M. Kennedy, *The German Campaign in Poland (1939)* (Washington, D.C.: US Army Center for Military History, Publication 104–20, US Government Printing Office, 1988), 120.

63 BA-MA H4/35.

64 Maier, Rohde, Stegemann and Umbreit, *Das deutsche Reich und der Zweite Weltkrieg*, Bd. 2, 133.

65 See file BA-MA RW 19/1933 for information on German equipment losses during the Polish campaign.

66 BA-MA RW 19/1938, Bl. 1–19.

67 Zaloga and Madej, *The Polish Campaign 1939*, 148.

68 XV Corps' war diary and annexes can be found on NARA T314, R550-552; for the war diary and annexes of XVI Corps, see NARA T314, R567-568; for the war

diary and annexes of XIX Corps, see NARA T314, R611-614; for the war diary and annexes of XXII Corps, see NARA T314, R665.

69 *Dowodztwo armii "Łódź", Sztab, L.dz. 155/1/III Op. M.p., dnia 7 wrzesnia 1939 r.godz.8-m a, Meldunek o polozeniu,* IPMS A.II 15/20, doc. 2; *Armia "Modlin' Sztab, L. 1324/3/III op., 2.IX., 00.30, Meldunek sytuacyjny wieczorny z dnia 1.IX.39,* IPMS, A.II 10/21, doc. 1.

70 Zaloga and Madej, *The Polish Campaign 1939,* 7.

71 According to Kennedy, *The German Campaign in Poland (1939),* 74, Fig. 4.

72 For more on this, see Niklas Zetterling, *Blixtkrig* (Stockholm: Försvarshögskolan, 2003) and Smedberg and Zetterling, *Andra världskrigets utbrott.*

73 See Williamson Murray, "The German Response to Victory in Poland—A Case Study in Professionalism," in *Armed Forces and Society* (Winter 1981), No. 2, Vol. 7, 285–298.

74 This is discussed in more detail in Smedberg and Zetterling, *Andra världskrigets utbrott,* particularly within Chapter 22.

75 Alexander B. Rossino, *Hitler Strikes Poland: Blitzkrieg, Ideology and Atrocity* (University Press of Kansas, 2003), 4.

76 Borodziej and Ziemer, *Deutsch-polnische Beziehungen 1939–1945–1949* (2000), 37f.

77 *Ibid.,* 71f.

Chapter 3

1 For more on the German attack on Norway, see M. Tamelander and N. Zetterling, *Den nionde april* (Lund: Historiska Media, 2000), 16–51, 61–69. For more on the German maritime strategy, see N. Zetterling and M. Tamelander, *Bismarck* (Drexel Hill, PA.: Casemate, 2009).

2 Tamelander and Zetterling, *Den nionde april,* 37–51.

3 Tamelander and Zetterling, *Den nionde april,* 41–51.

4 *Ibid.,* 41–51, 61.

5 *Ibid.,* 49–50.

6 Tamelander and Zetterling, *Den nionde april,* 61–67.

7 *Ibid.*

8 *Ibid.*

9 *Ibid.,* 61–69.

10 The story of Harald Zeller is based on *"Meine Erlebnisse bei der Besetzung Bergens,"* BA-MA MSg 2/2881. Harald Zeller is a fictitious name as the file is restricted for reasons of personal integrity.

11 *Gruppe XXI Ia Nr. 82/40 g-Kdos.Chefs., 16.3.40, Operationsbefehl für die Besetzung von Bergen,* NARA T312, R 980, F9172226-30; *Anlage 2 zu Gruppe XXI Ia (2) Nr. 38/40 g.Kdos, v. 11.3.40, Transport und Eintreffübersicht,* NARA T312, R980, F9172155. Also W. Hubatsch, *"Weserübung': die deutsche Besetzung von Dänemark und Norwegen 1940* (Göttingen: Musterschmidt Verlag, 1960).

12 'Meine Erlebnisse bei der Besetzung Bergens," BA-MA MSg 2/2881; Tamelander and Zetterling, Den nionde april, 77–79.

13 Edgar Alker, "So nahmen wir Drontheim, Steinkjer und Stören," BA-MA RH 37/6892.

14 Ibid.

15 Ibid.; Tamelander and Zetterling, Den nionde april, 76–77.

16 BA-MA RH 37/6892; Tamelander and Zetterling, Den nionde april, 76–77.

17 BA-MA RH 37/6892; Tamelander and N. Zetterling, Den nionde april, 76–77.

18 BA-MA RH 37/6892; "Gliederung, Stärken und Verteilung auf die Schiffseinheiten," BA-MA RH 37/6892; Weiss, "Erinnerungen an Norwegen 1940," 21–24, BA-MA RH 37/6892; Tamelander and Zetterling, Den nionde april, 76–77.

19 BA-MA RH 37/6892.

20 Ibid.

21 This narrative is based on Werner Boese, "Erlebnisbericht Blücher," BA-MA MSg 2/4922.

22 Ibid.; Tamelander and Zetterling, Den nionde april, 70–72, 83–87.

23 Tamelander and Zetterling, Den nionde april, 83–87.

24 Ibid., 41–56.

25 BA-MA MSg 2/4922.

26 Der Oberbefehlshaber det Luftwaffe, Führuungsstab Ic, No. 3343/40 g.Kdos (III), "Bericht über den Einsatz der Luftwaffe bei der Besetzung von Dänemark und Norwegen am 9.4.40," H.Qu., April 10, 1940, BA-MA RL 2 II/1027.

27 Tamelander and Zetterling, Den nionde april, 90–92.

28 Ibid.

29 Ibid.

30 BA-MA RL 2 II/1027; Tamelander and Zetterling, Den nionde april, 90–104.

31 Ibid., 93f, 103f.

32 Ibid., 113–119, 152–153.

33 OKW WFA Nr. 827/40 g.Kdos. Abt.L 19.4.40, NARA T312, R983, F9174915.

34 Andreas Hauge, Kampene i Norge 2 (Krigshistoriskt Forlag A.S, 1995), 113.

35 J. L. Moulton, The Norwegian Campaign of 1940 (Eyre & Spottiswoode, 1966), 169.

36 Luftwaffe Führungsstab Ia, order before the attack on Warsaw on September 17, 1939, BA-MA RL 2, II/51, 50.

37 Stellan Bojerud, "Norgefälttåget 1940—en studie i ett operativt misslyckande," in Urladdning (Stockholm: Probus förlag, 1990), 141–143.

38 Earl F. Ziemke, The German Northern Theater of Operations 1940–1945, (Department of the Army Pamphlet No. 20–271), 55–56.

39 Gruppe XXI Ia, Operationsbefehl für die Besetzung von Südnorwegen, 12.4.1940 (Mündl. Voraus 11.4 23.00 Uhr), NARA T312, R982, F9173670f.

40 I.R. 362 Ia, Unternehmen Norwegen, NARA T312, R989, F9181977-85.

41 Tamelander and Zetterling, Den nionde april, 134–141, 160–166.

42 *Gruppe Trondheim Ia, Lagebericht für die Zeit vom 22.—24.4.40, O.U., den 24.4.1940, 10.00 Uhr,* NARA T312, R983, F9175577.

43 *Gruppe XXI Ia Nr. 268/40 geh.* "*Befehl für Operationen im Raum Drontheim,*" *15.4.1940,* NARA T312, R982, F9174410.

44 *Gruppe XXI Abendmeldung 20.4.1940,* NARA T312, R982, F9173473; *Gruppe Detmold Ia, Lagemeldung für die Zeit vom 20.4 16.00 Uhr bis 21.4 17.00 Uhr,* NARA T312, R983, F9174858; *III./Geb.Jäg.Rgt. 138,* "*Gefechtsbericht Nr. 2 vom 21.4.1940,*" BA-MA RH 37/7063; *KTB III./Geb.Jäg.Rgt. 138,* 21.4.40, BA-MA RH 37/7063.

45 *Gruppe Detmold Ia,* "*Lagemeldung für die Zeit vom 20.4 16.00 Uhr bis 21.4 17.00 Uhr,*" NARA T312, R983, F9174858; *III./Geb.Jäg.Rgt. 138,* "*Gefechtsbericht Nr. 2 vom 21.4.1940,*" BA-MA RH 37/7063; *KTB III./Geb.Jäg.Rgt. 138,* 21.4.40, BA-MA RH 37/7063; P. Klatt, *Die 3. Gebirgs-Division* (Bad Nauheim: Verlag Hans-Henning Podzun, 1958), 33–37.

46 BA-MA RH 37/7063.

47 *Ibid.*

48 *Ibid.*

49 NARA T312, R983, F9174858; Tamelander and Zetterling, *Den nionde april*, 156.

50 NARA T312, R983, F9174858; Tamelander and Zetterling, *Den nionde april,* 156–157.

51 BA-MA RH 37/7063.

52 *Ibid.*

53 *Ibid.* The precise casualties suffered by the 359th Infantry Regiment have not been established, but it seems that four men were killed and ten wounded on April 22. See *Gruppe Drontheim Ia, Meldung an Gruppe XXI, 23.4.40, 09.45 Uhr,* NARA T312, R983, F9174742.

54 Until the morning of April 24, I and II Battalion (plus two platoons from the 14th Company) had arrived at Trondheim. In addition, I Battalion of the 359th Regiment had arrived, as well as around 300 men from II Battalion. Adding these units to the forces landed from the warships on April 9 gives a figure of 3,500 men. See NARA T312, R983, F9175577. With these resources, Woytasch had to face the Norwegian units in the area as well as the Allied units landed at Namsos and Aandalsnes, each amounting to around a brigade's worth.

55 *Gruppe XXI, Abendmeldung 18.4.40,* NARA T312, R982, F9173466; *Gruppe XXI, Abendmeldung 30.4.40,* NARA T312, R982, F9173502.

56 *Gruppe XXI, Morgenmeldung 4.5.40,* NARA T312, R982, F9173514.

57 *Tätigkeitsbericht der Abteilung IVa der 2. Gebirgsdivision über den Einsatz Norwegen,* NARA T315, R98, F000398.

58 *Tätigkeitsbericht der Divisionsarztes der 2. Gebirgs-Division,* NARA T315, R98, F000357.

59 NARA T315, R98, F000404.

60 *Gruppe XXI/Ia, mündl. durch Chef am 4.5 17.00 Uhr an Kdr. 2. Geb.Div. u. Kdr. 181. I.D.*, NARA T312, R1647, F000080.

61 *Gruppe XXI, Sondermeldungen vom 5.5.1940*, NARA T312, R982, F9173517.

62 *Gruppe XXI, Morgen und Abendmeldungen 7-10 maj 1940*, NARA T312, R982, F9173521ff.

63 The force that embarked *Nord-Norge* consisted of *1./Geb.Jäg.Rgt. 138*, one artillery battery and a heavy mortar squad, see *Kriegsgeschichte des I. Btl. Geb.Jäg.Rgt. 138, vom 5.3.–9.6.1940*, BA-MA RH 37/2781.

64 BA-MA RH 37/2781.

65 *Ibid.*

66 *Ibid.*

67 *Ibid.*

68 *Ibid.*

69 *Ibid.*

70 *Oberleutnant Rudolf, Gefechtsbericht des Unternehmens Wildente (7./138) vom 10.5, 16.00 Uhr bis 11.5. 03.00 Uhr*, NARA T312, R985, F9178051; *Hauptmann Holzinger, 1./138, Gefechtsbericht des Unternehmen Wildente vom 8.5.1940, 22.30 Uhr bis zum 15.5.40, 19.00 Uhr*, NARA T312, R985, F9178047ff; BA-MA RH 37/2781.

71 *Gruppe XXI, Morgenmeldung vom 12.5.1940*, T312, R982, F9173533; *Gruppe XXI, Abendmeldung vom 16.5.1940*, T312, R982, F9173543; *II./Geb.Jäg.Rgt. 137, "Vormarsch des verstärkten II./Geb.Jäg.Rgt. 137 von Trondheim—Finneidfjord (2.5— 16.5.40),"* BA-MA RH 37/7030; NARA T312, R985, F9178047ff.

72 The value of air reconnaissance is apparent from several of the sources given in the footnote above. In some cases, aerial reconnaissance was the only source of information for Sorko on the location of his own units.

73 BA-MA RH 37/7030; T. K. Derry, *The Campaign in Norway* (Sanders Phillips & Co. Ltd., 1952), 182–183; Trygve Sandvik, *Krigen i Norge 1940: Operasjonene til lands i Nord-Norge 1940 II* (Oslo: Gyldendal, 1965), 101.

74 BA-MA RH 37/7030. The company that remained at Mosjøen was *8./Geb.Jäg. Rgt. 137.* Sorko received the 7th and 8th Companies from the 136th Mountain Regiment.

75 *Ibid.*; *6./Geb.Jäg.Rgt. 137, "Bericht über den Einsatz der Schi-Stosstrupp-Kompanie,"* BA-MA RH 37/7030.

76 *II./Geb.Jäg.Rgt. 137, "Gefecht der Gruppe Sorko bei Stien—Mo am 17. und 18. Mai 1940,"* BA-MA RH 37/7030; *6./Geb.Jäg.Rgt. 137, "Bericht über den Einsatz der Schi-Stosstrupp-Kompanie,"* BA-MA RH 37/7030.

77 *II./Geb.Jäg.Rgt. 137, "Gefecht der Gruppe Sorko bei Stien—Mo am 17. und 18. Mai 1940,"* BA-MA RH 37/7030.

78 *Ibid.* The 7th Company was in the lead.

79 *Ibid.*

80 *Ibid.*
81 *Ibid.*
82 *Ibid.*
83 *Ibid.*
84 *Ibid.*
85 *6./Geb.Jäg.Rgt. 137, "Bericht über den Einsatz der Schi-Stosstrupp-Kompanie,"* BA-MA RH 37/7030.
86 *Ibid.*; *Sonderkommando Karolus, "Bericht zum Einsatz beim Vormarsch der Gruppe Sorko (16.–19.5.1940),"* BA-MA RH 37/7030.
87 *Ibid.*
88 *Ibid.*
89 *Ibid.*
90 *II./Geb.Jäg.Rgt. 137, "Gefecht der Gruppe Sorko bei Stien—Mo am 17. und 18. Mai 1940,"* BA-MA RH 37/7030.
91 *Ibid.*
92 *Ibid.*
93 *Ibid.*
94 *Ibid.*
95 *Sonderkommando Karolus, "Bericht zum Einsatz beim Vormarsch der Gruppe Sorko (16–19.5.1940),"* BA-MA RH 37/7030.
96 *Ibid.*; Sandvik, *Krigen i Norge 1940*, 102.
97 *II./Geb.Jäg.Rgt. 137, "Gefecht der Gruppe Sorko bei Stien—Mo am 17. und 18. Mai 1940,"* BA-MA RH 37/7030; *Sonderkommando Karolus, "Bericht zum Einsatz beim Vormarsch der Gruppe Sorko (16–19.5.1940),"* BA-MA RH 37/7030.
98 *II./Geb.Jäg.Rgt. 137, 'Gefecht der Gruppe Sorko bei Stien—Mo am 17. und 18. Mai 1940,"* BA-MA RH 37/7030.
99 *Ibid.*; J. Adams, *The Doomed Expedition* (London: Leo Cooper, 1989), 78.
100 Dietl was major-general when Operation *Weserübung* began, but he was promoted to lieutenant-general on May 9. For more on the fighting at Narvik, see Ziemke, *The German Northern Theater of Operations 1940–1945*, 87–104; Tamelander and Zetterling, *Den nionde april*, 79ff, 123ff, 199–272; A. Buchner, *Narvik, Die Kämpfe der Gruppe Dietl im Frühjahr 1940* (Neckargemünd: Kurt Vowinkel Verlag, 1958): *KTB Nr. 2 der 3. Geb.Div. (Gruppe Narvik) 6.4.40–10.6.40*, NARA T315, R174.
101 *Ibid.*
102 *Ibid.*
103 *Ibid.*
104 *I./Fallschirm-Jäger.Rgt. 1, "Einsatzbericht Narvik,"* BA-MA RL 33/37.
105 The description is based on *Stabsfeldwebel Fritz Scheuering, "Als Fallschirmjäger nach Narvik,"* BA-MA MSg 2/4032.
106 BA-MA RL 33/37; BA-MA MSg 2/4032.

107 Tamelander and Zetterling, *Den nionde april*, 241–244.

108 Ziemke, *The German Northern Theater of Operations 1940–1945*, 99–104.

109 *Erfahrungsbericht Gruppe XXI, 7.10.40*, NARA T312, R986, F9178783, 28f.

110 *Anlage zu 3. Geb.Div. Ia Nr. 241/40 geh. 16.7.40, Erfahrungsbericht*, NARA T312, R986, F9179062, 5–7.

111 NARA T312, R986, F9178783, 28f; NARA T312, R986, F9179062, 5-7.

112 James S. Corum, "The German Campaign in Norway 1940 as a Joint Operation," *Journal of Strategic Studies* (Vol 21.4, 1998), 50–77.

113 Tamelander and Zetterling, *Den nionde april*, 130–133, 163–183, 201–233, 231–241.

114 *Ibid.*, 130–133, 201–233, 231–241, 246–249. File RH 30/7 at *Bundersarchiv-Militärarchiv* contains a report on the actions fought by Group Feurstein in Norway.

115 Hans-Adolf Jacobsen, *Kriegstagebuch des Oberkommandos der Wehrmacht (Wehrmachtführungsstab) Bd. I* (Frankfurt am Main: Bernard & Graefe, 1965), 1166.

116 Adams, *The Doomed Expedition*, 175.

117 *Ibid.*

118 Hauge, *Kampene i Norge 2*, 296.

119 Hans-Martin Ottmer, *Weserübung* (Munich: Oldenburg Verlag, 1994), 145.

120 Francois Kersuady, *Norway 1940* (Bison Books, 1998), 225.

Chapter 4

1 Frieser, *Blitzkrieg-Legende*, 71ff.

2 Murray, "The German Response to Victory in Poland—A Case Study in Professionalism," 285–298.

3 *Ibid.*

4 *XV. AK. "Erfahrungsbericht über den Feldzug in Polen,"* NARA T314, R550, F298; *XV. AK. "Erfahrungsbericht,"* NARA T314, R551, F604. The fire damage to one of the reports resulted from a fire at the military history department of the German Army caused by an air raid in February 1942.

5 See Smedberg and Zetterling, *Andra världskrigets utbrott*, Chapters 11, 14 and 18. For the T/O&E of the German mechanized units in Poland, see Niehorster, *German World War II Organizational Series, Vol. I*.

6 *XV. AK., "Erfahrungen auf taktischem Gebiet,"* NARA T314, R550, F301.

7 For more on this issue, I recommend Alan R. Millett and Williamson Murray, *Military Effectiveness, Vol. II: The Interwar Period* (London: Allen & Unwin, 1988) and Robert A. Doughty, *The Breaking Point*.

8 Frieser, *Blitzkrieg-Legende*, 71ff.

9 *Ibid.*

10 *Ibid.*

11 *Ibid.*

12 *Ibid.*, 71ff.

13 An extensive report on the preparations and conduct of the attack on Eben-Emael can be found in file B-MA RL 33/97.

14 Frieser, *Blitzkrieg-Legende*, 71ff; Millett and Murray, *Military Effectiveness, Vol. II*, 241.

15 Frieser, *Blitzkrieg-Legende*, 71–135.

16 For force ratios, see Table 1. In 1940, Britain produced 7,771 combat aircraft and 1,399 tanks, which can be compared to the German production of 6,201 combat aircraft and 1,743 tanks. British production increased to 11,732 combat aircraft and 4,841 tanks in 1941. The Germans lagged behind at 7,642 combat aircraft and 3,701 tanks. The French capacity has to be added to this, emphasizing the German disadvantage. See Chamberlain, Doyle and Jentz, *Encyclopedia of German Tanks of World War II*, 261f and Ellis, *Brute Force*, 555–558 for production data.

17 *Erlebnisse der 3. Kompanie, Panzer-Regiment 35 im Westen von Hauptfeldwebel Hilpert*, BA-MA RH 39/373.

18 *Ibid.*; Neumann, *Die 4. Panzer-Division 1938–1943* (Bonn: Joachim Neumann, 1985), 98–107.

19 *XI. Fliegerkorps, Abteilung Ic, Br.B.Nr. 579/42 g.Kdos., 13.März 1942, "Abschriften von Unterlagen, Berichten und Schriftstücken zum Einsatz Eben-Emael und Albert-Kanal der Sturmabteilung Koch' (Versuchsabteilung Friedrichshafen)*, BA-MA RL 33/97.

20 Maier, Rohde, Stegemann and Umbreit, *Des deutsche Reich und der zweite Weltkrieg*, 284ff.

21 Frieser, *Blitzkrieg-Legende*, 119.

22 Wolfgang Paul, *Brennpunkte—Die Geschichte der 6. Panzerdivision (1. leichte)* (Krefeld: Höntges, 1977), 58ff; Frieser, *Blitzkrieg-Legende*, 271ff.

23 *Ibid.*

24 *Ibid.*

25 *Ibid.*

26 *Ibid.*

27 *Ibid.*, 273.

28 *KTB 11./Pz.Gren.Rgt. 4*, BA-MA RH 37/7515; *KTB und Anlagen II./Pz.Gren. Rgt. 4*, BA-MA RH 37/10; Paul, *Brennpunkte*, 60ff; Frieser, *Blitzkrieg-Legende*, 273–277.

29 *Ibid.*

30 *Ibid.* For the T/O&E of the 6th Panzer Division, see Niehorster, *German World War II Organizational Series, Vol. II*, 17ff.

31 BA-MA RH 37/7515.

32 *Ibid.*

33 *Ibid.*

34 *Ibid.*; Paul, *Brennpunkte*, 61f.

35 BA-MA RH 37/7515; Paul, *Brennpunkte*, 61f; Frieser, *Blitzkrieg-Legende*, 274.

36 Paul, *Brennpunkte*, 62–63.

37 *Ibid.*, 62–63.

38 This section is based on the war diary and appendices of *II./Pz.Gren.Rgt. 4*, BA-MA RH 37/10.

39 BA-MA RH 37/10; Paul, *Brennpunkte*, 66f.

40 Paul, *Brennpunkte*, 67f.

41 Frieser, *Blitzkrieg-Legende*, 275.

42 Frieser, *Blitzkrieg-Legende*, 275–294.

43 Jeffery A. Gunsburg, "The Battle of Gembloux, 14–15 May 1940: The 'Blitzkrieg' Checked," in *Journal of Military History* (January 2000), 97–140.

44 *Ibid.*, 100–102; Neumann, *Die 4. Panzer-Division 1938–1943*, 112–115.

45 BA-MA RH 39/373; Neumann, *Die 4. Panzer-Division 1938–1943*, 102–109.

46 BA-MA RH 39/373; Neumann, *Die 4. Panzer-Division 1938–1943*, 102–111. Hilpert mentions a village named "Jenruville," but no village with such a name can be found on the maps. He most likely meant Jandrenouille. There is no other alternative resembling "Jenruville."

47 BA-MA RH 39/373; Neumann, *Die 4. Panzer-Division 1938–1943*, 102–109; *KTB XVI. A.K. Ia, 13.5.40*, NARA T314, R569, F000391ff.

48 *Ibid.*

49 *Ibid.*; BA-MA RH 39/373; Neumann, *Die 4. Panzer-Division 1938–1943*, 102–109.

50 *Ibid.*

51 *Ibid.*, 122, 174f.

52 BA-MA RH 39/373.

53 Gunsburg, "The Battle of Gembloux, 14-15 May 1940," 138–139.

54 Frieser, *Blitzkrieg-Legende*, 51.

55 *Ibid.*, 292ff; Russel H. S. Stolfi, *A Bias for Action: The German 7th Panzer Division in France and Russia 1940–1941* (Quantico, VA.: Marine Corps Association, 1991), 11–17.

56 *Ibid.*; *KTB II./Pz.Rgt. 25*, BA-MA RH 39/753.

57 Anton Detlev von Plato, *Die Geschichte der 5. Panzerdivision* (Regensburg: Walhalla und Praetoria, 1978), 53–60; Frieser, *Blitzkrieg-Legende*, 294f; BA-MA RH 39/753; Stolfi, *A Bias for Action*, 11–17.

58 von Plato, *Die Geschichte der 5. Panzerdivision*, 57.

59 *Ibid.*

60 *Ibid.*

61 *Ibid.*

62 *Ibid.*

63 Frieser, *Blitzkrieg-Legende*, 295f.

64 *Ibid.*

65 von Plato, *Die Geschichte der 5. Panzerdivision*, 58f.

66 *Ibid.*

67 *Ibid.*

68 *Ibid.*

69 *Ibid.*

70 Frieser, *Blitzkrieg-Legende*, 188f, 194–197. For more on the German air support during the operation, see *Luftwaffe Lageberichten*, BA-MA RL 2 II/205; a report on experiences of cooperation between the Luftwaffe and Panzer Group Kleist can be found in BA-MA RH 21-2/83; *VIII. Fliegerkorps im Frankreich-Feldzug*, BA-MA RL 8/43.

71 *Ibid.*, 222–225.

72 Frieser, *Blitzkrieg-Legende*, 197–206.

73 *Ibid.*, 206–211.

74 Doughty, *The Breaking Point*, 324–332; Frieser, *Blitzkrieg-Legende*, 226–232.

75 Doughty, *The Breaking Point*, 202ff, 329f; Frieser, *Blitzkrieg-Legende*, 213ff; Hermann Balck, *Ordnung im Chaos* (Onsbabrück: Biblio Verlag, 1981), 269–279.

76 Doughty, *The Breaking Point*, 239ff; Frieser, *Blitzkrieg-Legende*, 216–220.

77 RHD 4/300/1 (*Heeresdienstvorschrift 300/1 'Truppenführung I. Teil' 1933*), 10–11.

78 Frieser, *Blitzkrieg-Legende*, 240–242, 315–317.

79 *Ibid.*, 316–317.

80 *Ibid.*, 316–318.

81 *Ibid.*, 318–324, 339–341.

82 *Ibid.*, 331–341.

83 *Ibid.*, 341–361; Stolfi, *A Bias for Action*, 35–37.

84 Frieser, *Blitzkrieg-Legende*, 359–365.

85 *Ibid.*, 365–379.

86 The description of this episode is based on BA-MA RH 39/753; *Gefechtsbericht 7. Pz.Div. 5.6.40*, NARA T315, R401, F716ff.

87 *KTB 2. Pz.Div. Ia, 9.6.40*, NARA T315, R92, F000647ff.

88 *Ibid.*

89 This entire narrative is based on NARA T315, R92, F000647ff; *Pz.Rgt. 3, Gefechtsbericht des Regiments vom 10.6.40*, BA-MA RH 39/653.

90 NARA T315, R92, F000647ff; BA-MA RH 39/653; *Verlustliste vom 5.6 bis einschl. 8.7.40 des Divisionsarzt 2. Pz.Div.*, NARA T315, R92, F678.

91 NARA T315, R92, F000647ff.

92 Frieser, *Blitzkrieg-Legende*, 64.

93 Ferdinand Otto Miksche, *Blitzkrieg* (London: Faber & Faber, 1941), 34.

94 Frieser, *Blitzkrieg-Legende*, 403.

95 For an excellent discussion on this, see Robert A. Doughty, *The Breaking Point— Sedan and the fall of France 1940* (Hamden: Archon, 1990), particularly 3–4 and 323–324.

96 Frieser, *Blitzkrieg-Legende*, 400.

97 *OKW/WiRüAmt*, BA-MA RW 19/1938, 1–19.

98 Jean-Paul Pallud, *Blitzkrieg in the West* (London: After the Battle, 1991), 607–609.
99 BA-MA H4/35.
100 Pallud, *Blitzkrieg in the West*, 607–609.
101 Doughty, *The Breaking Point*, 2–3.
102 Frieser, *Blitzkrieg-Legende*, 216–220.
103 An example is the 4th Panzer Division at Mokra on September 1, 1939, when retreating German tanks were mistakenly assumed to be advancing Polish vehicles by German infantry. The latter then panicked. See Smedberg and Zetterling, *Andra världskrigets utbrott*, 150f.
104 Frieser, *Blitzkrieg-Legende*, 431f.
105 *Ibid.*, 409–10.

Chapter 5

1 The Armed Forces Academy (*Wehrmachtakademie*) was instituted to train officers for inter-service operations. However, it would be short-lived. Few records have survived, but what remains can be found at section RW13 at *Bundesarchiv-Militärarchiv*, Freiburg.
2 For more on this, see M. van Creveld, *Supplying War* (Cambridge University Press, 1977), particularly Chapter 8.
3 The chief of the general staff, Franz Halder, noted the following in his diary (Vol. III, 48, July 6, 1941) after a meeting with General Gause on the situation in north Africa: "The personal relations are bleak owing to Rommel's character and his morbid ambitiousness. The kind of intimate relations sought for has not appeared. His defective character is clear, but nobody dare oppose him due to his brutal methods and his support from the top."
4 See *Einsatz Kreta, XI. Fliegerkorps*, BA-MA RH 20-7/124.
5 For more on the fighting on Crete, see I. G. Stewart, *The Struggle for Crete* (Oxford University Press, 1991). For British warship losses, see D. Brown, *Warship Losses of World War II* (London: Arms and Armour Press, 1990), 46–47.
6 Stewart, *The Struggle for Crete*, 475–476.
7 For more on this, see Ian Kershaw, *Fateful Choices* (New York: Penguin, 2007), Chapter 2.

Chapter 6

1 Frankson, "Summer 1941," 132–137.
2 Boog, Förster, Hoffmann, Klink, Müller and Ueberschär, *Der Angriff auf die Sowjetunion* (Frankfurt am Main: Schiffer, 1991), 359–363; Frieser, *Blitzkrieg-Legende*, 54–59.
3 Tessin, *Verbände und Truppen der deutschen Wehrmacht und Waffen-SS* (Osnabrück: Mittler & Sohn, Frankfurt am Main und Biblio Verlag, 1966–1975).
4 Frieser, *Blitzkrieg-Legende*, 44; Niehorster, *German World War II Organizational Series, Vol. III.*

5   This section is based on Hermann Türk's diary, BA-MA MSg 2/5354.

6   Boog, Förster, Hoffmann, Klink, Müller and Ueberschär, *Der Angriff auf die Sowjetunion*, 736–740, 832 (note 748).

7   *Ibid.*

8   N. Zetterling and A. Frankson, "Analyzing World War II East Front Battles," in *Journal of Slavic Military Studies* (March 1998), No. 1, Vol. 11, 193–194.

9   Boog, Förster, Hoffmann, Klink, Müller and Ueberschär, *Der Angriff auf die Sowjetunion*, 549; Grigori F. Krivosheev, *Grif Sekretnosti Sniat* (Moscow: Voenizdat 1993), 368.

10 Boog, Förster, Hoffmann, Klink, Müller and Ueberschär, *Der Angriff auf die Sowjetunion*, 574; Krivosheev, *Grif Sekretnosti Sniat*, 164, 368.

11 *KTB PzAOK 2 Ia*, NARA T313, R80, F7318479ff.

12 *KTB 4. Pz.Div. Ia*, NARA T315, R195, F468f.

13 *Panzer-Regiment 35 Abt. Ia, Bericht über Einsatz Staryi Bychoff, Rgts.Gef.Stand, den 4.7.1941, 20,00 Uhr.*, BA-MA RH 39/689.

14 For data on the German radio equipment fitted to tanks, see Chamberlain, Doyle and Jentz, *Encyclopedia of German Tanks of World War Two*, 254.

15 BA-MA RH 39/689.

16 *Ibid.*

17 *Ibid.*

18 *Ibid.*

19 *Ibid.*; *KTB 4. Pz.Div. Ia*, NARA T315, R195, F470.

20 *KTB Pz.Gruppe 2 Ia, 4-10 juli 1941*, NARA T313, R80, F7318508-8583.

21 Stolfi, *A Bias for Action*, 49–75; Thies, *Der Ostfeldzug, Heeresgruppe Mitte*, 7–20. Hoth's four Panzer divisions had 1,014 tanks, which can be compared to the 953 that the five Panzer divisions that Guderian's Panzer group possessed. See Niehorster, *German World War II Organizational Series, Vol. III*, 33.

22 Rolf Hinze, *19. Infanteri. und Panzer-Division* (Meerbusch: Verlag Rolf Hinze, 1997), 139–144; Thies, *Der Ostfeldzug, Heeresgruppe Mitte*, 7–20.

23 This narrative is based on *Gefechtsbericht über den Angriff der I. Abteilung (2. Komp) auf Peremerka am 7.7.1941*, BAMA RH 39/588.

24 Neumann, *Die 4. Panzer-Division 1938–1943*, 209–212, 225; *Oberleutnant Krause, 3./Pz.Rgt. 35, "'Bericht der 3. Kompanie über den Kampf bei Ryshkowka am 12.7.1941," Im Feld, den 22.Juli 1941*, BA-MA RH 39/743; *KTB 4. Pz.Div. Ia, 12.7.41*, NARA T315, R195, F463ff, 38–41.

25 This narrative is based on BA-MA RH 39/743.

26 NARA T315, R195, F463ff, 38–41.

27 Of course, it is conceivable that German ground units deliberately refrained from mentioning Luftwaffe efforts due to, for example, inter-service rivalry. However, this seems quite unlikely as air attacks often significantly impacted on how and when ground units acted. Air attacks usually affected attack directions, timing,

pauses and other matters that had to be discussed in the reports. It seems more likely that the Army unit reports would have played down the effects of the air attack, had they wished to do so, than pretended that they did not occur.

28 *KTB 4. Pz.Div. Ia, 17.7.41,* NARA T315, R195, F463ff, 58.

29 Erich von Manstein, *Verlorene Siege* (Bonn: Athenäum, 1955), 172ff; Boog, Förster, Hoffmann, Klink, Müller and Ueberschär, *Der Angriff auf die Sowjetunion,* 551–555.

30 Thies, *Der Ostfeldzug, Heeresgruppe Mitte,* 24–25.

31 Boog, Förster, Hoffmann, Klink, Müller and Ueberschär, *Der Angriff auf die Sowjetunion,* 541–574.

32 *Halder KTB, August 11, 1941,* 170; *Boevoy Sostav Sovetskoy Armii, chast I* (East View Publications).

33 Thies, *Der Ostfeldzug, Heeresgruppe Mitte,* 25–27; *Boevoy Sostav Sovetskoy Armii, chast I.*

34 Thies, *Der Ostfeldzug, Heeresgruppe Mitte,* 27–46.

35 *Ibid.; Halder KTB,* 106.

36 *Halder KTB,* 151.

37 This section is based on Georg Hoffmann's diary, BA-MA MSg 2/4539.

38 BA-MA, RH 2/1326, 231.

39 *KTB 4. Pz.Div. Ia, 21.7.41,* NARA T315, R195, F512.

40 Boog, Förster, Hoffmann, Klink, Müller and Ueberschär, *Der Angriff auf die Sowjetunion,* 586.

41 This section is based on *Rudolf Ruyter, Uffz., Stab I./Pz.Rgt. 35, "Ich fuhr in der I—Staffel, juni—Okt. 41," den 5.3.1942,* BA-MA MSg 2/4391.

42 Ruyter does not indicate any date, but another report describing the action suggests that September 9 is the most likely. See *5. Panzer-Brigade, "Gefechtsbericht für die Zeit vom 1.9.—5.9.1941,"* BA-MA RH 39/373. Despite its heading, the report also describes the actions fought on September 6–10.

43 For more on this, see *German Tank Maintenance in World War II* (Washington, D.C.: Center of Military History, US Army, 1988).

44 *Ibid.* See file BA-MA RH 2/1326 for information on the number of tanks in workshops.

45 BA-MA RH 2/1326.

46 German tank losses have been derived from BA-MA RH 2/1326, Soviet losses from Krivosheyev, *Grif Sekrenosti Sniat,* 368.

47 For more on the German siege of Leningrad, see Johannes Hürter, *"Die Wehrmacht vor Leningrad, Krieg und Besatzungspolitik der 18. Armee im Herbst und Winter 1941/42,"* in *Vierteljahrshefte für Zeitgeschichte* (July 2001).

48 H. Guderian, *Panzer Leader* (London: Futura, 1982), 196–205. See also *KTB Pz.Gruppe 2 Ia 21 August–26 August,* NARA T313, R86, F7326497ff.

49 This case can be compared to the battle in the Ardennes during December 1944, when US General Patton became famous for having switched three divisions on

short notice. These divisions (the 4th Armored, 26th Infantry and 80th Infantry) had been held in reserve for weeks. They received orders to redeploy on December 19, three days after the German offensive had been launched. On December 20, they assembled near Arlon and Luxembourg. They did not enter battle until December 22. They traveled a distance not exceeding 200 km (as the crow flies) through a well-known area with a better road network than could be found in Russia, encountering scant resistance. Compared to Guderian's change of direction in August 1941, this does not appear particularly impressive.

50 *KTB Pz.Gruppe 2 Ia, 22.8.1941*, NARA T313, R86, F7326496.

51 *KTB Pz.Gruppe 2 Ia, 21.8.1941*, NARA T313, R86, F7326486f.

52 *KTB Pz.Gruppe 2 Ia, 26.8.1941–7.9.1941*, NARA T313, R86, F7326528ff.

53 *KTB Pz.Gruppe 2 Ia, 8.9.1941–12.9.1941*, NARA T313, R86, F7326658ff.

54 *Ibid.*

55 Thies, *Der Ostfeldzug, Heeresgruppe Mitte*, 79–80.

56 *KTB Pz.Gruppe 2 Ia, 13.9.1941–15.9.1941*, NARA T313, R86, F7326705ff; Thies, *Der Ostfeldzug, Heeresgruppe Mitte*, 80–83; Boog, Förster, Hoffmann, Klink, Müller and Ueberschär, *Der Angriff auf die Sowjetunion*, 595–603; Guderian, *Panzer Leader*, 216–225 for precise data on the number of prisoners.

57 *KTB PzGruppe 2 Ia, 27.9.41*, NARA T313, R86, F7326837.

58 5. *Panzer-Brigade*, "Gefechtsbericht für die Zeit vom 29.9.–3.10.1941', O.U. 5.10.1941, BA-MA RH 39/373; 4. *Panzer-Division*, "Gefechtsbericht der 4. Panzer-Division für die Zeit vom 29.9.–6.10.1941," Div.Gef.Stand, 8.10.1941, BA-MA RH 39/373; Thies, *Der Ostfeldzug, Heeresgruppe Mitte*, 92–95.

59 5. *Panzer-Brigade*, "Gefechtsbericht für die Zeit vom 29.9.–3.10.1941," O.U. 5.10.1941, BA-MA RH 39/373; 4. *Panzer-Division*, "Gefechtsbericht der 4. Panzer-Division für die Zeit vom 29.9.–6.10.1941," Div.Gef.Stand, 8.10.1941, BA-MA RH 39/373.

60 *Ibid.* A large number of after-action reports from Eberbach's battle group can be found in file BA-MA RH 39/373, covering the period of August–December 1941. Rarely is any air support mentioned, which is a significant observation as Eberbach's battle group was often allotted very important missions.

61 5. *Panzer-Brigade*, "Gefechtsbericht für die Zeit vom 29.9.–3.10.1941," O.U. 5.10.1941, BA-MA Rh 39/373; 4. *Panzer-Division*, "Gefechtsbericht der 4. Panzer-Division für die Zeit vom 29.9.-6.10.1941," Div.Gef.Stand, 8.10.1941, BA-MA Rh 39/373.

62 *Ibid.*; Thies, *Der Ostfeldzug, Heeresgruppe Mitte*, 95.

63 'Ein Erlebnis beim Angriff auf Orel' von H. Schöffel, Münchberg, BA-MA RH 39/373.

64 For more on the German attack on Warsaw on September 9, 1939, see Smedberg and Zetterling, *Andra världskrigets utbrott*, 205–210.

65 'Ein Erlebnis beim Angriff auf Orel' von H. Schöffel, Münchberg, BA-MA RH 39/373.

66 *Ibid.*

67 *Ibid.*

68 *Ibid.*

69 *Ibid.*

70 *Ibid.*

71 5. *Panzer-Brigade, "Gefechtsbericht für die Zeit vom 29.9.-3.10.194," O.U. 5.10.1941,* BA-MA RH 39/373; 4. *Panzer-Division, "Gefechtsbericht der 4. Panzer-Division für die Zeit vom 29.9.–6.10.1941," Div.Gef.Stand, 8.10.1941,* BAMA RH 39/373.

72 5. *Panzer-Brigade, "Gefechtsbericht für die Zeit vom 29.9.–3.10.1941," O.U. 5.10.1941,* BA-MA RH 39/373.

73 Thies, *Der Ostfeldzug, Heeresgruppe Mitte,* 92–95.

74 *Gen.Kdo. XXXX. Panzerkorps Abt. Ic Br.B.Nr: 1831/41g., "Feindnachrichtenblatt Nr. 5," 1.10.1941,* BA-MA RH 39/99; *Gen.Kdo. XXXX. Panzerkorps Abt. Ic Br.B.Nr: 1825/41g., "Feindnachrichtenblatt Nr. 3," 1.10.1941,* BA-MA RH 39/99.

75 *KTB Pz.Rgt. 7 Ia,* BA-MA RH 39/99; *KTB 10. Pz.Div. Ia,* NARA T315, R561, F731ff.

76 *Ibid.*

77 *Ibid.*

78 *Ibid;* II./*Pz.Rgt. 7 Ia, Bericht über den Vorstoß der Abteilung vom 2. bis 7.10.1941, 9. oktober 1941,* BA-MA RH 39/99; Thies, *Der Ostfeldzug, Heeresgruppe Mitte,* 92–95.

79 *KTB Pz.Rgt. 7 Ia,* BA-MA RH 39/99; I./*Pz.Rgt. 7 Ia, Gefechtsbericht vom 2.10– 7.10.41, Abt. Gef.Stnd, den 9.10.41,* BA-MA RH 39/99; II./*Pz.Rgt. 7 Ia, Bericht über den Vorstoß der Abteilung vom 2. bis 7.10.1941, 9. oktober 1941,* BAMA RH 39/99.

80 *Ibid.*

81 *Ibid.* The 10th Panzer Division war diary (*KTB 10. Pz.Div. Ia,* 2.20.42, 08.05 *Uhr,* NARA T315, R561, F751ff) shows that the commander of the XXXX Panzer Corps, to which the 10th Panzer Division was subordinated, was present at the 10th Panzer Division's command post on the morning of October 2 and requested air support to halt Soviet reinforcements moving up via rail. Nothing more on air support is mentioned in the detailed war diary of the 10th Panzer Division. It does, however, show that communications with the lead elements were poor at this stage. It seems most plausible that the Stuka aircraft were committed independently to attack targets in the depth of the Soviet defenses and by chance happened to find the Soviet artillery and attack it.

82 *KTB Pz.Rgt. 7 Ia,* BA-MA RH 39/99; I./*Pz.Rgt. 7 Ia, Gefechtsbericht vom 2.10– 7.10.41, Abt. Gef.Stnd, den 9.10.41,* BA-MA RH 39/99; II./*Pz.Rgt. 7 Ia, Bericht über den Vorstoß der Abteilung vom 2. bis 7.10.1941, 9. oktober 1941,* BAMA RH 39/99.

83 *Ibid.*

84 *Ibid.*

85 *KTB 10. Pz.Div. Ia, 3.10.41,* NARA T315, R561, F770ff.

86 *Ibid.*

87 *Ibid.*; Thies, *Der Ostfeldzug, Heeresgruppe Mitte*, 94–97.

88 *KTB Pz.Rgt.* 7 Ia, BA-MA RH 39/99; *I./Pz.Rgt.* 7 Ia, *Gefechtsbericht vom 2.10-7.10.41, Abt. Gef.Stnd, den 9.10.41*, BA-MA RH 39/99; *II./Pz.Rgt.* 7 Ia, *Bericht über den Vorstoß der Abteilung vom 2. bis 7.10.1941, 9. oktober 1941*, BAMA RH 39/99.

89 *Ibid.*

90 *Der Oberbefelshaber der Heeresgruppe Mitte, Tagesbefehl, H.Qu., 19.10.1941*, BA-MA RH 19II/124.

91 E. F. Ziemke and M. E Bauer, *Moscow to Stalingrad* (New York: Military Heritage Press, 1988), 36–37 and M. Parrish, *Battle for Moscow—The 1942 Soviet General Staff Study* (Washington, D.C.: Pergamon-Brassey's, 1989), 203.

92 Thies, *Der Ostfeldzug, Heeresgruppe Mitte*, 94–97.

93 In the period of October 1–20, Army Group Center reported 57,363 killed, wounded and missing in action (*Wehrmacht Verlustwesen*, BA-MA RW 6/v. 556).

94 Thies, *Der Ostfeldzug, Heeresgruppe Mitte*, 97–98.

95 *Ibid.*; *Gefechtsbericht der I. Abteilung, Vorstoss auf Malojaroslawez am 17.10.1941*, BA-MA RH 39/588.

96 *Gefechtsbericht der I. Abteilung, Vorstoß auf Malojaroslawez, Protwa-Brücken und Worabji am 18.10.1941*, BA-MA RH 39/588; *Gefechtsbericht der I. Abteilung, Vorstoß am 18.10.1941 auf Malojaroslawez, Inbesitznehmen der Brücken an der Protwa und Bildung eines Brückenkopfes nordostw. Worabji*, BA-MA RH 39/588.

97 *Ibid.*

98 *Ibid.*

99 *Ibid.*

100 *Ibid.*

101 *Ibid.*

102 *Ibid.*

103 *Ibid.*

104 *Ibid.*

105 *Ibid.*

106 *Ibid.*

107 Rolf Hintze, *19. Infanterie-und Panzer-Division* (Düsseldorf: Rolf Hinze, 1997), 215–231.

108 *Ibid.*

109 Personal diary from *3./Sch.Rgt. 395*, BA-MA MSg 2/5353; Thies, *Der Ostfeldzug, Heeresgruppe Mitte*, 101.

110 This section is based on a personal diary from *3./Sch.Rgt. 395*, BA-MA MSg 2/5353.

111 *KTB Franz Halder*, Vol. III, 286.

112 *Pz.Rgt. 7, Regimentsarzt, "Bericht über den bei Lyskowa eingerichteten Rgts.-Verbandsplatz," O.U. 12.11.41*, BA-MA RH 39/99.

113 *Ibid.*

114 *Ibid.*

115 *Ibid.*

116 Guderian, *Panzer Leader*, 233ff.

117 According to *Anlagen zum Tätigkeitsbericht der Abt IIa & IIb der KTB des Pz. Gruppe 2*, BA-MA RH 21-2/v.756, the 3rd Panzer Division suffered 5,333 casualties from June 22 to November 22 and received 3,079 replacements.

118 This section is based on Hermann Türk's diary, MSg 2/5354.

119 Thies, *Der Ostfeldzug, Heeresgruppe Mitte*, 98–108.

120 For more on this, see van Creveld, *Supplying War*, Chapter 5.

121 *Schützen-Rgt. 40, Rgt.-Arzt, "Bericht über das Absetzen vom Feind in der Zeit vom 1.–26.12.41,"* BA-MA RH 37/7146.

122 *Ibid.*; Thies, *Der Ostfeldzug, Heeresgruppe Mitte*, 107.

123 BA-MA RH 37/7146.

124 *Ibid.*

125 *Ibid.*

126 *Ibid.*

127 *Ibid.*

128 For more on this, see Hans-Joachim Lorbeer, *Westmächte gegen die Sowjetunion 1939–1941* (Freiburg: Rombach, 1975).

129 Earl F. Ziemke in Millett and Murray, ed., *Military Effectiveness, Vol. II*, 14.

130 In June and July 1941, the first forty days of Operation *Barbarossa*, the Germans recorded 213,301 killed, wounded and missing (see *Wehrmacht Verlustwesen*, BA-MA RW 6/v.552). This can be compared to the casualties suffered during the campaign in the west, which amounted to 156,492 (see Pallud, *Blitzkrieg in the West*, 607–609). Considering that very little fighting took place during the final week of the campaign in the west and larger forces were involved in Operation *Barbarossa*, the casualty rates counted as losses per division and week were comparable.

131 See *Pz. Gruppe 2 IIa Verlustmeldungen*, BA-MA RH 21-2/757 for the 4th Panzer Division's casualties in 1941. Neumann, *Die 4. Panzer-Division 1938–1943*, 174 shows the losses sustained by the 4th Panzer Division during the campaign in 1940.

132 The German casualties on the eastern front in 1941 amounted to 831,0505 (see *Wehrmacht Verlustwesen*, BA-MA RW 6/v.552). Krivosheev shows that the Red Army lost 4,473,820 men in 1941 (Krivosheyev, *Grif Sekretnosti Sniat*, 146f). However, there are reasons to suspect that the latter figure may be too low. See Boris V. Sokolov, "The Cost of War: Human Losses for the USSR and Germany, 1939–1945," in *Journal of Slavic Military Studies* (March 1996), No. 1, Vol. 11; Zetterling and Frankson, "Analyzing World War II East Front Battles."

Chapter 7

1   The notion that the Germans had revolutionized warfare by adopting new technology was advanced in the 1990s as an argument for the trend known as "Revolution in Military Affairs." This was a misunderstanding that was unsupported by military history. For more on this, see Stephen Biddle, "The Past as Prologue: Assessing Theories of Future Warfare," in *Security Studies* (Fall 1998), No. 1, Vol. 8, 1–74.

2   While working on this book, I went through many reports and war diaries. The pattern that emerged was fewer complaints about friendly-fire incidents and more comments on effective cooperation as the Germans gained experience. Also, two articles by Joel Hayward may be worth reading: "A Case Study in Early Joint Warfare: An Analysis of the *Wehrmacht's* Crimean Campaign of 1942," in *Journal of Strategic Studies* (December 1999) and "Von Richthofen's 'Giant fire-magic': The Luftwaffe's Contribution to the Battle of Kerch, 1942," in *Journal of Slavic Military Studies* (June 1997).

3   For more on the German development before World War I, see Robert M. Citino, *The German Way of War* (University of Kansas Press, 2005).

4   See also Doughty, *The Breaking Point*, 323.

5   Millett and Murray, *Military Effectiveness, Vol. II*, 244. See also Martin van Creveld, *Fighting Power* (Westpoint, CT.: Greenwood Press, 1982) for more on this.

6   For more on this, see Niklas Zetterling, "*Ledning genom uppdragstaktik*," in *Kungliga Krigsvetenskapsakademins Handlingar och Tidskrift* (May 1995) and "*Uppdragstaktik och tidsfaktorn*," in *Kungliga Krigsvetenskapsakademins Handlingar och Tidskrift* (February 2000).

7   On Israeli advance rates, see Niklas Zetterling, "*Behandlingen av erfarenheter från Gulfkriget*," in *KKrVAHT* (June 1994), 115–124. On Israeli command methods, see Niklas Zetterling, "*Ledning genom uppdragstaktik*," in *KKrVAHT* (May 1995), 93–104 and, of course, Martin van Creveld's *Command in War* (Harvard University Press, Cambridge 1985), where the chapter "Masters of Mobile Warfare' is devoted to Israeli command methods.

BIBLIOGRAPHY

The sources used for this book include archival records, articles and books. Documents are indicated in the notes. They have been taken from four different archives. The two most important are *Bundesarchiv-Militärarchiv* in Freiburg, Germany (abbreviated BA-MA in the notes) and National Archives and Records Administration in Washington, D.C. (abbreviated NARA in the notes). Also, a few Polish documents have been used in Chapter 2. They were found at the General Sikorski Institute in London. The abbreviation for this institute is IPMS. Finally, there are a few documents from the war archives in Stockholm (abbreviated "Kra" in the notes).

The printed sources that were useful in the writing of this book are listed below.

Rüdiger Alberti, *Als Kriegspfarrer in Polen* (Dresden: C. Ludwig Ungelenk, 1940)

Hermann Balck, *Ordnung im Chaos* (Osnabrück: Biblio Verlag, 1981)

Ulf Balke, *Der Luftkrieg in Europa 1939–1941* (Augsburg: Bechtermünz Verlag, 1997)

Kurt Bernhard, *Panzer packen Polen* (Berlin: Mittler & Sohn, 1940)

Stephen Biddle, "The Past as Prologue: Assessing Theories of Future Warfare," in *Security Studies* (Fall 1998), No. 1, Vol. 8, 1–74

Mieczyslaw Bielski, *Grupa Operacyjna Piotrków 1939* (Warszawa: Bellona, 1991)

Fedor von Bock, *The War Diary 1939–1945* (Atglen, PA.: Schiffer, 1996)

Horst Boog, Jürgen Förster, Joachim Hoffmann, Ernst Klink, Rolf-Dieter Müller and Gerd Ueberschär, *Der Angriff auf die Sowjetunion* (Frankfurt am Main: Fischer, 1991)

David Brown, *Warship Losses of World War II* (London: Arms and Armour Press, 1990)

Alex Buchner, *Narvik, Die Kämpfe der Gruppe Dietl im Frühjahr 1940* (Neckargemünd: Kurt Vowinkel Verlag, 1958)

Peter Chamberlain, Hilary Doyle and Thomas Jentz, *Encyclopedia of German Tanks of World War Two* (London: Arms and Armour Press, 1978)

Robert M. Citino, *The German Way of War* (University Press of Kansas, 2005)

James S. Corum, The Roots of Blitzkrieg (University Press of Kansas, 1992); "The German Campaign in Norway 1940 as a Joint Operation," in *Journal of Strategic Studies* (December 1998), No. 4, Vol. 21

Martin van Creveld, *Supplying War* (Cambridge University Press, 1977); *Fighting Power* (Westpoint: Greenwood Press, 1982); *Command in War* (Harvard University Press, 1985)

Norman Davies, *White Eagle, Red Star: the Polish-Soviet war, 1919–20* (London: Orbis, 1983)

Len Deighton, *Blitzkrieg—From the Rise of Hitler to the Fall of Dunkirk* (London: Triad/Granada, 1980)

Wilhelm Deist, Manfred Messerschmidt, Hans-Erich Volkmann and Wolfram Wette, *Das deutsche Reich und der Zweite Weltkrieg, Bd. 1* (Stuttgart: Deutsche Verlags-Anstalt, 1979)

Wolfgang Dierich, *Kampfgeschwader 55 "Greif"* (Stuttgart: Motorbuch Verlag, 1994)

Robert A. Doughty, *The Seeds of Disaster: The Development of French Army Doctrine, 1919–1939* (Hamden, CT.: Archon Books, 1985); *The Breaking Point—Sedan and the Fall of France, 1940* (Hamden, CT.: Archon Books, 1990)

Antulio J. Echevarria, *After Clausewitz, German Military Thinkers Before the Great War* (University Press of Kansas, 2001)

Fritz Fechner, *Panzer am Feind* (Gütersloh: Bertelsmann, 1941)

A. Frankson, "Summer 1941," in *Journal of Slavic Military Studies* (September 2000), No. 3, Vol. 13

B. H. Friesen, "The Battle of Aire, German Flank Guard Actions During the 1940 French Campaign," in *Armor* (Jan–Feb 1994)

Karl-Heinz Frieser, *Blitzkrieg-Legende—Der Westfeldzug 1940* (Munich: Oldenbourg Verlag, 1996)

Brian I. Fugate, *Operation Barbarossa* (Novato, CA.: Presidio, 1984)

German Tank Maintenance in World War II (Washington, D.C.: Center of Military History, 1988)

David Glantz, "Excerpts on Soviet 1938–40 operations from *The History of Warfare, Military Art and Military Science,* a 1977 textbook of the Military Academy of the General Staff of the USSR Armed Forces," in *Journal of Slavic Military Studies* (March 1993), No. 1, Vol. 6, 85–141

Rudolf Gschöpf, *Mein Weg mit der 45. Infanterie-Division* (Linz: OÖ Landesverlag, 1955)

Jeffrey A. Gunsburg, "The Battle of Gembloux, 14–15 May 1940: The 'Blitzkrieg' Checked," in *Journal of Military History* (January 2000), 97–140

Heinz Guderian, *Panzer Leader* (London: Futura, 1982)

Bruce I. Gudmundsson, *Stormtroop Tactics—Innovation in the German Army, 1914–1918* (Westport: Praeger, 1992)

Franz Halder, *Kriegstagebuch*, 3 vols. (Stuttgart: Kohlhammer, 1962–64), volume I, II, and 3

Bernd Hartmann, *Geschichte des Panzerregiments 5 1935–1943 und der Panzerabteilung 5 1943–1945* (Erfstadt: Bernd Hartmann, 2003)

Andreas Hauge, *Kampene i Norge 2* (Sandefjord: Krigshistoriskt Forlag, 1995)

Rolf Hinze, *Hitze, Frost und Pulverdampf, Der Schicksalsweg der 20. Panzer-Division* (Meerbusch: Rolf Hinze, 1996); *19. Infanteri. und Panzer-Division* (Meerbusch: Verlag Rolf Hinze, 1997); *Löwendivision, 31. Infanterie- und Grenadier-Division* (Meerbusch: Verlag Rolf Hinze, 1997)

Alistair Horne, *To Lose a Battle* (London: Papermac, 1990)

Hermann Hoth, *"Mansteins Operationsplan für den Westfeldzug 1940 und die Aufmarschanweisung des O.K.H. vom 27.2.40,"* in *Wehrkunde 1958*, 127–130; *"Das Schicksal der französischen Panzerwaffe im I. Teil des Westfeldzuges 1940,"* in *Wehrkunde 1958*, 367–377.; *"Die Verwendung von Panzern in der Verteidigung und die Neugliederung der deutschen NATO-Divisionen 1959,"* in *Wehrkunde 1959*, 631–638.

Walther Hubatsch, *"Weserübung': die deutsche Besetzung von Dänemark und Norwegen 1940* (Göttingen: Musterschmidt Verlag, 1960)

Bo Hugemark (ed.), *Urladdning* (Stockholm: Probus, 1990)

Johannes Hürter, *"Die Wehrmacht vor Leningrad, Krieg und Besatzungspolitik der 18. Armee im Herbst und Winter 1941/42,"* in *Vierteljahrhefte für Zeitgeschichte* (July 2001)

Hans-Adolf Jacobsen, *Kriegstagebuch des Oberkommandos der Wehrmacht (Wehrmachtführungsstab) Bd. I* (Frankfurt am Main: Bernard & Graefe, 1965)

Robert M. Kennedy, *The German Campaign in Poland (1939)* (Washington, D.C.: US Army Center for Military History, Publication 104–120, US Government Printing Office, 1988)

Ian Kershaw, *Fateful Choices* (New York: Penguin, 2007)

Christian Kinder, *Männer der Nordmark an der Bzura* (Berlin: Mittler & Sohn, 1941)

Grigori F. Krivosheyev, *Grif Sekrenosti Sniat* (Moscow: Voenizdat, 1993)

Fritz Kühlwein, *Gefechtstaktik des verstärkten Bataillons* (Berlin: Mittler & Sohn, 1936); *Die Gruppe im Gefecht (Einheitsgruppe)* (Berlin: Mittler & Sohn, 1936)

Hans Kürsten, *Panzer greifen an* (Leipzig: Desse & Becker, 1940)

Stephan Leistenschneider, *Auftragstaktik im preußisch-deutschen Heer 1871 bis 1914* (Hamburg: Mittler & Sohn, 2002)

Stanislaw Maczek, *Avec mes blindés* (Paris: Presses de la cité, 1967)

Klaus Maier, Horst Rohde, Bernd Stegemann and Hans Umbreit, *Das deutsche Reich und der Zweite Weltkrieg, Bd. 2* (Stuttgart: Deutsche Verlags-Anstalt, 1979)

Erich von Manstein, *Verlorene Siege* (Bonn: Athenäum, 1955)

Alan R. Millett and Williamson Murray, *Military Effectiveness, vol. II: The Interwar Period* (London: Allen & Unwin, 1988); *Military Effectiveness, vol. III: The Second World War* (Boston: Unwin Hyman, 1988)

Klaus-Jürgen Müller, *General Ludwig Beck* (Boppard am Rhein: Harald Boldt Verlag, 1980)

Williamson Murray, "The German Response to Victory in Poland—A Case Study in Professionalism," in *Armed Forces and Society* (Winter 1981), No. 2, Vol. 7, 285–298; *The Luftwaffe 1939–45—Strategy for Defeat* (Washington, D.C.: Brassey's, 1996)

Williamson Murray & Allan Millett (ed.), *Calculations—Net assessment and the Coming of World War II* (New York: The Free Press, 1992)

Williamson Murray & Allan Millett (ed.), *Military Innovation in the Interwar Period* (University of Cambridge Press, 1996)

Joachim Neumann, *Die 4. Panzer-Division 1938–1943* (Bonn: Joachim Neumann, 1985)

Leo Niehorster, *German World War II Organizational Series*, 5 vols. (Hannover: Leo Niehorster, 1990), vols. I, II, and II

Richard J. Overy, *War and Economy in the Third Reich* (Oxford: Clarendon Press, 1995)

Hans-Martin Ottmer, *Weserübung* (Munich: Oldenburg Verlag, 1994)

Wolfgang Paul, *Brennpunkte—Die Geschichte der 6. Panzerdivision (1. leichte)* (Krefeld: Höntges, 1977)

Anton Detlev von Plato, *Die Geschichte der 5. Panzerdivision* (Regensburg: Walhalla und Praetoria, 1978)

Roger R. Reese, *Stalin's Reluctant Soldiers* (University Press of Kansas, 1996)

Herbert Reinecker, Karl Georg von Stackelberg and Wilhelm Utermann, *Panzer nach vorn!* (Berlin: Verlag der Heimbücherei, 1940)

The Rise and Fall of the German Air Force 1933–1945 (Kew: Public Record Office, 2001)

Florian K. Rothbrust, *Guderian's XIXth Panzer Corps and The Battle of France, Breakthrough in the Ardennes, May 1940* (Westport, CT.: Praeger, 1990)

Martin Samuels, *Command or Control? Command, Training and Tactics in the British and German Armies, 1888–1918* (London: Frank Cass, 1995)

Lennart Samuelson, *Soviet Defence Industry Planning—Tukhachevskii and Military-Industrial Mobilisation 1926–1937* (Stockholm School of Economics, Stockholm Institute of East European Economies, 1996)

Trygve Sandvik, *Krigen i Norge 1940; Operasjonene til lands i Nord-Norge 1940 II*, (Oslo: Gyldendal, 1965)

Oskar Schaub, *Aus der Geschichte Panzer-Grenadier-Regiment 12* (Bergisch Gladbach: Selbstverlag, 1957)

Herbert Schindler, *Mosty und Dirschau* (Freiburg: Rombach, 1979)

August Schmidt, *Geschichte der 10. Division* (Bad Nauheim: Podzun, 1963)

Hans Schäufler, *So lebten und so starben sie—Das Buch vom Panzer-Regiment 35* (Bamberg: Kameradschaft ehm. Pz.-Rgt. 35, 1968)

Marco Smedberg and Niklas Zetterling, *Andra världskrigets utbrott—Hitlers anfall mot Polen 1939* (Stockholm: Norstedts, 2007)

Boris V. Sokolov, "The Cost of War: Human Losses for the USSR and Germany, 1939–1945," in *Journal of Slavic Military Studies* (March 1996), No. 1, Vol. 11

Fritz Sternberg, *Germany and a Lightning War* (London: Faber & Faber, 1938)

I. G. Stewart, *The Struggle for Crete* (Oxford University Press, 1991)

Russel H. S. Stolfi, *A Bias for Action: The German 7th Panzer Division in France and Russia 1940–1941* (Quantico, VA.: Marine Corps Association, 1991); *Hitler's Panzer East* (Phoenix Mill: Alan Sutton, 1992)

Rolf Stoves, *1. Panzer-Division 1939–1945* (Bad Nauheim: Podzun, 1961); *Die gePanzerten und motorisierten deutschen Grossverbände 1935–1945* (Friedberg: Podzun-Pallas, 1986)

Franz Josef Strauß, *Die Geschichte der 2. (Wiener) Panzer-Division* (Eggolsheim: Dörfler, 2005)

Michael Tamelander and Niklas Zetterling, *Bismarck—Kampen om Atlanten* (Stockholm: Norstedts, 2004); *Den nionde april* (Lund: Historiska Media, 2000)

G. Tessin, *Verbände und Truppen der deutschen Wehrmacht und Waffen-SS* (Osnabrück: Mittler & Sohn, Frankfurt am Main und Biblio Verlag, 1966–1975)

Klaus-Jürgen Thies, *Der Polenfeldzug—Ein Lageatlas der Operationsabteilung des Generalstab des Heeres* (Osnabrück: Biblio Verlag, 1989); *Der Ostfeldzug, Heeresgruppe Mitte—Ein Lageatlas der Operationsabteilung des Generalstab des Heeres* (Bissendorf: Biblio Verlag, 2001)

Harold R. Winton and David R. Mets (ed.), *The Challenge of Change—Military Institutions and New Realities, 1918–1941* (University of Nebraska Press, 2003)

Timothy A. Wray, *Standing Fast: German Defensive Doctrine on the Russian Front During World War II, Prewar to March 1943* (Fort Leavenworth: US Army Command and General Staff College, 1986)

Stephen Zaloga and Victor Madej, *The Polish Campaign 1939* (New York: Hippocrene, 1991)

Kurt Zeitzler, "*Die Panzer-Gruppe v. Kleist im West-Feldzug 1940*," in *Wehrkunde 1959*, 182–188; "*Die Panzer-Gruppe v. Kleist über Sedan nach Abbeville und Dünkirchen im Mai 1940*," in *Wehrkunde 1959*, 239–245; "*Erkenntnisse und Erfahrungen der Panzer-Gruppe v. Kleist im West-Feldzug 1940*," in *Wehrkunde 1959*, 366–372

Niklas Zetterling, "*Ledning genom uppdragstaktik*," in *Kungliga Krigsvetenskapsakademins Handlingar och Tidskrift* (1995), No. 5; "*Uppdragstaktik och tidsfaktorn*," in *Kungliga Krigsvetenskapsakademins Handlingar och Tidskrift* (2000), No. 2

Niklas Zetterling and Anders Frankson, "Analyzing World War II East Front Battles," in *Journal of Slavic Military Studies* (March 1998), No. 1, Vol. 11

Earl F. Ziemke, *The German Northern Theater of Operations 1940–1945* (Washington, D.C.: Department of the Army Pamphlet, No. 20–271, 1960)

INDEX OF PLACENAMES